SACRED CIRCLES,
PUBLIC SQUARES

THE POLIS CENTER SERIES ON RELIGION AND URBAN CULTURE

DAVID J. BODENHAMER AND ARTHUR E. FARNSLEY II, EDITORS

SACRED CIRCLES
PUBLIC SQUARES

The Multicentering of
American Religion

Arthur E. Farnsley II,
N. J. Demerath III,
Etan Diamond,
Mary L. Mapes,
Elfriede Wedam

INDIANA UNIVERSITY PRESS   BLOOMINGTON AND INDIANAPOLIS

This book is a publication of

Indiana University Press
601 North Morton Street
Bloomington, IN 47404-3797 USA

http://iupress.indiana.edu

Telephone orders 800-842-6796
Fax orders 812-855-7931
Orders by e-mail IUPORDER@INDIANA.EDU

Library of Congress Cataloging-in-Publication Data

Sacred circles, public squares : the multicentering of American religion / Arthur E. Farnsley II . . . [et al.].
p. cm. — (The Polis Center series on religion and urban culture)
Includes bibliographical references and index.
ISBN 0-253-34472-7 (cloth : alk. paper)
1. Indianapolis (Ind.) — Religion. I. Farnsley, Arthur Emery. II. Series.
BL2527.I6S23 2004
200'.9772'52 — DC22
2004009430

1 2 3 4 5   09 08 07 06 05 04

CONTENTS

PREFACE AND ACKNOWLEDGMENTS   vii

1. INTRODUCTION   1

2. THE CIRCLE CITY ON THE PLAINS   15

3. RELIGIOUS CIVILITY, CIVIL RELIGION   46

4. RELIGIOUS TRADITIONS DIVERSIFIED AND
   DOMESTICATED   76

5. TYPES AND TENSIONS OF CONGREGATIONAL LIFE
   113

6. BACK HOME AGAIN: RELIGION IN THE
   NEIGHBORHOODS   150

7. CONCLUSION: RELIGION AND URBAN CULTURE   188

NOTES   211

BIBLIOGRAPHY   221

CONTRIBUTORS   227

INDEX   229

PREFACE AND ACKNOWLEDGMENTS

Sacred Circles, Public Squares is the capstone of the Project on Religion and Urban Culture (PRUC), which was housed at The Polis Center on the Indiana University–Purdue University Indianapolis campus. The PRUC was a multiyear, multimillion-dollar attempt to engage the city of Indianapolis in a public conversation about religion's role in the city. Along the way, the project produced seven books, four of which are included in this Indiana University Press series. In addition to the present volume, Arthur E. Farnsley II's *Rising Expectations: Urban Congregations, Welfare Reform and Civic Life* and Etan Diamond's *Souls of the City: Religion and the Search for Community in Postwar America* have already been released. Mary L. Mapes's *A Public Charity* is forthcoming. The project also produced two video series: *Religion as a Window on Culture* and *Faith and Community: The Public Role of Religion.* There were, of course, scores of newsletters and research reports and dozens of public presentations and conversations. Finally, the PRUC spawned an annual civic festival called *Spirit and Place,* which still brings important writers and thinkers to Indianapolis each fall to discuss the intersection of religion, community, and geography.

Neither this city-wide conversation nor its products would exist without the generosity of the Lilly Endowment and the wisdom of its staff, the patient guidance of evaluators and colleagues, and the literally tens of thousands of hours worked by staff at The Polis Center. Special thanks to Craig Dykstra, vice president for religion at Lilly Endowment, and Jim Wind, formerly of the Endowment and now president of the Alban Institute. Thanks also to Kathleen Cahalan, Carol Johnson, and John Wimmer, all of whom headed our evaluation team at one time or another.

David Bodenhamer is director of The Polis Center and also directed the PRUC. He is co-editor of this series along with Art Farnsley, and was also a content editor for this manuscript. Kevin Armstrong was a project evaluator and then senior public teacher for the project. *Sacred Circles, Public Squares* and the video series *Faith and Community* drew heavily from one another because of constant conversation between Kevin and Art.

Of the researchers and authors in this book, only Art Farnsley was raised in Indiana and still lives there. But each of us brought directly relevant research experience to the table. Art is the author of *Southern Baptist Politics* (Pennsylvania State University Press, 1994), but his more immediately relevant experience was as research manager and contributing author in Nancy Ammerman's *Congregation and Community* (Rutgers Press, 1997) project. That project's pioneering research on congregations in a variety of urban communities paved the way for the fieldwork in the Project on Religion and Urban Culture. Jay Demerath, the senior scholar of our group, has written too many books to list here, but one he wrote together with Rhys Williams, *A Bridging of Faiths* (Princeton University Press, 1992), was a prototypical attempt to look at religion's role in shaping a New England city. Etan Diamond is an expert on suburbanization, having already written a book about Toronto: *And I Will Dwell in Their Midst: Orthodox Jews in Suburbia* (University of North Carolina Press, 2000) in addition to the new volume named above. Mary Mapes did her dissertation work on historical connections between religion and social service in Chicago before shifting her focus to Indianapolis. Finally, Elfriede Wedam was an integral part of the Religion and Urban America Project based in Chicago. Her work from that project appears in *Public Religion and Urban Transformation* (Lowell Livezey, ed., New York University Press, 2000), among other places, and she has returned to Chicago-based research.

The five of us obviously had help from many scholarly colleagues, but three deserve special mention. Jan Shipps was a regular part of our conversations throughout. Indeed, she is completing a manuscript of her own comparing Indianapolis to four other mid-size American cities. David Vanderstel was a key advisor to the project's historians from the very beginning; Bill Mirola became part of the sociology team in later years. None of those three deserve any criticism for this book's shortcomings, but they should certainly share the credit for any strengths it possesses.

Beyond these is a list of people who made enormous contributions administrating, conducting, and disseminating the research. This very long list is still much too short to thank the many student researchers and staff people who played important roles. Our apologies to anyone who deserved, but failed to receive, mention. We did our best: Nancy Ammerman, Tess Baker, Robert Cole, Kevin Corn, Vicki Cummings, Cynthia Cunningham, Kim Cronin, Jim Dowling, Marjorie Estivil, Tommy Faris, Allen Federman, Karen Feitl, Amanda Fisher, Karen Frederickson, Michelle Hale, Emma Hall, Monty Hulse, Sharon Kandris, Jason Lantzer, David Licht, Alexis Manheim, Susan McKee, Sonia Meisenheimer, Kevin Mickey, Terri Murray-Whalen, Heather Nakonezny, John Neal, Dawn Parks, Margaret Puskar, Edward Queen, Susannah Quern, Brad Sample, Shaun Scholer, Alexis Simmons, Tyrone Simpson, Jason Skelton, Ted Slutz, Carl Smith, Debbie Springer, Jim Stout, Sarah Wagner, Susan Walcott, R. Stephen Warner, Yolanda White, Sherri Wilson, Pat Wittberg, and Eric Wright.

We also offer our grateful thanks to the staff at the IUPUI library, the Indiana State Library, the Indiana Historical Society, the Christian Theological Seminary Library, and the archivists at denominations and congregations throughout Indianapolis. Thanks also to the staff at the mayor's office during the Goldsmith administration. Continuing thanks to the editorial staff at Indiana University Press for their work on this manuscript and in the series.

As with any authors, the five of us owe personal debts too large to repay. Art would especially like to thank Gail, Sarah, and Caleigh for their patient encouragement. Editing five authors' work into one voice was a significant challenge; his apologies to his colleagues for places where he got it wrong. Jay wants to note that although he was a latecomer to the project after its data were collected, his participation marked a prodigal's grateful return to the site of an important chapter of his childhood during World War II and the longtime home of his mother's family, the Tituses of Woodruff Place. Etan thanks his wife, Judy, for all her love and support, and his children, Eli, Shira, and Avi, for making his life so much fun. (A special thanks for Avi, who now has a book dedication of his own!) Mary wishes to thank her parents, Dorothy and Lynn Mapes, her sisters, Kathy Mapes, Lynne Mapes-Riordan, and Christine Mapes-Pearson, and her husband, Peter D'Agostino. And Elfriede wanted to thank her co-authors for the opportunity to collaborate with them in a meaningful learning community.

Beyond that, each of us, and all of us, want to thank the people of Indianapolis — and especially the members of congregations and other religious organizations — who so graciously allowed us to observe, question, and otherwise bother them over the course of several years. Some of their specific activities, ideas, and even quotes made it into this book, but the huge majority did not. Nonetheless, we hope they realize that we learned piece by piece, conversation by conversation. If Indianapolis were not the city it is—with gracious residents and generous community institutions—this project and this book would not have been possible. We sincerely hope we have been able to give back to the city some small measure of all that was given to us.

SACRED CIRCLES,
PUBLIC SQUARES

1

INTRODUCTION

Commerce, art, education, religion, labor, the professions,
literature, the forces of war, and the forces of peace, all passed
along in a long procession, illustrating in a graphic manner
a century of the faith, the hope, and the progress
that make a real city.

— *Indianapolis News,* June 8, 1920,
on Indianapolis's Centennial Celebration parade

The plan was straightforward, both in symbolism and in substance. When Governor Jonathan Jennings and his fellow commissioners sought a location for the Indiana state capital in 1820, they selected an area along Fall Creek in the very center of the state. This was to be, quite literally, Indiana's city: *Indianapolis.* It was not a fort, a trading post, a river port, or the end of a railroad line. Indianapolis was created out of nothing to be the seat of government.

The equally straightforward design for the city came from Alexander Ralston, a colleague of Pierre L'Enfant, the surveyor who designed Washington, D.C. Ralston had similar visions for this new capital: a one-mile-square city, bounded by the unsubtly named North, South, East, and West Streets. The street pattern followed a traditional grid, with sixty-foot streets alternating with thirty-foot lots. Spaces were set aside for a State House and a Court House, as well as two city markets. Breaking the grid like a big "X" were four diagonal streets that were primary transportation routes in and out of the city.

At the center of it all was the eighty-foot-wide Circle Street, circumscribing a 333-foot lot on which the governor's house was to sit — at the center of the center, given Indianapolis's location relative to the rest of the state. By 1840, four of the city's most prominent churches — all part of the Protestant establishment — surrounded the Circle, with a fifth Protestant church just one block away. The vision was clear. At the heart of both the city and the state, the political and religious establishments were comfortably inter-twined. A deeply symbolic symmetry balanced the church alongside the state, the sacred with the secular, the Circle within the Square.

At the end of the twentieth century, the Circle still centered downtown Indianapolis, but the city's neat, compact symmetry was long since skewed. Throughout the city's history, the suburbs grew and expanded ever out-ward. Starting in the 1960s, the inner city's population dwindled. Said Ste-phen Goldsmith, mayor of Indianapolis from 1992 to 2000,

> As in all of the other large cities east of the Mississippi, we suffered many of the same problems in the 60's, 70's, and 80's . . . essentially, the flight of the middle class, the concentration of urban poverty, the typical reaction that as wealthy people moved out of the city, tax rates were increased in order to more aggressively redistribute wealth. . . . I often say that on a very bright, clear day — my office is on the 25th floor of the City/County Building — I can actually see dollar bills float across the city line and land in the sub-urbs where the tax rates are less, the crime is less, and the education is often better.[1]

In this massive urban realignment, both the trappings of traditional reli-gion and its formative cultural power gradually faded from the old center. All but one of the churches left the Circle, and that remaining church is dwarfed by the towering office buildings that surround it. Government and commerce claimed the mile square, and they were gradually separated, in principle at least, from the old religious establishment. There was still cross-fertilization within the city's leadership elite, who often shared both church membership and board membership, joined in subtle bonds forged by prox-imity. But the separate institutions grew ever less proximate due in part to an increasingly rigorous legal separation of church and state. By the end of the 1990s, Goldsmith could describe the relationship thus:

> [W]e pretended the government was neutral with respect to faith-based organizations. In fact, our experience was that it wasn't neutral at all. It was hostile. And it was hostile at almost every level of government.

In 1997, Mayor Goldsmith launched the Front Porch Alliance (FPA), an ambitious attempt to build partnerships among faith-based organiza-tions, civic groups, and local government. He appointed a director and staff whose job it was to keep local religious groups — mostly churches — informed about funding opportunities for their outreach ministries. He looked for ways the city could offer a helping hand to civic-minded con-

Fig. 1.1. Historic Photo of Circle, ca. 1865. Courtesy Indiana Historical Society C7666.

regations, perhaps through extra neighborhood police patrols or small zoning or traffic changes.

Goldsmith's goal was not to have religion somehow recreate the old symmetry for the city as a whole. Instead, he envisioned the Front Porch Alliance as a component of his Building Better Neighborhoods program. Religion's role, as he saw it, was not about revitalizing the city center, not about the city's metropolitan identity. Religion's role concerned relatively small groups joined in specific communities throughout the city. And faith-based organizations, especially congregations, were defined as community insiders, crucial to the dream of "rebuilding communities from the inside out." These local, supposedly indigenous, faith communities were the true focus of faith-based welfare reform, the targets of the "charitable choice" laws enacted in 1996.

At one level, the kind of small, personal religious presence imagined in welfare reform had always been a key part of the city. It was local — practiced in communities defined by ethnicity, race, social class, geographic boundaries, and, to greater and lesser degrees, personal choice. The practice of real religious communities — both in worship and in mission — had always been specific and particular virtually by definition.

But if traditional religious practice was as local as ever, religion's larger cultural role had changed. The establishment Protestantism that had acted as a cultural template informing moral living and good citizenship in the city had declined. In its place was a combination of many different religious traditions on the one hand and an evolving common civic faith on the other. Traditional religion was still vital in the lives of most of the city's residents, and still crucial, in changing ways, to the city's public life. But the religion of the white Protestant establishment would never again be the de facto religion of the city imagined as a common enterprise. The churches would never again assume their central place around the Circle.

Religion and Urban Realignment

Questions about religion's role in a city's public life, about religion's relationship to urban culture, are far from academic. Understanding religion's role gives us clearer insight into many of the topics that scholars, policy makers, and other civic leaders have recently put on the public agenda.

Throughout the 1990s, few concepts energized foundation officials and civic leaders more than the notion of *social capital*. Robert Putnam most famously used James Coleman's phrase in his essay, and later book, *Bowling Alone*,[2] which charged that America was losing a sense of community because it had lost many of its community-building institutions and practices. Putnam claimed that Americans were becoming more insulated and solitary, that they favored playscapes, decks, and swimming pools in their backyards over front porches that connected them to their neighbors. Americans still bowled, indeed in record numbers, but they did so with their immediate family and friends, not in organized leagues.

As the supposed community-building qualities of various organizations assumed center stage, considerable debate arose concerning the role of churches, synagogues, and mosques in creating social capital. Some scholars and practitioners rose to the defense of congregations, claiming they were one of the last bastions of social capital, producing a strong sense of community among their members and teaching social and civic skills that contributed to public life.[3] Religious organizations were praised, moreover, as community builders not just for their members, but for the neighborhoods that surrounded them. They were defined as long-standing, indigenous community organizations, a characterization that fit hand-in-glove with attempts to mobilize these faith-based groups in the service of welfare reform.

But to focus on religion's community-building role at the level of congregations, or even at the level of denominations and entire religious traditions, was to see only one side of the story. Religious groups surely did build community, unfailingly for their own members and to varying degrees for the wider geographic areas they served. But religion, in this traditional characterization, seemed ever less capable of building a strong sense of metropolitan community. As the city became more diverse and more spread out, it was clear that Indianapolis's identity did not depend on, and could not be defined by, any one religious tradition.

One brief example illustrates this point nicely. From 1920 to 1960, city fathers held sunrise services on the Circle each Easter Sunday morning to celebrate the city's Christian heritage. In 1930, 15,000 people attended these services. At the center of the festivities on the Circle was a cross, built from rugged logs, that was visible to those sitting blocks away. The assembly was entertained by a 500-member children's choir and a rendition of "Jesus, the Children's Friend." By 1955, just twenty-five years later, eighty-seven people attended the downtown services, by then being held in local theaters. By the mid-1960s the services were abandoned altogether. Mayor Richard Lugar tried to reinstate the practice in the 1970s as part of his larger effort to rejuvenate the downtown, but the proposal was met with such indifference that the idea was abandoned.

This change in Easter rituals represents a significant religious shift, but it also signals a shift in the very nature of urban community. To understand social capital, we must first understand how religion helps to build and sustain it. To understand how social capital has changed, we must see those changes in relationship to religion's public role. It is clear enough that religion still plays a vibrant part in the lives of individuals and their defined communities, which in turn has some effect on the city as a whole. But it is also clear that a certain kind of religion no longer plays the formative civic role it once did. Questions about community, about our lives together, come into clearer focus when we ask them in appropriate historical and institutional context.

Social capital is not the only contemporary public concern that can be illuminated by deeper contextual understanding. Public debate about the appropriate relationship between *church and state* also comes into focus when seen "on the ground" as it is manifested in real beliefs and practices. Current dialogue about faith-based welfare reform, so-called "charitable choice," is the most recent example of the ongoing struggle to define what is legitimately public and necessarily private.

The relationship between church and state is difficult to pin down be-cause it occurs at many different levels. The presence of five Protestant churches around the governor's mansion in the Circle provides potent sym-bolism and strongly suggests that church and state were closely related, but mere presence is not the same thing as giving public funds collected through taxation to private religious groups for the provision of social ser-vices. When Mayor Goldsmith said that government had become hostile toward religion, he was talking about the latter phenomenon. Government had, in his view, cut all administrative and financial ties to religion to avoid any structural entanglements. Cultural entanglements, including overlap among the leadership of elites joined by political, economic, and religious interests, are not so easily addressed through legislated avoidance.

But the two—religion's cultural relationship to government and direct funding or administrative ties—are certainly related. When religion and government are symbolically and culturally intertwined, when many values are widely understood to be shared by both, then there is less need to enforce their administrative separation so rigorously. The decision to avoid entanglements, whether characterized as healthy separation or as hostility, is an acknowledgment of religious pluralism, an admission that the same religious values are not necessarily shared by most of the community. In that context, religious values are left to the personal sphere, not only to private individuals, as some like to emphasize, but also to their particular groups. Different, less sectarian, values must undergird the common, public deci-sions made in government. Diverse religious groups make their case in the public square—sometimes contending, sometimes negotiating—but they do so within a secular framework that attempts to treat a multitude of view-points fairly.

Much of the debate about church and state, and about its contemporary incarnation as faith-based welfare reform, revolves around the interpreta-tion of constitutional questions. While those legal questions are extremely important, they too often point us away from other very important ques-tions about religion and public life. Why have some government and civic leaders turned to smaller, more local faith communities—especially congre-gations—as social service organizations? Why do proponents of faith-based reforms think these smaller organizations and the individuals within them are the appropriate venue for community building? What does this say about us as a people, about our common interests and shared values? Questions like these are not answered by appeal to legal principle, but by examination of contemporary practice in its broadest historical and social context. Dur-ing the 1990s Indianapolis was home to many pioneering experiments in faith-based reform. To see those experiments in their real-life context is to get a glimpse into religion's changing role in our lives together.

Discussions about church and state, as well as those concerning social capital, are truly "big picture" issues whose relevance is immediately apparent. But just below the surface of these issues are several smaller ones, each of which points us toward the need for a deeper understanding of religion's role in our common lives, each of which can be better understood when the appropriate social context serves as the basis for our theories.

Pluralism is a defining feature of America — *E Pluribus Unum* — but it also presents an abiding social concern. Can we be a community, can we define our shared goals and values, if we cannot even say who *we* are? America has always welcomed new immigrants, some more enthusiastically than others. Religion — both the faiths of recent arrivals and the faiths already established at their destinations — plays an important role in bridging the gap between new and old. But is the "melting pot" the right metaphor, or does "separate but equal" (or even unequal) come closer to the truth?

The Islamic Society of North America (ISNA) lies just west of Indianapolis in the suburb of Plainfield. After the horrific events of September 11, 2001, local officials called the ISNA administrative offices to ask whether they wanted special police protection. They were told "no thank you." The gist of the ISNA message was that their doors would stay open and that they would do what they could to respond to their neighbors' questions and concerns. This was, after all, their community, and they did not wish to be cut off at such a difficult time.

Although that vignette paints a rosy picture of a pluralism that works, Indianapolis's history contains other less flattering stories. Indianapolis was a hotbed, in many ways a capital, for the revitalization of the Ku Klux Klan in the 1920s. It was a white, Protestant city that drew hard distinctions between natives and foreigners. Reflecting that history, Indianapolis today houses a very small Jewish population, an even smaller number of Muslims, and numbers of other non-Christian religions nearly too small to count. But even in the supposedly whitebread, Christian Midwest, something happened between the Klan days of the 1920s and the events at the ISNA in 2001. To understand how pluralism works in our lives, we must consider not only the role that religion plays in defining who we are, but also the shared values that make it possible for Muslims, Jews, and Christians to live together even during times that could not be more tense. We must understand the ways in which traditional religion centers people's lives in their personal elective communities, but we must see how those many centers are joined together in a larger, common enterprise symbolized by the city's one center.

One way to frame those shared values symbolizing the common enterprise is to imagine them as a *civil religion*. The term "civil religion" is unpopular today for a number of good reasons. It is ill-defined, making it risky for scholars. Many liberals find it distasteful because they fear the uncritical linkage of patriotism with isolationism and aggression. Conservative Christians sometimes veer away from it because it requires uncomfortable reflection on an often unspoken bond between Christian theology and American nationalism.

Despite those concerns, though, something that looks and acts very much like a civil religion seems to fill the downtown cultural space once occupied by the Protestant establishment. Downtown Indianapolis is defined by war memorials; the lieutenant governor claimed it had the greatest number of patriotic monuments of any city outside Washington, D.C. Government buildings, crowned by the domed capitol, are also defining features of the mile square. Some of the most striking downtown buildings are the sports facilities, including the RCA Dome, home to the NFL's Colts, and Conseco Fieldhouse, home to the NBA's Pacers. And, of course, a multitude of high-rise office buildings signify the city's commitment to business.

A visitor from Europe who knew only cities built around grand cathedrals would be hard-pressed to pick out the "cathedral" in Indianapolis, though the state capitol building, the RCA Dome, and the full-scale copy of Mausolus's tomb set amid blocks of urban parkland as a World War memorial would be leading candidates. Some ideas and values hold the city together despite differences in race, ethnicity, socioeconomic class, and religion. There are still strands of social capital that link the city at its center, despite the centrifugal movement of its population and its growing cultural pluralism.

The realignment of the city that saw patriotic shrines, businesses, and sports facilities gradually displace churches from the city center might be assumed to be evidence for *secularization,* the gradual waning of religion's role due to advances in more rational-scientific ways of thinking. There are, in fact, good reasons to see urban change as a kind of secularization, especially insofar as religion exercises continually less *authority* in our public lives.[4] But a city with 1,200 congregations, where at least half the population maintains membership in a faith community, could hardly be described as secular or irreligious. In fact, religion plays a crucial, often primary, role in the life of many of the city's citizens.

Religion's influence is widespread. In every neighborhood, in every parish, in every region, there are dozens of congregations where people worship, reflect, transmit values to their children, and serve through missions. Religion holds people together in small groups, but it also binds them in much larger faith traditions linked by ethnicity, race, and theology. Congregations are, by a considerable distance, the largest group of volunteer organizations in the city. Their members are involved in literally every level of civic life, from neighborhood groups, to non-profit organizations, to business, to government. Beyond congregations, though, are the schools, hospitals, and universities that have religious support and deep religious roots.

The story of religious change at the city center during urban realignment is not, then, the story of religion's disappearance. But it would be pointless to think that traditional religion — the faith practiced in congregations, schools, and hospitals — was immune to the effects of the city's structural and cultural realignment. To understand religion's role in our public lives we must look carefully at both sides of the equation: the broadening of our shared, common values symbolized at the city center and the continuation of traditional religious belief and practice in the city's multiple different communities, whether defined geographically or culturally. Changes in the city center, both literal and symbolic, have meant change for the multiple religious centers throughout the metropolis.

National Issues, Local Context

In the mid-1990s, we set out to understand religion's changing role in public life with support from Indianapolis's own Lilly Endowment, Inc. To do this, we attempted to create a public dialogue that allowed the widest possible variety of people to explain not only how religion shaped their lives as individuals but, more importantly for us, how it shaped their communities. The Project on Religion and Urban Culture (PRUC) was always imagined as a public conversation. The data it collected were always meant to be public information, and so they were disseminated in two video series, ninety newsletters, multiple public presentations and festivals, and a variety of non-academic books containing spiritual biographies, short stories, essays, and photographs. More academic discussion took place within The Polis Center Series on Religion and Urban Culture from Indiana University Press.

We chose to run the project as a public conversation rather than as a specifically sociological or historical research project because we believed that both the city and the nation would benefit from a broad understanding of religion's public role. But most importantly, we wanted the work to be a resource in the communities we were studying. Given the national trend led by Kretzmann and McKnight[5] toward focusing on assets rather than liabilities, we hoped to provide the occasion for open discussion about religion as a community asset. We wanted to see how community discussions and a better flow of public information might *build* social capital as well as to reflect upon it. This was also an important goal of the Lilly Endowment, which wanted both to describe religion's public role and to raise public awareness of it.

As we began our work, intellectual interest in congregations was hitting its peak. Ammerman et al.'s *Congregation and Community* as well as Wind and Lewis's *American Congregations* were current intellectual topics. Mark Chaves was just cranking up his seminal national survey. Government was moving toward partnership with congregations at the local, state, and national level. Everyone, it seemed, was interested in religion's ability, and especially congregations' ability, to build community. Again, Lilly Endowment was providing the lion's share of support for many of these efforts.

Even with these pragmatic, community-oriented goals, we needed reliable information about the local context in order to stimulate public discussion and to develop useful public products. Discussion about religion and community was already occurring at the level of big ideas, driven by normative definitions of what *should* be. Indianapolis's public conversation needed to be driven by an accurate picture of what was. The project's research component used historical and sociological methods—some traditional and some experimental—to produce the kind of contextual information that would shape the public conversation.[6]

The research involved historians who specialized in suburbanization and in religion's relationship to social welfare and sociologists who conducted field research in eighteen Indianapolis neighborhoods, selected to represent the many sides of the city, from the inner city to "in-town" to the outer suburbs. Student researchers were provided training in the use of detailed census forms and sent to local congregations to retrieve relevant data, though they also conducted hundreds of interviews, both formally and informally. Numbers in this book about congregational membership size, percentage of members who live in the neighborhood, budgets, and mission spending are self-reported by representatives of the congregations, usually the pastor, during formal interviews. In all, a total of 413 congregations completed census forms, representing well over 75 percent of the congregations in the neighborhoods studied.

Other methods were less traditional. In a pilot phase, high school students interviewed older residents of their inner-city neighborhoods—again as a way to increase information sharing and to build social capital. In one neighborhood, students from a local high school class conducted the canvas, even making a videotape of religion's role in the community.

We also conducted three more traditional surveys. The first was a 1997 survey of 600 inner-city residents, 150 in each of four selected neighborhoods. The second was a 1999 city-wide survey of 806 respondents on questions of religion and community life. A third was a 2000 survey of 260 Indianapolis clergy members. All were conducted by the Indiana University Center for Survey Research.

SETTING THE STORY

Much of the information created by the Project on Religion and Urban Culture is available in the individual monographs of team members, as well as in the research notes, newsletters, and video series. This book, though, offers our broadest reflection on the big picture. Here we hope to use our city and our project to contextualize some important national concerns.

Providing context through case study is something of a Hoosier tradition. The famous *Middletown* studies took place just up the road from Indianapolis.[7] While we are by no means trying to assume such a prestigious mantle for ourselves, we are trying humbly to emphasize the value of taking a longer look at one place in order to understand the interrelationship between many different issues. Indianapolis is a good place to take that long look. Without question it lacks the cultural complexity, the sheer heterogeneity, of a New York, Los Angeles, or Chicago. But much has been written already, and is being written still, about those great cities. Books like Robert Orsi's *Gods of the City*[8] display the dazzling religious diversity of large cities. Indianapolis is a mid-size city and is, in many ways, more representative of the places where the majority of Americans live. There must, after all, be some reason why advertising agencies and large corporations continue to choose to test market their products in Indianapolis, the "crossroads of America" in the center of the "Hoosier heartland."

Although Chapter 4 will describe the city's religious landscape in some detail, it is important to see the rough contours at the outset. Indianapolis has traditionally been a Protestant town. During its first century and beyond, it was dominated by the traditions that came to make up the Protestant mainline: Methodists, Congregationalist Christians, Presbyterians, Lutherans, Baptists, and Episcopalians. In the contemporary denominational configuration, United Methodists and the Christian Church (Disciples of Christ) are the largest among these denominations. The Christian Church is headquartered in the city and Christian Theological Seminary is also located here. At the turn of the twentieth century, mainline Protestants constituted a majority of religious adherents in the city. Today, the mainline Protestant denominations combine to make up just under a quarter of those adherents.

Through the course of the twentieth century, other religious groups grew both in raw numbers of members and in terms of their "market share" within the total population. Catholics grew from a small minority to be the largest single religious body in the city. Although there are more Protestants than Catholics — which separates Indianapolis from many other midwestern cities — there are more Catholics than members of any single Protestant denomination. Today Catholics make up just over a quarter of Indianapolis's religious adherents.

If mainline Protestants and Catholics together make up one-half of the religious pie, a broad mixture of religious traditions makes up the other half. White evangelicals are the largest slice. Indiana has long been a seedbed for independent Christian reformers, including the movements that produced the many churches that are simply called "Christian." The Black Church — comprising the Methodist traditions as well as Baptists and Pentecostals — has also been strong in the city from the Great Migration forward. There is a scattering of other religious traditions, with a higher proportion of holiness churches than in the nation as a whole. Finally, Indianapolis has a relatively small Jewish tradition representing around 1 percent of the population, less than in many comparably sized midwestern cities.[9]

Even the briefest description of the religious landscape would not be complete without further mention of Lilly Endowment, Inc., our project's sponsor. Lilly Endowment is historically the largest foundation funder of religious activities and religious research in the U.S. Their clear mission is to support congregations and their pastors and to aid in the development of Christian character among church members of all kinds. Leadership in the Endowment is today, as it has always been, primarily drawn from the Protestant mainline. In the reflections that follow, the Endowment, as it is called in Indianapolis, plays an unmistakable and formative role in the evolution of religion's relationship to the city's public life.

Urban Realignment and Multicentering

This book tells the story of religious traditions, of how the individuals and congregations within them shaped and were shaped by the changing city. That story of religious change sheds needed light on practical issues like social capital and faith-based welfare reform, with a few rays illuminating the dark corners of more philosophical concepts such as secularization, civil religion, and pluralism. But it is important not to get so caught up either in the details of the case study or in reflection on these civic issues that we miss the big story of urban and religious realignment that animates our reflections. A constant tension produces the energy from which the story of religious change and its effect on our public lives emerges.

At the broadest level, that tension can best be described as countervailing *inward* and *outward* pressures. As in most American cities, Indianapolis has experienced growth as a movement outward, witnessed by the constant development of new and ever more distant suburbs and exurbs. Nothing defines the current shape of the city like this continual flow of population, and trends toward desegregation in the 1950s, 60s, and 70s only accelerated the process. Both in town and around the edges, Indianapolis developed into a collection of many different, and often distant, communities. It developed multiple "centers" of urban community.

Pushing back against this outward pressure, though, have been repeated attempts to assert and establish — and to re-establish — the city center. From Ralston's original design to concerted efforts in the 1970s to redefine the city limits, civic leaders have continued to imagine Indianapolis as one community anchored by its downtown mile square. Decisions about where to put state government, city government, sports facilities, entertainment venues, the combined Indiana University–Purdue University Indianapolis urban campus, and virtually everything else were determined by the long-time insistence that Indianapolis *is* a center and that it *has* a center.

These countervailing trends manifest themselves in the city's built environment, but they are also apparent in people's lives. On the one hand, people see themselves as southsiders, northsiders, eastsiders, and westsiders. They identify themselves as members of neighborhoods, congregations, and other local groups. Individuals choose their own communities and draw their own mental maps of those communities that include schools, work-places, and shopping centers. No two maps are necessarily alike, even for next-door neighbors. The outward pressure allows for families and small communities that are custom-built and personal.

At the same time, though, those individuals, families, and small groups still participate in the city as a common enterprise. They vote for and pay taxes to the same government. They read the same newspapers, cheer for the same professional sports teams, and are inspired by the same memorials and monuments. They are at once members of their many small communities and citizens of Indianapolis.

The tension that links many communities to the one community and creates identities that are at once both local and metropolitan also shapes religious belief and practice. When critics complain that "the churches are all country clubs," they are saying something about religion's personal, elective nature. When others say that religion has been increasingly relegated to the private sphere, or take the even stronger view that religion has devolved into a kind of individual mysticism, they are acknowledging the force of the outward pressure that creates small, personal, elective communities.

But to see only that side of the story is to miss the myriad ways that traditional religion, practiced in multiple communities of faith, affects our common, public lives as the members of those small communities interact elsewhere throughout the city. And it is to ignore the ideas and practices that make up the civil religion that binds the city as one metropolis. Neither the story of the city's structural realignment nor the story of religious culture in Indianapolis can be told as a straight line running in one direction.

Both Indianapolis as a city and the religious life within it can be accurately described as multicentered. At first blush, "multicentering" seems an oxymoron. If something has more than one center, then it has no center at all. But the relationship among the city's many centers and its one metropolitan center is precisely the issue at hand. If we hope to understand religion's role in urban community, we must first understand that community is formed at many different levels: in families, in neighborhoods, in urban regions, in voluntary organizations, in historic traditions, and in the metropolis imagined as a whole. Religion plays a role in shaping community at each of those levels, but it is stronger at some levels than at others, and that relationship has changed over time. One of our foremost goals is to describe the dual process by which urban religion lost its formative power at the metropolitan center — it was, literally, decentered — but continued to shape the many different communities that make up the city as it was just as literally recentered in multiple specific settings. Thus urban religion is itself multicentered: it builds and sustains community in a pluralism of urban centers without having a center of its own.

Indianapolis residents will, we trust, be able to see their lives in the pages that follow and be helped to reflect on the relationship between the religious change and urban realignment that they experience daily. But the tension between the one center and the many centers, between individuals and communities, between the parts and the whole, is hardly limited to Indianapolis. Many of our common concerns about how we live together in community have religious roots, and we understand them better when we understand both the historical antecedents and the contemporary social context of religious change.

2

THE CIRCLE CITY ON THE PLAINS

I think that even in the city the definition of a neighborhood has
changed, because at one point people lived in proximity while the kids
all went to the same school. There were little markets all over the place.
You saw each other at the market, the barber shop, the beauty shop.
The church was just one entity where people crossed paths all the time.
But now, even within the city, we have kids in different schools. We go
shopping outside the place where we live. There are many cases in my
church where people see each other on Sunday and then don't see
each other again until next Sunday.

— an inner-city Catholic priest

Religion cannot be separated from the economic, racial, and cultural
issues that have transformed our urban centers. The highways built in
the 50's and 60's allowed for mobility, while the civil rights movement
lowered the boundaries and allowed minorities to live, for the most
part, where they would like to live. Folks were saying,
"ok, I can still go to this church but I can also begin to
live the American dream. I want my 40 acres and a mule."

— African American community liaison in
the Indianapolis mayor's office

In October 1944, as World War II was entering its final months, Indianapolis department store magnate Meier S. Block invited a group of 350 local businessmen to a dinner at his downtown store to hear a presentation on postwar planning for Indianapolis, offered by George A. Kuhn, chairman of the Mayor's Committee on Post-War Planning. In his speech, Kuhn outlined dozens of large and small proposals to advance Indianapolis as a modern industrial city. Included were proposals to expand the road and highway system, increase parking space, improve air quality through smoke abatement programs, redevelop slums, clean up and beautify area streams and rivers, and construct a large public auditorium. The underlying premise of these transformations was to reverse a "trend toward decentralization." All the Committee's efforts, Kuhn argued, would "make Indianapolis more attractive, not less so," thus promoting a "successful integration of old and new suburban areas with the city proper."[1]

In the half-century following George Kuhn's speech, most of his proposals came to fruition. The road and highway system evolved into a comprehensive interstate highway layout. Smoke abatement programs succeeded in improving the city's air quality. Neighborhood redevelopment on the city's west and northeast sides removed slums. Proposals for stream and river beautification resulted in several city parks and greenways. The "large public auditorium" evolved into the Market Square Arena. And beginning in the late 1970s, downtown Indianapolis underwent a revitalization that reaffirmed its status as the region's economic and recreational hub.

During that same period when civic leaders sought to keep downtown Indianapolis at the top of the metropolitan pyramid, Shirley Volz proceeded to build a life for herself on the far west side of Marion County. Having grown up in a neighborhood just north of downtown, Volz married in 1955 and moved into a home in the Farley Addition, a new suburban subdivision near West 10th Street. Volz was Catholic, and after attending the downtown parish of Saints Peter and Paul as a child, she joined the rapidly growing St. Christopher parish, which at the time encompassed the town of Speedway and vast tracts of rural farmland along almost the entire western third of Marion County. Although she worked downtown for a while, much of Volz's life was centered on her neighborhood and her Catholic parish. She watched the west side grow from "dirt roads" and "cows and roosters" to a sprawling suburban landscape, and her church evolve into a congregation of more than six thousand members. Throughout the changes, however, Volz remained a westsider — and a St. Christopher parishioner — through and through. Did she remember when a nearby parish was split off from St. Christopher's? Did she have a sense of the larger growth of the city and of Catholicism in Indianapolis? Don't ask her about other neighborhoods, she pleaded with an interviewer. "Get me out of Speedway and I'm lost. I just know the west side pretty well, you know." After all, Indianapolis is so large that "it's mind-boggling. You can get lost on the east side of the city."

George Kuhn and Shirley Volz likely did not know each other, but they are nevertheless connected by their contrasting experiences in Indianapolis in the second half of the twentieth century. On one side was Kuhn, who sought dozens of physical improvements that would ensure a degree of cohesiveness within the Indianapolis region, with a strong downtown holding the region together. On the other side was Volz, happily ensconced in her west side life, centered not on downtown but on her suburban parish. Kuhn and Volz symbolized the realignment underway in Indianapolis, and they represented two sides of a significant divide in the way Americans thought about cities. Are cities best thought of as single places, unified by some common culture and symbols? — a view taken by Kuhn in his desire to stop decentralization and refocus activity on downtown. Or are cities primarily decentralized collections of smaller groups and ideas only collected in a loose fashion? — a view represented by Volz and her west side parish insularity. More broadly, do cities have one true center — whether real or symbolic — that holds residents together, or do cities have multiple centers that may overlap but are not truly concentric?

It is pointless to deny that every city has a center and that, at some level of abstraction, they are unified as a metropolitan whole. But to focus only on this common, often abstract, center and to make common citizenship the focus of urban analysis can be misleading. A large city like Indianapolis must also be understood as a collection of hundreds of thousands of individuals who individually have their own social networks, but who collectively weave those networks into a fabric of metropolitan life. The urban historian Robert Fishman recognized this duality in cities by describing the twentieth-century metropolis as a "city a la carte," an environment within which residents construct individualized networks of work and play.[2] Fishman's point was echoed by the geographer Charles Leven, who described how he lives his life at a number of different "scales" and "densities" simultaneously. At once he is a resident of his subdivision, municipality, county, and metropolitan region, and depending on the particular issue or even time of day, one affiliation matters more than another.[3]

Each resident in a metropolitan area has his or her own set of networks and no two persons' sets are exactly the same. Yet when layered on top of one another, the aggregation of individual networks reveals the multiple connections that make up the metropolis. When enough individualized networks of behavior overlap and converge in particular places, when enough people make a particular place — say, the mall — a regular part of their lives, then that place becomes what urban planner Kevin Lynch calls a "node." These nodes need not be universal.[4] Airports are nodes for business travelers, schools are nodes for children, office parks are nodes for office workers. Any place that enough people frequent can become a node. To recognize the existence of such places, then, is to recognize that the city is a complex and dynamic environment where the independent decisions of thousands of individuals combine to produce a collective hierarchy of spaces and places. From city block to neighborhood to subdivision to township to city limits to metropolitan area, a contemporary city centers and aligns people's lives at a variety of levels.[5]

The stories of Shirley Volz and George Kuhn dramatize two opposing, concurrent trends that defined Indianapolis over the twentieth century. One trend was a realignment of personal space, where individuals and families chose to define their own particular communities and particular cultures, usually increasingly farther away from the city center. The counter-trend was an ongoing effort to imagine the city as one community, drawn together and symbolized by one city center. To understand the role of religion in Indianapolis, to gain insight into big questions about church and state, cultural pluralism, civil religion, or secularization, we must first understand how religion helped to shape and was shaped by these countervailing trends. In the massive urban realignment of the twentieth century, religion's role was redefined both in the particular communities where people lived and in the city center that symbolized their common lives and shared values. So although this book is primarily about religious change in the city, it must begin with an explanation of the urban realignment that formed the context for religious restructuring.

URBAN CENTERS AS LANDSCAPES AND CULTURESCAPES

Cities are centers unto themselves, particularly when considered in their national context. At the broadest level, we tend to conceive of the United States and even the world as having distinct "capitals" for specific activities. Hollywood is the "entertainment capital of the world," New York the "financial capital." At the beginning of the last century, Carl Sandburg cemented Chicago's reputation as "Hog Butcher for the World."

Indianapolis is the country's twelfth largest city, but it is far more typical of urban America than behemoths like New York, Los Angeles, and Chicago. Like many mid-sized cities, Indianapolis has long lacked a definable industrial reputation. In the early twentieth century, the city ranked second to Detroit for automobile manufacturing and was home to several headquarters including the Stutz Motor Car Company and the Duesenberg Motors Company. But many of these closed down or were relocated over the years and, although the buildings remained, the reputation did not. The same might be said of insurance, as Indianapolis ranks second to Hartford for the number of insurance company headquarters. But insurance does not define Indianapolis the way it does Hartford.

In the 1970s, Indianapolis's civic leadership sought to bolster its national reputation by imagining the city as the nation's "amateur sports capital." Heartened by an apparent lack of competition, the city embarked on a plan to attract national sports federations and to build several world-class sporting facilities that could hold national and international events. The plan succeeded with a combination of public and private financing. Following construction of a new track and field stadium, a new natatorium, and a new soccer field, the sports vision was realized in the 1987 Pan American Games, which presented the "new" Indianapolis to the world. But even with this notoriety, a reputation as amateur sports hub somehow lacked the zing of being the country's automobile or entertainment capital. In fact, by the 1990s, the term was rarely used to market Indianapolis, despite the city's ongoing efforts that eventually resulted in the NCAA headquarters relocating there. "Amateur sports" seemed at times like the large-city equivalent of a small town's boast of having the largest corn silo. Nice, but not quite big-league.

To many, the desire to recreate Indianapolis as a national capital for something, for anything, seems to have been the number one priority of civic boosters for the past half-century. Support for these efforts frequently came from the Lilly Endowment, perhaps the strongest institution supporting the inward, centering forces that insisted Indianapolis would have a unified metropolitan identity. The Endowment is legally separate from, but the largest single stockholder in, the city's largest employer and taxpayer, pharmaceutical manufacturer Eli Lilly and Company. The company has a workforce of several thousand, including many professional researchers, scientists, marketers, and executives. It therefore has a substantial stake in making Indianapolis a place where such people would want to live. The Lilly Endowment has the resources to make this a reality by sponsoring or subventing the construction of sporting arenas, convention centers, museums, and public gathering places in downtown shopping malls. What benefits the company benefits the Endowment, and vice versa, and both provide enormous economic resources to Indianapolis as a whole.

Civic Centers Symbolizing Common Bonds

No matter how spread out contemporary cities may seem, they always contain civic centers that are identifiable locally, and perhaps even recognizable nationally or globally. One or two classical images usually come to mind for most major cities: for New York, Times Square; for Washington, D.C., the U.S. Capitol; for Paris, the Eiffel Tower; for London, the Clock Tower and Houses of Parliament. These are central civic spaces recognized as symbols by insiders and outsiders alike; they show up on postcards and are featured in the coffee table books produced by chambers of commerce. Indianapolis has three such civic symbols: Monument Circle, the War Memorial Mall, and the Indianapolis Motor Speedway.

Monument Circle's history as Indianapolis's pre-eminent civic space dates to the original founding of the city, as described in the introduction. It was part of the symmetrical plan to build the symbolic circle within the mile square. But it is worth noting that the founders' vision was never fully realized. No first family ever actually lived in the governor's house. Esther Ray, wife of Governor James Grown Ray, refused to live in the house because she felt uncomfortable living "in the round," having no privacy to hang her

Fig. 2.1. Soldiers and Sailors Monument with Christmas Decorations, ca. 1960.
Bass Photo Company Collection, courtesy Indiana Historical Society.

laundry. The Circle's interior experienced many uses, most notably as a public park, before the construction of the Soldiers and Sailors Monument in the late 1880s cemented the Circle's reputation as the symbol of Indianapolis. An elaborate obelisk set amid fountains and statuary, the Monument quickly became the city's dominant civic space, hosting parades, public celebrations, political rallies, and even religious services like those at Easter sunrise.

Over the twentieth century, Monument Circle had an up-and-down career: down when the energy and money seems to move away from the city center, but up during periods of central revitalization. A city ordinance in 1905 declared that no building should be built higher than the Monument, a law similar to Philadelphia's informal agreement not to build structures higher than William Penn's statue. After World War I, commercial interests spurred the city council to amend this regulation and allow buildings to rise above the Monument. Over the next few decades, new buildings on the Circle and beyond began to dwarf the Monument, and by the 1950s, the place had lost much of its symbolic value. In the 1970s, as part of a larger attempt to revitalize downtown, civic leaders announced plans to brick the Circle and restore its elegance with plans that included the annual lighting of the World's Largest Christmas Tree. That revitalization continues to the present and Monument Circle has regained its symbolism as the center of Indianapolis.

A few blocks north of Monument Circle sits Indianapolis's second important civic center, the Indiana World War Memorial Plaza. In 1919, shortly after the American Legion was founded, Indiana campaigned to bring the group's headquarters to Indianapolis. As part of the agreement to build a memorial to World War I veterans, the city set aside two city blocks for the future site. By 1926, construction began on the Memorial, which was situated immediately between two of the city's historic churches. Construction occurred intermittently over the next three decades, stalled occasionally by a lack of funding. In the 1950s, amidst a new push to complete the Memorial, the city bought the land of First Baptist and Second Presbyterian Churches, both of which relocated to the city's northern suburbs. With the church land now available, the Memorial was expanded and completed by 1965. In addition to the Memorial itself, the Plaza included fountains and open green spaces with walkways. One area was set aside for flying state flags. In the 1990s, the Plaza was further expanded to include memorials to veterans of World War II, the Korean War, and the Vietnam War.

Originally envisioned as a place to remember national events, the War Memorial has evolved into a civic rallying point. It serves as home for Fourth of July festivals, Memorial Day and Veterans Day services, and is a prime location along the city's downtown parade routes. Although it is not as easily recognizable as Monument Circle, the Plaza is still the locus for events of special civic significance, a place where the civic memory can be brought to the fore for a few brief moments during the year.

Indianapolis's third civic center is of an entirely different breed from the neoclassical architecture of the monuments and memorials. The Indianapolis Motor Speedway, located in the west side suburban town of Speedway, is the city's most famous, most globally recognized landmark. Although dedicated to a narrow segment of the population interested in auto racing, the Speedway has a wider appeal as a symbol of Indianapolis. For much of the twentieth century, the Speedway held only one race, the Indianapolis 500 on Memorial Day weekend. For one month out of the year, the attention of the entire world of auto racing focused on Indianapolis and the Speedway. Hundreds of thousands of fans made the pilgrimage to the open lots at 16th Street and Georgetown Road, parking their campers and trailers for the month of May. They watched as legends were made and technology advanced. On qualifying day, and even more on race day, the throngs of fans

Fig. 2.2. Indiana War Memorial. Bass Photo Company Collection, 228146, courtesy Indiana Historical Society.

made local streets impassable. Journalists transmitted the local activities to audiences around the world. By the mid-1990s, fractures in the auto racing world threatened to reduce the significance of the Indianapolis 500, but the addition of two new races from the NASCAR and Formula One racing series brought renewed attention to the Speedway in other months.

Although the Speedway's primary activities — racing — occupy the facilities for only three months out of the year, in the other nine months the structure stands empty but not forgotten. Instead, the Speedway serves as the city's defining feature, a "must-see" destination for out-of-town guests. Tourists can visit a museum documenting the history of the Speedway and can even take a tour bus around the famed racetrack. The route of Indianapolis's annual mini-marathon includes a circuit around the 2.5-mile oval. Business conventions often use a racing theme in their logos. When the U.S. Treasury decided to mint quarters recognizing each of the fifty states,

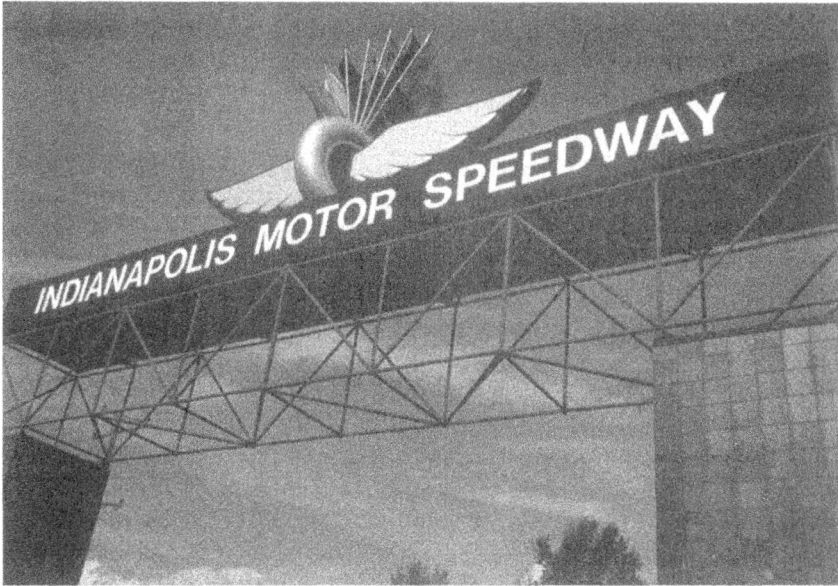

Fig. 2.3. Indianapolis Motor Speedway. Courtesy Indiana Historical Society.

there was little doubt that the Hoosier quarter would feature an Indy-style racing car.

Monument Circle, the War Memorial Plaza, and the Indianapolis Motor Speedway are touchstones by which the city is identified. In many ways, they represent the inward push toward centralization, toward imagining the city as a shared, common enterprise. But few people's everyday lives and activities revolve around these public symbols. Lives are lived in the work, commercial, and recreational spaces that are part of each daily routine. The urban realignment of the twentieth century has meant that these spaces are less and less tightly tied to the city's symbolic center.

Work and Commerce

As in most cities, Indianapolis's downtown was the region's employment hub for most of the twentieth century. Here stood the city's only high-rise office buildings, which housed the major banks, insurance companies, and law firms. On the western edge of downtown, the entire machinery for Indiana's state government employed thousands of people. But if downtown Indianapolis was the primary location for office-oriented employment, factory work was always located elsewhere in the county. Industrial zones, including stockyards, automobile factories, chemical firms, and other manufacturing concerns rising from the landscape, rose up on the west and south sides of the city in the early 1900s. When the New York Central relocated its rail yards from Brightwood to Beech Grove, the locus of railroad-connected employment shifted as well. In the 1950s, an industrial complex was created on the far east side along Shadeland Avenue, where workers manufactured cars for Chrysler and Ford and telephones for Western Electric.

By the 1980s, new office parks on the northwest and northeast side of the county were created to house light industry, warehousing, and office employment. About the same time, Indianapolis's only "edge city" type of development was created on the far north side at Keystone at the Crossing, a combination office park–shopping mall–hotel complex located at the crossroads of I-465, Keystone Avenue, and 82nd Street. All of these outlying developments meant that, by 1986, the amount of suburban office space surpassed that of downtown's office space.[6] While downtown remained the single largest employment center, it was only one of many in the county at the end of the twentieth century. Work had literally been decentered in the new alignment of population and infrastructure.

Commercial activity realigned even more drastically during this period. By the 1920s, local neighborhood commercial districts had developed on the periphery of Indianapolis, including small commercial corridors along 38th Street on the north side, along Washington Street in Irvington on the east side, and in Fountain Square on the south side. These districts allowed local residents to obtain goods and services without traveling downtown. For higher order goods and services, however, people still had to travel to the city center to department stores such as L. S. Ayres or William Block's. As late as 1957, more than 80 percent of consumers in Indianapolis made most of their major household purchases at downtown stores. That year, a survey of consumer spending habits showed that shoppers overwhelmingly went downtown to purchase home furnishings, women's shoes and dresses, and men's shirts and ties. Interestingly, the only two categories with a sizable number of neighborhood shoppers were "major appliances" and "children's shoes." By 1960, the city's central business district brought in an estimated $260 million in retail sales.[7]

But even as the 1957 data were being published, the opposite trend was gaining steam. In 1950, the Town and Country Shopping Center opened at 4400 North Keystone. A small shopping outlet by contemporary standards at only 100,000 square feet, Town and Country nonetheless offered a different shopping experience than could be found downtown. In a single compact area, one could find a variety of stores—and park for free. Two years later, a larger project was studied by the national urban planning firm of Homer Hoyt Associates. The Meadows shopping center at 38th Street was portrayed as a potentially strong competitor to the downtown shopping district, particularly "if shoppers can buy here practically everything that is available both in downtown Indianapolis and in local neighborhood centers, and if they can avoid central business district congestion and park near the stores." According to Hoyt, with the presence of Indianapolis's major department stores, together with apparel stores new to the city and a handful of other smaller specialty shops, "there would be little reason for families in northern and eastern Indianapolis or in Washington, Lawrence, Pike or Warren Townships to go to downtown Indianapolis for any major purchases. The convenience of ample free parking and the ease of shopping in one location with stores grouped around a mall from which all automobile traffic is excluded, would be a powerful attraction that would bring most of the middle and higher income families in northern and eastern Indianapolis to the Meadows for most of their shopping needs."[8]

Hoyt's predictions proved on target. Within the next decade and a half, almost twenty shopping malls opened around Indianapolis. The typical mall was located about five and a half miles from downtown, offered more than 260,000 square feet of selling space, and made almost 2,000 free parking spaces available to shoppers. By 1967, downtown's share of area retail sales had declined to $214 million, only one-fifth of the retail activity in the region.[9] The siphoning of economic activity was further hastened in 1968 with the opening of Lafayette Square, Indianapolis's first major enclosed shopping mall. Located at 38th Street and Lafayette Road on the city's northwest side, Lafayette Square had more than a million square feet of shopping space spread over an eighty-five-acre site. The success of Lafayette Square was followed by the opening of Castleton Square on the northeast side in 1972 and Washington Square on the far east side in 1974.

Today, Indianapolis has four major regional malls, one on each side of the county, as well as dozens of smaller shopping malls scattered throughout the region. In the 1990s, a fifth mall was added to this mix, located in the very place where the city's commercial activity began. Circle Center Mall had been envisioned as the retail anchor that would spark downtown's revival in the 1980s and 1990s. After much delay and several years as a big hole in the ground, the project was completed in 1994. As expected, Circle Center Mall became a major commercial concern and downtown has once again become a hub of commercial activity, though now one among many.

Recreation

Recreational opportunities have been scattered around Indianapolis and Marion County even longer than work and commerce. Some of the most popular recreational facilities in the early twentieth century were amusement parks. Riverside Amusement Park, located at 30th Street and the White River, opened in 1903 with mechanical rides and attractions similar to those found in New York City's Coney Island amusement parks. Three years later, two other parks opened, Wonderland Amusement Park on the east side and White City Amusement Park on the north side in Broad Ripple Park. Capitalizing on the national amusement park craze, all three parks tried to provide the scariest rides and most exotic exhibits. But as was true throughout the national amusement park craze, they were not built in the safest manner. An electrical short caused the mostly wooden White City to burn down in 1908, and a similar accident destroyed Wonderland in 1911. A later incarnation of White City, renamed Broad Ripple Amusement Park, appeared in the 1920s. For the next few decades, both parks provided space for recreation, as they added swimming pools, roller skating rinks, and dance halls to their assortment of rides and attractions. In 1945, however, Broad Ripple Amusement Park closed. Riverside lasted for three more decades, but a combination of rising crime in the Riverside neighborhood and a history of protests from blacks who never forgot the park's former "whites only" policies led to the park's closing in 1970.

Part of the initial popularity of amusement parks came from providing some of the few leisure opportunities in Indianapolis. But by the 1920s other recreational institutions were emerging around the city. Bowling became popular, with more than eighty-eight different leagues operating during a typical winter season in the 1920s. A local survey of recreation and leisure reported that Indianapolis had 280 billiard rooms, more than any other city of its size. One of the most popular leisure activities was attending movies. According to the survey, more than 200,000 patrons attended the theater each week, a sizable number for a city with about 350,000 people. As happened in other cities like Chicago, where movie theaters played a prime role in linking local life to a national mass culture, Indianapolis's movie theaters brought the world into the city's neighborhoods.[10] More than two-thirds of the city's sixty-four theaters were scattered throughout the city, with the rest concentrated downtown. The downtown theaters, such as Circle Theatre on Monument Circle and the Murat on North New Jersey Street, tended to be more opulent and larger, with ten having seating capacities of more than a thousand. In contrast, neighborhood theaters were smaller (eighteen local theaters held fewer than 500 people each, and none held more than 1,500) and less extravagant. They were, however, nearby, and for the average moviegoer a trip to the theater was not a major excursion downtown, but rather a part of neighborhood life. Many of the theater buildings still exist as symbols of an earlier phase of urban community. In Indianapolis, as in other cities, local entrepreneurs routinely attempted theater renovations in hopes of creating renewed space for community socializing.

The landscape of Indianapolis's professional non-motor sports has followed a somewhat different pattern. Apart from the Speedway, its first professional stadium (for baseball) — Victory Field (later renamed Bush Stadium) — was located northwest of downtown on the banks of the White

River at 16th Street, tucked between an industrial warehouse district and a residential neighborhood. There, the Indianapolis Indians played at the country's highest minor league level. From the 1930s to the 1970s, Indianapolis's minor-league hockey franchise played in the Coliseum, located on the Indiana State Fairgrounds at 38th Street North.

Today, the city's sports scene continues to have multiple locations, but, in the end, professional sports came to be defined as a common, public enterprise, and the centralizing trend determined their downtown location in the mile square. A new Victory Field on the western edge of downtown stands as one of minor league baseball's best stadiums. Across the street from Victory Field is the RCA Dome, formerly known as the Hoosier Dome, home to the National Football League's Indianapolis Colts since the team moved from Baltimore in 1984. Like football stadiums across the nation, in major cities and college towns, the Dome becomes the city's focal point on Sunday afternoons, as fans converge for tailgating parties and a game.

Also downtown, the new Conseco Fieldhouse has replaced Market Square Arena as home to the National Basketball Association's Indiana Pacers and has become the symbolic heart for basketball throughout basketball-crazed Indiana. Critics have applauded the Fieldhouse's throwback décor and its steadfast refusal to look like a cookie-cutter stadium. A basketball museum fills the corridors of the Fieldhouse and allows fans to revel in their state's pride and joy.

CULTURAL ALIGNMENT

So far we have seen — in work, commerce, and recreation — the countervailing inward and outward trends as they defined the literal space of the city. Some things, like shopping malls and movie theaters and office buildings, arose away from the downtown, becoming part of the city's regions and neighborhoods where people lead their lives in their personal, elective communities. Other things, like sports, government, the city's patriotic memorials, and many of the larger business headquarters, occupied the city's center and helped to define the metropolis as a common concern.

To focus only on the use of space would be misleading, though. Cities have cultural centers, or perhaps more accurately they have different social groups that occupy, organize, and align cultural, economic, political, and civic life. Two related, countervailing trends are also at work here. On one side is a set of elite civic leaders, the pillars of community around which twentieth-century Indianapolis was built. On the other side are the multiple other cultural groups, many of which were generally excluded from civic and political power, who have gradually assumed their places at the table. If spatial realignment in the city is born of the interplay between inward-moving, centralizing forces and outward-moving, personalizing ones, cultural realignment is driven by the ongoing negotiation between the old establishment and the city's many other cultural blocs.

Upper-class, native-born Protestant whites have long sat at the cultural core of Indianapolis. As the city's "founding fathers" and their heirs, this group controlled the city's civic and economic life for the first half of the twentieth century and continues to wield great influence. These individuals attended the same churches and social clubs, sat on the same philanthropic boards, and felt responsible for the direction of the city. The extent to which this group was interconnected is seen through analysis of their business and social networks. Throughout the twentieth century, at least one-quarter to one-half of the city's elite, defined here as members of boards of directors of several leading civic and economic institutions, belonged to either the Columbia Club or the Indianapolis Athletic Club. They sat on each other's boards, including those of the Lilly Endowment, the Indianapolis Water Company, the Chamber of Commerce, and the city's various banks. They also shared religious orientations, mostly revolving around the most prestigious Presbyterian, Methodist, Episcopalian, or Baptist churches. They used these formal and informal relationships to transform Indianapolis over the twentieth century.

Consider two examples. In 1932 Fred G. Appel, a member of the Indiana National Bank board of directors, borrowed $25,000 in cash from the institution to buy savings books from individuals who were anxious about their money's security. The accounts Appel bought that day were held by the Railroadmen's Savings & Loan, a financial firm he also served as a member of its board of directors. While certainly a generous personal gesture on his part, Appel's efforts to buy the savings books made smart business sense, since he halted a run on the Savings & Loan that might have crippled the institution and led to serious credit problems throughout Indianapolis.[11]

In 1979, James E. Browning, president of one of Indianapolis's largest architectural firm, and William K. McGowan, Jr., president of the Indianapolis Convention and Visitors Association, flew to Syracuse to look at the Carrier Dome, the large domed stadium on the campus of Syracuse University. They thought a similar dome would fit into an open lot just south of the Indiana convention center. They worked with James Morris, vice president of the Lilly Endowment and president of the Indianapolis Water Company, to facilitate a $25 million grant from the Endowment for the construction project. They worked with Deputy Mayor David Frick to assemble the land parcels. And within five years, Indianapolis had a new domed stadium and a new football team relocated from Baltimore.

Both of these examples make clear the way Indianapolis's elite networks influence the city's public choices. In the former, Fred Appel used his own relationships to accomplish his goal of security for the city's financial institutions. In the latter, the participation of several individuals and groups helped oversee the revitalization of downtown Indianapolis through the construction of a sports stadium. In both cases, the activities were facilitated by the informal relationships built on shared social and economic backgrounds.

Simultaneous with the direction of Indianapolis by its elite core, other cultural groups — defined by race, ethnicity, and often religion — continued to grow, and the activities of each of these groups revolved around an axis that served as its own center. The city's African American community, for example, was largely peripheral to the machinations of those at the civic core, yet the community had a recognized, if sometimes ill-defined, axis organized around religious and political participation in the civil rights movement of the 1940s through the 1960s. From NAACP leader William B. Ransom to Baptist minister and social critic Dr. Andrew J. Brown, a coalition of activist churches and political groups spoke on behalf of African Americans as an interest group.

Two other similar cultural blocs deserve special note. Throughout the period of mainline Protestants' social and cultural power, Indianapolis's Catholics built their own "shadow" institutions capable of supporting a large community that had been ostracized by the Ku Klux Klan in the 1920s and largely left out of civic leadership until the post–World War II period. Parochial primary schools in most neighborhoods, multiple high schools with metropolitan-wide reach, Catholic hospitals, and a growing Catholic Charities movement that came to embrace a wide range of social services were all part of an institutionalized, separate-but-formidable Catholic presence in the city. Smaller but also well-organized was the Indianapolis Jewish community. Through the development of a Jewish Federation, a Jewish Community Center, retirement housing, facilities for immigrants and refugees, and eventually a Hebrew Academy, the city's Jews also created a set of shadow institutions that allowed them to operate as a separate religious and cultural center.

URBAN REALIGNMENT AND MULTIPLE METROPOLITAN CENTERS

As we have already glimpsed, the relationship between urban culture and urban space is constantly being renegotiated and realigned due to changing tastes and behaviors, to be sure, but also due to historical circumstance beyond any individual's control. An athletic stadium might act as a focus of regional identity when the home team wins championships on a regular basis; when the local team plays poorly and attendance declines, the arena can lose that role. A local pub can act as a community organization in a working-class neighborhood, serving as the place for locals to unwind at the end of the day. But if the nearby factory shuts down and the jobs disappear, that same pub gradually loses its ability to generate social capital.

The nodes around which communities gathered in the early twentieth century were rarely the same as those operating at the end of the century. Other intervening factors, such as highway construction, slum clearance, suburbanization, and deindustrialization, all changed patterns of behavior and disrupted people's social and economic networks. Cultural blocs change too. Elite groups in one period might not wield the same influence a generation later. Immigration and assimilation contribute to these changes, as do national and local migration patterns.

The experience of the Indianapolis elite demonstrates the often ephemeral nature of centrality, both cultural and physical, as it underwent considerable change and even fragmentation over the course of the twentieth century. Consider that in 1930, Indianapolis stood out as Indiana's largest and most important city, but was relatively unconnected to a larger national network of metropolitan regions. It might have functioned as the central point of information and materials for Indiana, but cities like Chicago, Detroit, and St. Louis surpassed Indianapolis in terms of national relevance. The city was big enough to have several major industries and financial institutions, but unlike larger cities, Indianapolis's major companies were primarily homegrown and focused on the Indianapolis and Indiana markets. In 1930, more than 90 percent of the city's elites worked for an Indianapolis-based company, and more than half were members of these companies' founding families. Because there were fewer large-scale firms compared to a larger metropolis, the number of men at the top of the economic ladder was relatively small. In addition, the city's small size also limited the number of social institutions for elite participation. As "big fish in a small pond," Indianapolis's elites were a tight-knit group whose business and social activities overlapped in many places.

After World War II, Indianapolis's connections to the rest of the United Sates began to grow. The city remained a dominant force in Indiana, but the local economy was connected not only to Fort Wayne, Evansville, and Terre Haute, but also to St. Louis, Detroit, and Chicago. As industrial and financial leaders sought to increase Indianapolis's national connections, they created a situation that led to their own fragmentation. Non-local companies discovered Indianapolis and began to increase their presence in the city by transferring "white-collar" executives to Indianapolis to oversee branch offices of national firms. In some cases, non-local owners bought out Indianapolis's homegrown companies and brought in new management. Although these kinds of activities raised Indianapolis's stature, they also meant that different kinds of people would be leading the changes.

These new "captains" of Indianapolis were less likely to have been raised in Indiana, to have imbibed "Hoosier" values, or to have embraced a traditional midwestern sense of "localism" that pervaded the region earlier in the century. In addition, the fact that these companies were no longer locally owned meant that their leadership was less tied to local activities. For example, in 1960, when the Indianapolis Civic Progress Committee was formed as the forerunner of the Greater Indianapolis Progress Committee (GIPC), three-quarters of the group's board of directors were native Hoosiers and were involved in an average of eleven economic, social, and civic activities outside of the workplace. By 1976, only half of the thirty members of GIPC's executive committee had been born in Indiana, and the number of activities had fallen to nine. By 1990, only about one-quarter of GIPC's executive committee were Indiana natives and their local economic, social, and civic groups fell to an average of only five activities. As their collective local ties decreased, the cohesion of this elite core declined as well. Participation in social organizations outside of the workplace — such as country clubs, fraternal lodges, or other service organizations — fell between 1930 and 1990. Participation in Masonic lodges was particularly hard hit. In 1930 almost one-third of elites belonged to the same Masonic lodge and maintained ties to several other lodges. By 1990 the most popular Masonic organization captured only 5 percent of the cohort, and overall membership in any Masonic lodge was extremely low compared to 1930. This decline in association meant that elites had fewer opportunities to interact with one another outside of their workplace. This in turn created fewer opportunities for the informal networking that created links among elites. Intermarriage among elite families, a sure sign of informal relationships, decreased over time. Furthermore, the concentration of elites in a handful of churches, where they would have opportunities to "talk shop" on Sunday mornings, had dissipated by the 1990s.

To be sure, the changing nature of Indianapolis's elite reflected wider societal trends away from social participation. Since 1970 the average time spent at work for Americans has increased, and it is likely that local leaders simply had less time to devote to social organizations in 1990 than they might have had in 1930 or 1960. In addition, increasing emphasis on gender equality has reduced the social acceptance of single-sex social clubs such as fraternal organizations or Masonic lodges. With such organizations less accepted by society as a whole, elites might have consciously moved away from them, choosing instead to participate in family-oriented, or at least socially diverse, social activities.

Yet as Indianapolis's core became increasingly pluralistic, the elites who occupied that core were finding fewer reasons to come together. A network analysis of the city's elites revealed the growth in "cliques," or factions within the elite cohort, since 1930, when Indianapolis had only a few civic leadership groups, such as the Chamber of Commerce. That year, the cohort of elites formed one large network with no discernible cliques to drain power and resources away and affect the social cohesion of the larger body. By the 1970s, 1980s, and 1990s, the individuals who led Indianapolis were coming from different backgrounds, with new ideas and with sometimes

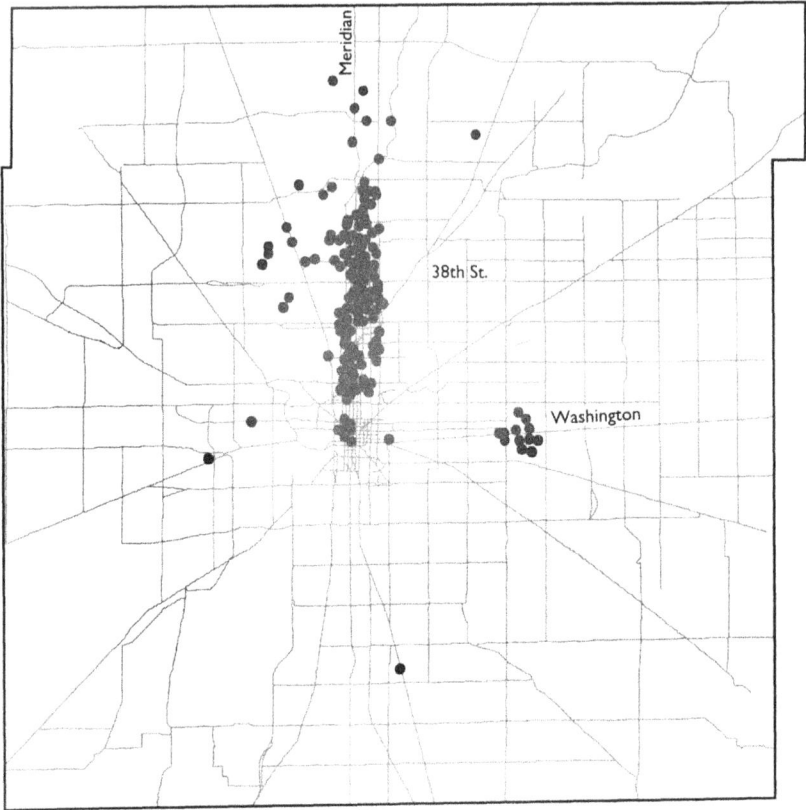

Map 2.1. Residences Listed in the Indianapolis Social Register, 1931.
Courtesy The Polis Center.

competing agendas. New organizations, such as the GIPC or the Corporate Community Council (CCC), and philanthropic bodies such as the Lilly Endowment or the Indianapolis Foundation, while not necessarily at odds with one another, nonetheless offered multiple venues for Indianapolis's civic leadership to wield influence.

Most recently, the emergence of a "new economy" has resulted in yet another evolution in the city's elite. With high-tech businesses replacing industrial companies or more traditional service firms, especially in insurance and banking, a new generation of civic leaders is poised to take over. Paralleling the nature of high-tech commerce, these leaders will likely have even less to do with each other on an ongoing basis, but rather will come together temporarily over single issues. Particular causes might rally groups of leaders who will then dissolve to form other groups for other causes.

In short, as Indianapolis became more global, the number of local businesses, and local people who headed these businesses, declined, a fact that did not go unnoticed in civic circles. In 1992, a plane crash took the lives of four of the men who had done the most to develop Indianapolis as a sports capital. A decade later, the city was still bemoaning the loss. Said the head of the Central Indiana Corporate Partnership, "There has been a significant decline in that kind of involvement and leadership. I don't think we have the group of dedicated, committed civic leaders we had 25 years ago."

The leadership of Indianapolis has changed, involving more people from outside the city and outside the old establishment network. Yet it is this very broadening, under the leadership of new and even "foreign" elites, which helped the city deal with the two tensions that define its realignment. The breaking of parochialism meant new growth and a broader picture of the world, one in which Indianapolis became a more cosmopolitan city rather than a great midwestern town.

It is important to note that this urban realignment is by no means simply a matter of one group taking over while another group recedes. Here the prime example is Unigov, the 1970 consolidation of Indianapolis and its surrounding suburban areas into a single unified metropolitan government. As a direct response by elites to what they perceived to be regional decentering and destabilization, its story deserves telling in some detail.

Unigov

As with virtually all American cities in the 1940s and 1950s, postwar suburban growth was changing the demographic and economic balance of power between Indianapolis and its surrounding suburbs. In 1940, only 16 percent of Marion County's population lived outside the Indianapolis city boundaries. Ten years later, the proportion rose to 23 percent, and by 1960, 32 percent of the county population lived outside the city. Along with the movement of people went the movement of institutions and — more important — social, cultural, and financial resources.

The impact on the downtown was dramatic. As mentioned earlier, the growing suburban ring was beginning to drain the downtown business core of much economic activity. The shifting population was also leaving a demographic mark on the central city, as entire neighborhoods flip-flopped racially and socioeconomically during the 1950s and 1960s. For example, in one census tract on the near north side, a black population of only 18 in 1960 grew to almost 4,400 people in 1970. While going from 99 percent white to 92 percent black, the proportion of two-parent families fell from 80 percent to 65 percent, the level of education fell from 12.2 to 11.4 years, and the poverty rate rose to 12 percent — well above the 7 percent rate for the rest of Indianapolis.

This decentering realignment of population affected not only Indianapolis's inner-city neighborhoods, but also the smaller rural areas on the metropolitan periphery. But as suburbanization took hold, many of the smaller rural communities that had existed as independent communities outside of Indianapolis through the first half of the twentieth century were woven into the larger metropolitan carpet. Even into the early 1940s these small towns had remained generally untouched by the big city. A 1941 description of the town of New Augusta, about ten miles northwest of downtown Indianapolis along Michigan Road, noted that many residents worked in defense industries elsewhere in Indianapolis. Although New Augusta was "practically a suburb" of Indianapolis, "the quiet of its shaded streets and the simplicity of its town life it appears to be an oasis of content in the midst of traffic, hurry-up, and confusion."[12] Within a few years, however, this quiet disappeared, largely because suburbanization brought a degree of middle-class cosmopolitanism that had been absent in these rural areas earlier.

As early as 1950, the differences between the old-timers and the newcomers were already becoming evident. That year, census data revealed that rural non-farm residents averaged more years of education than did rural farm residents (11.4 years to 10.1 years), and a higher proportion of non-farm residents had some high school or college education. The higher levels of education corresponded with a much higher proportion of non-farm residents working in professional or managerial positions (23.2 percent to 11.7 percent for men). It was also clear that Marion County's farms were unable to retain their young adults. In 1940, more than 20 percent of the rural farm population was between ages ten and nineteen. Ten years later, the cohort between ages twenty and twenty-nine accounted for only 10 percent of the population. At the other end of the age spectrum, the proportion of rural farm population over age sixty-five grew from 14 to 18 percent between 1940 and 1950.[13]

Some in the small communities were pleased to become part of the expanding city. Proponents of suburban expansion in the southeastern town of Wanamaker claimed that the town "can hardly wait to become a city and it isn't hesitating until the last minute to prepare for the change. It's willing — and eager — to expand into the metropolis. It would turn flip-flops in welcoming new industry and residents."[14] In Trader's Point, in the northwest part of the county, a new four-lane U.S. 52 highway that connected Indianapolis to Lafayette and beyond to Chicago sliced "the hamlet though the middle. All night, every night, huge trucks with the names of distant cities on their sides come roaring down into the village from the hills bordering each side of the Big Eagle Creek valley." When they passed through the village, these trucks found "filling stations, a garage, restaurants — all catering chiefly to whatever part of the highway traffic stops at their door."[15]

Others looked less kindly at the loss of independence and isolation. Those same trucks rumbling through Trader's Point also brought other problems. As new suburbanites move out, "an air of almost mutual suspicion" arose between newcomers and old-timers. Though they lived in the country, the newcomers were not fully of the country, preferring instead to maintain links to the city. Similarly, while some in Wanamaker were doing cartwheels over the new ties to Indianapolis, others lamented the disappearance of "one of the few places near Indianapolis where you can stand on your front porch and hear nothing but birds singing and the faint trickling of the brook that twists through the neighborhood and always seems nearby."[16]

For the most part, the language used by those in Marion County's rural communities focused on being economically and socially integrated into the larger Indianapolis region. They were not, however, thinking about political integration. Fifty years earlier, they might have been. In the late nineteenth and early twentieth centuries, the towns of Brightwood, Haughville, Mount Jackson, West Indianapolis, Irvington, Broad Ripple, and University Heights all merged with Indianapolis through annexation.[17] Over time, however, resistance to annexation increased and the city only occasionally added pieces of unincorporated and often undeveloped land. Thus, few in either the city or the changing suburbs spoke of formally joining city and suburb.

This changed in 1964, however, with the election of Democrat (and Catholic) John Barton as mayor. Barton had run on a platform of increasing the power of the office, and emphasized increasing the powers of annexation to strengthen the city center. Barton's election and his plans to expand the city outward raised eyebrows, particularly among suburban residents who had left the city and did not want to be dragged back into it. The Republican Party, which dominated the suburban areas of Marion County and was mainly mainline Protestant, also did not look kindly at the prospect of a strong Democratic mayor expanding his strongly Democratic central city into the periphery. Yet even among Republicans there was a sense that something had to be done to address the changing dynamics between the central city and the growing suburbs. They also realized that something had to be done to resurrect their political fortunes in the aftermath of Barry Goldwater's national presidential debacle and the local fragmentation of the Republican Party. The Republican Action Committee (RAC) was formed in 1966 to develop a plan both to win back the mayor's office and to find a solution to metropolitan change that was better than piecemeal annexation. Their conversations evolved into an idea for metropolitan consolidation whereby the city of Indianapolis and the suburbs of Marion County would be fused into a single governmental entity. Successful metropolitan consolidation had occurred in a number of cities in the 1950s and 1960s, including Toronto, Nashville, and Jacksonville, Florida. Bringing city and suburbs into a single unified government was seen as a way to achieve administrative efficiency, and was, in fact, an idea that had been talked about for Indianapolis in the 1940s and 1950s. To the RAC, however, consolidating city and county would also consolidate their party's power by bringing the mostly white and Republican suburban townships into a city political landscape dominated by mostly African Americans and the Democratic Center Township.

The RAC's short-term goal was accomplished over a three-year period beginning in 1966 when Republicans won control of the county council. The following year, Richard Lugar defeated Barton in the mayoral election and in 1968 Republicans swept the electoral slate for Marion County representatives to the Indiana General Assembly. With this mandate, Lugar set out to reorganize the city-county relationship. Through their study of Indiana's statutes concerning cities, Lugar and the RAC realized that metropolitan consolidation could be effected through the state legislature rather than through a vote of the participating municipalities. With Republican control of city and county and with strong influence in the state legislature, Lugar now had the ability to make his dream of consolidation a reality.[18] He wasted little time in launching his effort for consolidation, now referred to as Unigov or Unified Government.[19] The Indiana General Assembly's Unigov bill (c.173 SB 543) was sponsored by State Senators Borst and Rubin and Representatives Lamkin and Mills. The bill passed with mostly Republican support, but also with the support of Indiana's other metropolitan counties. Legislators from Allen, Delaware, Lake, Marion, St. Joseph, and Vanderburgh counties all voted for the measure, and their county chairmen started dreaming of the day when they could request similar legislation.[20]

On January 1, 1970, Unigov became a reality. No longer were the city and county separate entities. Instead, a single mayor oversaw the entire area. In place of forty separate municipal departments, Unigov introduced five executive departments, including departments of Capital Asset Management, Metropolitan Development, Public Works, Public Safety, and Parks and Recreation.[21] Additionally, Unigov merged the city and county councils into one legislative body. And it increased the city's population by 50 percent, thus boosting Indianapolis into twelfth place on the list of largest cities in the country. Unigov seemed to solve the "decentering" of Indianapolis by redefining and enlarging the center to include the periphery as well. It seemed as if there would no longer be a center and periphery since they were now one and the same.

Not surprisingly, because Unigov was pushed through by a coalition of civic and political elites looking to place their stamp on Indianapolis, it was not met with universal acclaim. Many outside the city's elite understood that making Indianapolis into a larger administrative unit meant their own influence would be even more diluted. African Americans viewed Unigov as a plan to reduce their political opportunities since they made up a much smaller percentage of the newly united county than they had of the old central city. As whites were leaving downtown, blacks were gaining a strong-hold and, although not a majority in the old city boundaries, they still had the potential of being an important political force. Had Unigov not been enacted, for example, African Americans would have made up about 30 percent of the city population in 1970. With the larger metropolitan India-napolis bringing the white suburbanites into the same voting pool as the black city residents, the black proportion fell to 18 percent of the whole county. It is hard to measure the dilution of Catholic voting strength in such a straightforward manner, but it is worth noting that Unigov was fol-lowed by six consecutive mayoral terms — twenty-four years in total — shared by two mayors from the Methodist and Presbyterian wings of the Protestant establishment.

To be sure, Unigov reformed the election of the Common Council, switch-ing from at-large elections to single-member districts. The concentration of African Americans on the north side ensured that at least some districts would be heavily black and that some black candidates would be elected. In addition, Unigov's supporters claimed, the widening of the Indianapolis tax base to include the wealthier suburbs would have trickle-down benefit to the poorer parts of the old city. But these changes notwithstanding, other areas that did not get changed had an even greater impact on African Americans. For all its consolidation, Unigov did not merge the city and county school districts. This meant that the wealthier (and whiter) school districts of the northern part of Marion County did not have to share their resources with the poorer (and blacker) Indianapolis public schools. Police and fire protec-tion also remained in the hands of the local townships, ensuring that the city and county crime statistics would not be merged. Finally, welfare and social service provision remained a township responsibility rather than a city re-sponsibility, also ensuring that resources would not be transferred from wealthier to poorer areas. In short, from the perspective of the African American community — a group that was clearly outside the center of power in Indianapolis — Unigov represented a decision by those in civic leadership to realign the metropolitan center for their own good rather than for a larger common good.[22] Unigov suggested a new, shared center for an even larger city. In practice, though, it increased the sense that the city had multiple centers, each competing for their share of the civic pie. It acknowl-edged the outward, personalizing flow away from the downtown at the same time it tried to bring the farthest reaches of the metropolitan area into the fold.

Realignment through Multiple Regional Centers

Over the next two decades, Indianapolis centrophiles articulated their vision for a revitalized downtown through a series of Regional Center Plans. The idea for a planning strategy for downtown Indianapolis originated in a grant awarded to the Department of Metropolitan Development in 1970 by the federal Department of Housing and Urban Development. The main goal of the project, known as the Unified Planning Program, was to combat deterioration in the urban core by creating an environment hospitable to new development. Proposals in the program included creating more green space along the White River, renovating Union Station and Monument Circle, and redeveloping the City Market and the surrounding area. By 1978, with several of these proposals either completed or in process, a new Regional Center Plan was commissioned. Three years later, the new document, titled "Indianapolis 1980–2000 Regional Center General Plan," proposed to continue the downtown redevelopment through office construction, expansion of the convention center, creation of White River State Park, and a retail mall in the downtown core.

These downtown revitalization projects were developed in conjunction with the initiative to recreate Indianapolis as the nation's amateur sports capital, as discussed earlier. The proposed new sporting facilities would not only boost Indianapolis's national reputation, but would also provide a base around which other downtown development might occur — new restaurants, hotels, and nightlife. Between 1979 and 1989, the city, with the support of the Lilly Endowment, spent more than $125 million to develop a comprehensive sports infrastructure. This included a new natatorium and track and field stadium on the campus of Indiana University–Purdue University Indianapolis (IUPUI), a downtown skating pavilion, and the aforementioned Hoosier Dome.[23] In the 1990s, more money went to build a new minor league baseball stadium on the western edge of downtown and a new basketball arena on the southern edge.

As happened with Unigov, the Regional Center Plan and the emphasis on downtown sports facilities met with considerable opposition, especially from those who saw it as benefiting only a small core of civic and economic elites and a small portion of the region's physical space. One particularly biting critique came from the Downtown Development Research Committee, a private-citizens group who questioned the wisdom of downtown redevelopment programs. "The supposed benefits of Downtown Development for inner-city neighborhoods are non-existent," the committee argued. Downtown development was "merely pushing the poor into already-crowded neighborhoods in order to make room for richer residents of the projects themselves." The committee's report went on to criticize the cozy financial relationships between Indianapolis's economic and political powers, claiming, for example, how various downtown projects financially benefited those at the highest levels of the city, while the surrounding neighborhoods received nothing of value.

Although the Downtown Development Research Committee's report failed to stop the redevelopment of the business core, its criticism, along with that of other prominent officials such as United States Congressman Andy

Jacobs, was enough to give the civic powers pause in their plans for a third Regional Center Plan. In the RCPIII, the authors shifted their focus away from the downtown core and toward the neighborhoods, where they proposed to improve the everyday spaces in which Indianapolis residents lived. Other signs also pointed to a shift away from a downtown-focused planning program. In 1991, Stephen Goldsmith was elected mayor after running on a platform that included a desire to redirect attention into "Building Better Neighborhoods." Near the end of his administration, Goldsmith created the Front Porch Alliance, a program designed to foster close communication between the mayor's office and multiple local communities.

The rhetoric of Goldsmith's administration and of the new Regional Center Plan notwithstanding, many projects in the 1990s continued to have a strong central focus. That decade saw the development of Circle Center Mall adjacent to Monument Circle, the construction of a new downtown baseball stadium, and the expansion of White River State Park. If there was a difference in this phase of downtown development, it was that the newly revitalized downtown was now just one center among many throughout the Indianapolis region. Circle Center Mall provided downtown with just one of several regional malls spread around the county. The revitalization of the canal and the construction of White River State Park, Victory Field, an IMAX theater, and botanical gardens offered recreational activities in the core. Finally, downtown became more residential once again, with the erection of apartments and condominiums along the water on the west side of downtown and the gentrification of the Old Northside and the east side's Lockerbie Square. Now, those wanting an urban lifestyle found downtown as an appealing residential choice among many others in the county.

THE ONE AND THE MANY URBAN CENTERS

The shift in the 1990s away from downtown redevelopment toward the neighborhood reminds us that the tension runs both ways. Different — though not necessarily exclusive — communities will recognize different spatial boundaries and different sets of elites and leaders. To some identifiable degree, whites and blacks frequent different places in Indianapolis, as elsewhere. High- and low-income groups meet in different places. Immigrants have their own spaces, as do Jews, ethnic Catholics, and so on. Moreover, even when different groups see the same space as central, they will likely experience that space differently, imbuing it with different meanings and symbolism. Thus, an inner-city church that provides a food pantry for local residents means one thing for the church members who drive in from suburbia every Sunday morning, but something else for the neighborhood clients who receive food.

In contrast to the civic elite's orientation toward "downtown," many Indianapolis residents saw the revitalization of downtown as peripheral to their daily lives. We have already noted that with residential outward realignment came a realignment in work and commerce, which prompted the leadership's desire to strengthen the common, urban center. But for those whose lives were reconfigured on the periphery, downtown was just one more place in an increasingly sprawling region. More pertinent to their daily routine was the neighborhood, the residential spaces in which they lived.

In any city, the residential spaces serve as the primary locales for the lives of the individuals who live there. More to the point, neighborhoods represent central spaces where the physical and cultural aspects of a city come together. This is most evident in ethnic neighborhoods, places that have identifiable boundaries and a homogeneous population. Neighborhoods are often typified by their dominant racial or socioeconomic group. In earlier generations, one could speak of religious neighborhoods, although with the exception of one Jewish neighborhood, this is decreasingly so in Indianapolis. Few American cities now reflect the sharply defined religious neighborhoods of a Belfast or a Jerusalem.

Over the past half-century, American neighborhoods have undergone a considerable change due largely to mobility. In the 1960s, scholars described neighborhoods as "communities of limited liability" to suggest the replacing of deep social bonds among neighbors with more superficial temporary or single-issue relationships. Neighbors come together to address problems with crime or trash removal or school funding, but then go their separate ways. Yet even if people have fewer attachments to their particular residential spaces, neighborhoods still function as important centers, not the least because people still have to live somewhere. The fact remains that a house or apartment exists in a particular place in proximate relationship to other houses or apartments as well as to schools, businesses, factories, hospitals, churches, roads, parks, trash dumps, or any other physical entity. Plus, those physical spaces are filled with a variety of people who might or might not be the same as one another and who each have their own personal networks and cultural identities.

Finally, history plays a role, reminding us that physical spaces and cultural populations might or might not be the same as they were five, ten, or fifty years before. No city is static, and perhaps with the exception of small villages in remote settings, every place has undergone some sort of change. In America's inner cities, the most common transformation of the twentieth century has been the white-to-black, middle-class-to-lower-class change. On the rural edges of metropolitan areas, changes also occurred as farming towns became residential suburbs, and, in time, those suburbs themselves changed. As the novelist W. D. Wetherell described in his 1985 short story "The Man Who Loved Levittown," those who settled the suburban community in the 1950s watched as a new generation of suburbanites changed their town in the 1970s and 1980s.

Neighborhood life is easily overlooked in Indianapolis because the city lacks the geographical or ethnic cues that identify neighborhoods in other metropolitan regions. Unlike Cincinnati or Pittsburgh, where hills and rivers carve the city into distinct spaces, Indianapolis is topographically flat, and the few waterways that run through Marion County only occasionally interrupt the tabletop-like landscape. Unlike Chicago or Detroit, where hundreds of immigrant groups clustered in their own areas and developed distinct "ethnic" neighborhoods, Indianapolis is more socially homogeneous. The high point for the city's foreign-born population was 1910, and even then foreigners accounted for only 10 percent of the entire population. For the rest of the twentieth century, Indianapolis consistently ranked among the largest American cities with the lowest proportion of foreign-born residents. Yet despite the lack of cultural or geographical features that often contribute to neighborhood identity and solidarity, Indianapolis residents have still been able to create neighborhood centers to organize their lives. In 2000, almost 500 neighborhood associations were officially registered with the Indianapolis Neighborhood Resource Center.

As we shall see in Chapter 6, there is considerable variety among these neighborhoods and various ways of capturing it conceptually. As in virtually all American cities, a first cut might involve the four axes of history, geography, socioeconomic status, and race and ethnicity. Geographical categories include inner city, inner suburban, and outer suburban. These overlap with the historical categories of the oldest urban concentration, the early suburbs, and the more recent suburbs. Socioeconomic status includes high, middle, and low. Racial divisions are white, black, and mixed, since Indianapolis lacks any further ethnic separation. Our study focused especially on eighteen neighborhoods selected to represent a fair mixture of these categories, as described very briefly in the accompanying table.

Although Table 2.1 and the accompanying map (Map 2.2) seem clear enough in their own terms, there is an additional aspect of neighborhood life that is not included, namely, the recurring issue of multicentering through urban realignment — the tension between one urban center and the many locales where people choose to live their personal lives — at the core of this book. As we shall see later, some neighborhoods are far more cohesive — both centered and centering in their own right — than others. Moreover, different neighborhoods provide different kinds of "centers" for different sorts of people.

The term "multicentering" captures here again the tension surrounding urban realignment. Changes that some would say have decentered and destabilized the city seem to others to have recentered and restabilized it in a balance among multiple centers. The process of suburbanization, for instance, is sometimes described as destabilizing and decentering. People move *out* from the central city to the peripheral suburbs. Population declines in the center and grows on the margins. Businesses and other institu-

Table 2.1

Name	Geography	Socioeconomic Status	Race	Historical Trajectory
Mapleton–Fall Creek	Inner city	Low	Black	White, upper-class to black, lower-class
Martindale-Brightwood	Inner city	Low	Black	Separate white and black working-class to all-black lower-class
United Northwest Area	Inner city	Low	Black	Black middle-class to black lower-class
Near East Side	Inner city	Low	Mixed	Stable
Near West Side	Inner city	Low	Mixed	Stable
Mars Hill	Inner city	Low	White	Stable
Greater Southeast	Inner suburban	Low-Middle	White	Stable
Irvington	Inner suburban	Middle	Mixed	Stable
Crooked Creek	Inner suburban	Middle	Mixed	Stable
Butler-Tarkington	Inner suburban	Middle	Mixed	Stable
Broad Ripple	Inner suburban	Middle	White	Stable
Speedway	Inner suburban	Middle	White	Stable
Lawrence-Geist	Inner suburban/ Outer suburban	Middle-High	Mixed-White	Suburban/ Rural area to suburban
Carmel	Outer suburban	High	White	Rural town to suburban
Cumberland–Far East Side	Outer suburban	Middle	White	Rural to suburban
Greenwood	Outer suburban	Middle	White	Rural to suburban
Plainfield	Outer suburban	Middle	White	Rural to suburban

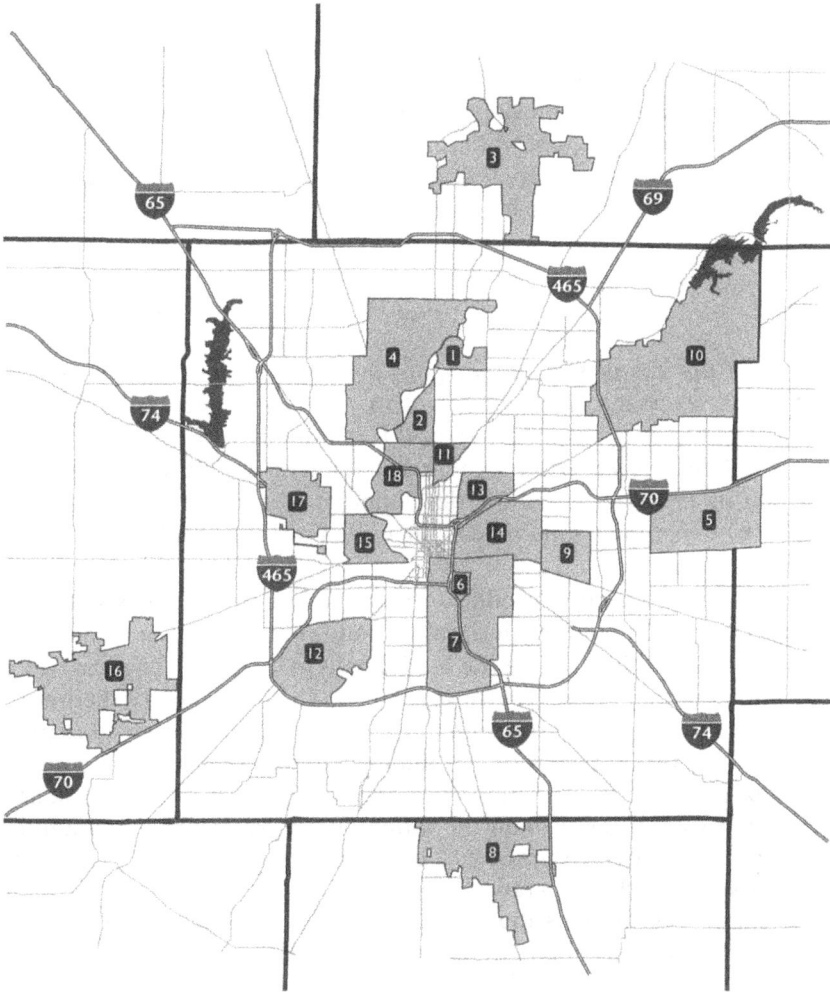

1.	Broad Ripple	10.	Lawrence
2.	Butler-Tarkington	11.	Mapleton–Fall Creek
3.	Carmel	12.	Mars Hill
4.	Crooked Creek	13.	Martindale-Brightwood
5.	Cumberland	14.	NESCO
6.	Fountain Square	15.	WESCO
7.	Southeast Side	16.	Plainfield
8.	Greenwood	17.	Speedway
9.	Irvington	18.	UNWA

Map 2.2. Eighteen Neighborhoods Studied by the Project on Religion and Urban Culture. Courtesy The Polis Center.

tions leave urban neighborhoods for suburban ones. But suburbanization can also be described as a recentering form of realignment. Rather than looking at the movement of individuals or institutions outward, we can look at the regions they were moving *to*. Such places might once have been isolated and independent, but with new growth they became absorbed into a growing metropolitan region, losing some of their individual identity while assuming a new identity as part of a whole that is larger, if more diffuse.

MOVING AHEAD

Most of the changes in Indianapolis over the last century occurred in other cities across the country too. Indianapolis saw its geographical center rise, fall, and rise again in importance. It saw its circle of elite civic leadership broadened, even at the expense of some of the old establishment's centralizing leverage. It saw the development of multiple communities — bound by geography, sometimes, but united also by ethnicity, race, and theological tradition.

Some readers may find it odd to focus so much on the city's structural changes in a book about religion, culture, and community. But we believe it would be odder still to ignore the hard details of the city's historical trajectory when thinking about just those subjects. The discussion of theoretical issues like pluralism or civil religion or secularization too often takes place in a historical vacuum. How can we understand the contemporary configuration of urban community until we understand how it came to look as it does? How can we understand the difference between local communities and the metropolis envisioned as a common enterprise unless we see the forces that forged that separation at work?

Even practical concerns about the relationship between church and state or about the purported loss of social capital cannot be considered apart from structural changes in the city. "Religion" and "community" are not merely abstract ideas. They are embodied in real practices that are intimately intertwined with facts about where people reside, what institutions they live their lives in, and how those institutions have changed over time.

The city's structural realignment raises important questions about the city's culture. Did Indianapolis retain a coherent civic identity tied to the centralizing trend, and if so, did that identity shift from one set of meanings and symbols to another? Or is identity now found only in the multiple centers, the smaller, elective, personal communities defined by the outward trend? It is here that the specific story of religion in Indianapolis moves toward the fore. As the city realigned, much everyday religious practice moved outward with the flow of population, helping to forge the identity of particular communities with specific sets of interests. At the same time, though, the city's broadest civic identity continued to be shaped both by the religious traditions of its leaders and by an evolving civil religion that mixed those traditions with others that had once been outside the fold, only to have both blended with less traditionally religious ideas and sentiments. To understand the cultural response to urban realignment, we must see religion's changing role first in civic life, then in the multiple faith traditions, and finally in the local congregations and neighborhoods where life is played out.

3

RELIGIOUS CIVILITY,
CIVIL RELIGION

As a community, Indianapolis has stood, and still stands, for the best
things in life, for the broad culture that includes all the elements of
good education, religion, law, patriotism, self-sacrifice, helpfulness for
the poor and unfortunate, and the abiding idea of leaving the world
better than they found it. This is the character of Indianapolis. Let our
slogan for the future be "a bigger city if God wills, but always and under
all circumstances a better city."

—speech at Centennial Celebration, June 5, 1920

In the summer of 1915, the leaders of the Indianapolis Church Federation — representing mainline Protestants throughout the city — published
an "open letter" to the mayor in the *Indianapolis News*. Describing the city as
"wide-open," they complained in dramatic fashion that "the saloons are
generally permitted to remain open at will. The unlawful winerooms, which
are veritable death traps to scores of young boys and girls, continue their
nefarious business unmolested." Most disturbing, "the houses of prostitution and assignation, with few exceptions, have been undisturbed, though
they are outlawed in this city and state."[1] The leaders of the Church Federation knew of what they spoke, for they had literally taken to the streets in
their investigation of the city's seamier side.

Seventy-five years later, on an August day in 1990, a group of African
American clergy gathered at the front steps of the city's central police station, where together with laymen and laywomen they protested police vio-

lence against African Americans.[2] Established in the 1960s at a time of rapid social and political change, Concerned Clergy has for the past four decades provided a voice for African Americans in the public square. And in their quest to be heard, the clergy have frequently taken their religion to the streets.

Although these episodes both represent expressions of religion in Indianapolis's public life, they would seem to have little else in common. In 1915 the city's most prominent white Protestant laymen and clergy, men who wielded heavy political, economic, and social clout, led the Church Federation. By contrast, in 1990 the Concerned Clergy was led by African American ministers who held considerable moral authority within their own communities but who exerted much less influence on the wider public than the Church Federation leaders had. Even more revealing, the Church Federation used its power to bring city vices to the attention of public authorities; the Concerned Clergy's object of protest was public authority itself. Despite these differences, both groups shared one important element: *both claimed the city, the entire city, as their responsibility*. The Church Federation never questioned that it was their right and responsibility to shape the public order, and much like their Puritan forefathers they envisioned the city as a single corporate body over which they held moral guardianship. Although Concerned Clergy did not assume that theirs was the only or even the most authoritative voice in the public square, its members also believed that the civic life of the city was a domain over which they should wield moral authority, and like the Church Federation leaders, they demanded that civic leadership listen to them.

In recent years there has been extensive discussion of the actual and appropriate roles of religion in public life, but the importance of moral civic leadership is rarely explored. Instead, headlines are given to controversial issues such as prayer in the public schools, Christmas crèches on public property, the government's role concerning religiously freighted issues like abortion, and most recently, the rightful place of "faith-based initiatives" in providing social services and amelioration. For most people, conceptions of religion and civic life include only those attempts to infuse religious practices and symbols into public life, or to use the power of the state to promote a particular religious viewpoint or practice. But social justice campaigns such as the 1960s civil rights movement were also expressions of religion in the public arena. When we imagine the "public presence" of religion more broadly to include, among other things, efforts to "help shape the public morality on the basis of which public decisions about policy are made," we find that the effect of religion on civic life is not only diverse but that it varies across the country, from region to region and from city to city.[3]

Over the twentieth century, religion in Indianapolis has had much to say about the city's civic life, as is true in most American cities. But those from the old establishment — white, liberal mainline Protestants — have had very different things to say than those from the peripheral concentrations of religious and civic power, especially Catholics, Jews, and black Protestants. To understand religion's role in our public lives, we must consider the relationship between those at the core of cultural and social power, those on the periphery, and the changing nature of their relative positions. This tension between core and periphery is yet another important facet of the competing inward and outward forces that have shaped the city.

Three central issues highlight this changing relationship: public religious celebration; religion and the delivery of educational and social services; and the influence of religion on public policy and social movements. These issues are neither merely local nor are they specific to particular geographical spaces. They extend across the entire city, beyond congregational walls and parish boundaries. But in doing so they take on different meanings and shadings. It is precisely because these issues cross so many boundaries that they provide a useful window onto the ever-evolving public role of religion. Only when we understand religion's role in defining the city at this broadest level, when we see how religion's ability to center the city has changed, can we tunnel deeper inside to understand how religion operates within the city's myriad subcultures, communities, neighborhoods, and institutions.

THE ALL-AMERICAN CITY

In the late nineteenth and early twentieth centuries, native-born white Protestants discussed with great concern the changes occurring in the nation's cities. Beginning in the 1880s, large numbers of eastern European Jews and Catholics migrated to the United States, with most settling in urban areas. For example, in Chicago and Detroit, two of the nation's largest cities, Jews and Catholics together made up numerical majorities not long after the turn of the century. Leading religious writers such as Josiah Strong and Samuel Loomis debated amongst themselves whether these new immigrants could become fully American while still retaining their own faiths. Similar questions were discussed also among the general population, with many coming to the conclusion that the only way to become a good American was to embrace some form of Protestantism.

Native-born Protestants also expressed concern about other significant changes taking place in urban America. Industrial strikes were becoming commonplace in American cities as workers who were forced to work twelve to sixteen hours a day for low wages challenged the inequalities of the marketplace. New and suspect forms of leisure were also becoming popular, including vaudeville, theater, Sunday sports, and taverns. Together with the growing industrial unrest, they provided a stark contrast to the vision of the small, well-ordered town for which many urban Protestant leaders longed. One historian has described this as a time when the notion of the city as a hotbed of "disorder" became the lens through which Americans viewed the new urbanism.[4] This was especially true of the nation's Protestant clergy, who expressed anguish over their inability to control these momentous changes and lamented what they perceived as their declining religious authority.

The history of Indianapolis in the early twentieth century is different from those of the nation's largest cities. In this city—the "Crossroads of America"—immigrants constituted less than 10 percent of the population, so pluralism did not seem as pressing a problem here. Native-born Protestants celebrated the fact that Indianapolis was a "100 percent American town," where "there is almost a total absence of the foreign floating element."[5] Given such conditions, one might expect that fears of urban disorder would be muted and questions concerning Americanization and good citizenship irrelevant. In fact, the opposite was true. Believing their city's strongest virtue to be its true "Americanism," city leaders took seriously their responsibility to define the parameters of proper citizenship and to enforce those boundaries vigilantly. The boundaries applied not only to the few immigrants who found their way to Indianapolis, but also to all of the city's native-born residents. In 1916, the superintendent of the city's largest denomination, the Methodists, said, "The opportunity is at hand to grip this city religiously as it has never been gripped before."[6] But even then, Protestant leaders could feel control of the city slipping from their grasp.

In their quest to keep hold of the city's civic identity, the clergy focused considerable attention on Sunday closings. In 1905 they actively supported the passage of a new Sunday closing law that would explicitly forbid the new forms of entertainment that were becoming popular in the city. In particular, they targeted vaudeville and theater productions as well as Sunday baseball games. Anyone found participating in such activities on Sunday would be subject to a five-dollar fine. This new closing law built on the state's earlier Sunday closing law, which dated from the early nineteenth century and had forbade, "hunting, fishing, quarreling," and any work defined as "common labor."[7]

Protestant clergy were confident that they had a right and responsibility to act as guardians of the city's secular life, but others in the city begged to differ. Fans of Indianapolis's minor league baseball team, the Indians, clearly liked Sunday baseball, and attendance at the games regularly numbered in the thousands. Supporters of Sunday baseball games hoped to evade the 1905 law by passing the Brolley bill, which legalized Sunday baseball. In addition to fighting the clergy on the legal front, supporters of Sunday baseball also waged a rhetorical war, making the argument that baseball led to the development of good personal character.[8] Supporters of Sunday theater productions also joined the war of words, claiming that "it is entirely consistent from a religious viewpoint for a man to attend church in the morning and attend a decent theater in the afternoon."[9] Not persuaded by such arguments, the city's ministers responded by attempting to pass a more expansive Sunday closing law that would have outlawed all forms of recreational activity on Sunday. They failed at this last attempt, making clear that their hold on the city was weaker than they had assumed. But even the attempt at such an initiative demonstrated that they viewed themselves as guardians not only of their parishioners but of the city as a whole. Moreover, it signaled that for them, secularization was not a theory but a threat.

Reflecting on their waning influence, the clergy warned that the city was risking a "distinct let down in the moral tone for which Indianapolis has a reputation."[10] It was this fear about the "moral tone" of Indianapolis and a belief that the city should represent the "best" that America could offer that led the men who had been active in the Sunday closing campaigns to establish the Indianapolis Church Federation (ICF). Across the nation, Protestant clergy and laymen began establishing such federations through which they could articulate a single voice as they attempted to control the changes occurring in their cities. Indianapolis was no different. More than one hundred men representing forty of the city's white mainline Protestant churches attended the Federation's first meeting held at the YMCA on the evening of June 7, 1912. From the very beginning the concerns that these clergy and laymen held about the health of the city's public life dominated the Federation's activities. And it was probably because of these concerns that the Federation's members decided to elect Vinson Carter, a former judge in the Marion County Superior Court, as their first president. Carter's experiences in the city's judicial system had given him a close look at Indianapolis's vices and virtues. How best to fight the vices and promote the virtues became the Federation's most popular undertaking, through its Public Morals Committee.[11]

The beginning of the twentieth century was a time when Indianapolis's elite self-consciously attempted to bring greater order to the city by championing inward, centralizing tendencies in the face of constant outward pressure. In fact, the Church Federation was formed the same year that the city's economic elite, many of whom were involved in the Federation, joined together to reorganize the existing Chamber of Commerce. Businessmen seeking to create a climate conducive to business growth believed that they needed to bring the major economic players in the city together. These businessmen sought also to systematize and centralize their charitable work through the Community Chest, the precursor to the city's United Way charities, in 1920. Rather than have each of the city's charitable organizations run its own fund-raising drives, the Community Chest would hold one grand drive and then disburse the funds to the city's charities.

Although the Church Federation was a religious organization, the Chamber of Commerce an economic one, and the Community Chest a charitable one, these three groups shared much in common. Many of the same men sat on the boards of all three and none of these private organizations was subject to the democratic mandates of the formal political system. In fact, the city's elite were drawn to these private organizations because it had become more difficult to direct an increasingly diverse society through public channels. They realized that they could best maintain their civic influence by centralizing their efforts in private associations that could speak more powerfully than individuals acting alone or small associations representing only a small number of citizens. The city's Protestant elite was engaged in a process of realignment, with various voluntary groups drawing on modern bureaucratic forms both to shape and to express their collective interests. Together these collective interests created the vision of the city as a singular, unified place, precisely the vision that would reappear with the introduction of Unigov.

A speech to the city's Centennial Celebration in 1920 summed up the vision:

> As a community, Indianapolis has stood for the best things in life, for the broad culture that includes all the elements of good education, religion, law, patriotism, self-sacrifice, hopefulness for the poor and unfortunate, and the abiding idea of leaving the world better than they found it. This is the character of Indianapolis. Let our slogan for the future be "a bigger city if God wills it, but always and under all circumstances a better city."

Religious guardianship of that better city fell to the Church Federation. Concern about what its leaders viewed as secular threats to the city's civic soul occupied the Federation in its early years, especially the Public Morals Committee, which focused on passing new legislation as well as monitoring legislation already on the books. The particular concerns were with gambling, prostitution, and the liquor trade. Church Federation leaders conducted what they referred to as monthly vice campaigns in which they used laymen and "detectives" to go undercover to see for themselves the city's "growing immorality." During one such campaign, the Church Federation visited nine well-known "winerooms." Disguised as patrons, the men described how they saw liquor being sold illegally and men and women of questionable character fraternizing in inappropriate ways. Especially disturbing was the large number of girls "coming and going alone," with its intimation of prostitution.[12]

In addition to speaking to the police about its discoveries, the Federation published the names and addresses of the winerooms in the local papers. By criticizing the political authorities for failing to enforce existing laws, the Church Federation had a strong justification for proclaiming itself as the only real force in the city standing up for "civic righteousness."[13] The Federation members' diligence in engaging and shaping Indianapolis's larger secular culture demonstrates clearly that they saw themselves as the city's guardians.

At a time when many Protestant leaders believed that Protestantism was

America's driving moral force, no aspect of urban life escaped their attention. Across the nation, Protestant leaders expressed strong concern about
the Catholics and Jews emigrating from southern and eastern Europe. Even
though few immigrants migrated to Indianapolis, the native-born residents
expressed concern about the supposed threat these groups posed to the
larger body politic in Indianapolis, both literally and figuratively. Historian
Ruth Crocker has described how the native-born men and women who ran
Foreign House, a social settlement house located on the city's southwest
side, took it upon themselves to "Americanize" these new immigrants. They
provided civic and English classes to the immigrant men with the hope that
these newest of the city's residents would not be attracted to the radical political messages that often appealed to immigrants who worked long hours
for incredibly low wages. At the House's mothers' clubs, immigrant women
were discouraged from cooking their traditional meals and instead taught
how to make "American pies." Children who attended the vacation bible
school learned that Protestantism was the only true faith. Finally, Foreign
House's public health clinic's primary role was not to attend to the health
needs of individual immigrants but rather to protect the city's native-born
residents from the diseases immigrants were assumed to harbor.[14]

The native-born Protestant men and women running Foreign House were
obviously concerned with inculcating new immigrants with the "proper"
values of good American citizenship. However, concerns about Americanism and good citizenship were not limited to those who worked with foreigners; they extended to those who provided social services to native-born
poor Americans. The more affluent sought to shape the citizenship of the
less affluent. This led the congregation at Fletcher Place Church to establish
Fletcher Place Community Center and the congregation at Second Presbyterian to establish Mayer Neighborhood House. In both cases, the native-born
poor whites who received services learned that Protestantism and good
citizenship went hand in hand. This was true not only for the children who
attended bible schools or who played in the gymnasiums, but also for the
adults who attended the health clinics or received emergency aid.

Indianapolis did not have many immigrants to "Americanize." However,
even a brief glance at Fletcher Place and Mayer demonstrates that the city's
elite took good citizenship seriously and made sure that the city's residents
accepted its parameters. Indianapolis's Protestant establishment believed
that it was precisely because most of their city's residents were native-born
that their city could embody the traits of true Americanism. And they never
questioned that Protestantism provided the moral fiber upon which that
American identity rested.

The belief that some form of Protestant Christianity was central to the
larger task of making good citizens also had an effect on the city's public
school system. As early as the 1880s, students in the Indianapolis public
schools participated in daily recitation of Bible verses. However, a proposal

in 1913 to teach the Bible in both history and literature classes sparked a round of heated debates as the city's growing Catholic and Jewish communities successfully challenged the curriculum as an affront to their own religious traditions. When the Church Federation revisited the question of religious instruction in public schools in 1925, it creatively entitled the new course "Americanization and Education."

By linking Bible education to the Americanization of immigrants, the city's leaders hoped to block opposition and appeal to the patriotic and religious concerns of its majority population. Even more important, the course's title suggests a shift in the strategy of Indianapolis's religious leaders. They could exert greater influence on the city generally, and education specifically, if they focused less on what it meant to be a good Methodist, Baptist, or even Protestant and more on what it meant to be a good American. By claiming guardianship over the body politic, the city's Protestant leaders drew on the moral authority they held as religious spokesmen, but redefined their religious concerns as civic concerns. By blurring the line between religion and citizenship, the Church Federation aided the development of a civic equivalent to the nation's "civil religion," where religion was a patriotic duty and patriotism was expressed through one's religious devotion.

Enter the KKK

The belief that Protestantism and Americanism represented two sides of the same coin led some to evangelize the city's non-Protestants or to encourage greater religiosity among their own. But it also paved the way for hardliners to attempt to exclude non-Protestants altogether. The Ku Klux Klan, which thrived in Indianapolis during the 1920s, gained control of most of the city's important political offices and institutions, including the board of school commissioners, the city council, and even the mayor's office.[15] The rise of the Klan at this time has generally been attributed not only to racism, but also to the fears of native-born whites about the large influx of Catholic and Jewish immigrants into America's cities. Exactly why Indiana, the state with the highest Klan membership, became so hospitable a breeding ground has proved a conundrum of sorts. Indiana as a state and Indianapolis as a city had far fewer immigrants, and far fewer Catholic and Jews, than most other northern states and cities. But if one looks both at what the Klan opposed as well as what it supported, its broad appeal in Indiana becomes clear.[16]

Klan members believed they were fighting for the future of a Christian America, a nation where one could not be fully American without embracing some brand of Protestantism. In this "ideal" Catholics and Jews would not be part of the larger body politic. This idea appealed to those Indianapolis residents who had little or no contact with immigrants and wanted to

Fig. 3.1. Street scene with Cadle Tabernacle. Larry Foster Collection, 22, courtesy Indiana Historical Society.

keep it that way. Because the Klan was a strong supporter of vice reform and prohibition, it also appealed to those men and women who believed that America in general, and urban America in specific, needed to be morally "pure."

In a city that prided itself on being all-American, the Klan proved especially appealing. Somewhere between 27 and 40 percent of all native-born white men officially joined the Klan, including many of the city's clergy. Howard Cadle, who had built an 11,500-seat auditorium called Cadle Tabernacle, was an especially strong supporter, and his Tabernacle had a reputation for being a hotbed of KKK activity. The city's congregations also expressed their support. For example, cross burnings were a frequent occurrence at Brightwood Congregational and served as a signal to all who passed by the church's lawn that the KKK was welcome there.[17] In fact, a church's association with the Klan could prove very appealing to potential congregants. For example, less than six months after Reverend Wilhelm, a known Klan supporter, joined Calvary Baptist Church, the church's membership rose from 166 to 260. That this particular congregation's sympathies for the Klan were common knowledge in the larger community was made clear when more than 2,500 people showed up at the church to witness the "unveiling" of the "illuminated cross."[18] No doubt many of these same people participated in the Klan's parades, including one that took place in May of 1924 when more than 7,000 gathered at the Indiana State Fairgrounds and marched through the city's black neighborhoods before finally ending downtown.[19]

SACRED SPACES AND PUBLIC PLACES

Of course, the Protestant establishment housed diversity of its own. Some gravitated to the message of hatred generated by the KKK, and others embraced a more tolerant Americanism, embodied in the Church Federation, that made room for "Americanized" immigrants. In addition to confronting the forces that they feared, the Protestant community also attempted to fortify the civic-sacred connection by claiming the city's public spaces for their religious celebrations.

Public celebrations like the Easter sunrise services on the Circle contain important clues about the societies that sponsor them. Through these public performances, a community celebrates its "common social identity," both to affirm the ties that bind its members and to publicize these ties to the larger community. Equally significant, public performances provide an opportunity for a people to express non-verbally "look, this is how things should be, this is the proper, ideal pattern of social life."[20]

The sunrise Easter services held at the Circle for nearly forty years reveal much about Indianapolis's mainline Protestant community. The decision to celebrate Easter Sunday, the most holy of all Christian holidays, in such a grand public fashion was hardly random. The fact that the mainline Protestant community chose the Circle as the site for this celebration makes clear its civic importance. This was a very public announcement of the city's civil religion, and that religion was grounded in Protestantism.

As we saw in the previous chapter, the Circle has been the most prominent of all public spaces in the city since the first settlers arrived in the city in the early nineteenth century. Because the Circle was literally the center of the city, public celebrations occurring there were identified with the city as a whole rather than with just a neighborhood. Events that took place on the Circle thus received widespread attention and gained a kind of civic legitimacy that was unequaled. And at a time when making use of public space was in effect making a kind of claim on the civic body itself, claiming the Circle for the Easter celebration was the grandest of all claims. The Protestant establishment's use of Monument Circle not only transformed religious beliefs and rituals into civic ones, it sacralized the Circle itself. The Circle and the war memorials that eventually moved up Meridian Street then over into Whitewater Park became important parts of the city's emerging civil religion, though the explicit connection to Protestantism would gradually decline, leaving the patriotic and nationalist elements to stand for themselves.

Of course, not all of Indianapolis's public life centered on the Circle and its evident symbolism. Mainline Protestants also took to the side streets and byways in their attempts to bring religion into the city. One of the first proposals considered by the Church Federation was an open-air evangelism campaign. This was not surprising since open-air revivals had long been an important part of the city's life. In 1905 the German Methodist Church set up a revival tent at the corner of New York and Arsenal and invited people passing by to come in to participate. Thus, when the Federation set up a revival tent across the street from city hall and encouraged clergy to speak out on urban woes, there was little doubt about the religious claim on Indianapolis's public space.[21]

Catholics and Jews on the Periphery

Even as the Protestant establishment worked diligently to combine Protestantism and Americanism, Catholics and Jews struggled both to avoid Protestant evangelical efforts and to prove the compatibility of their own faiths with larger American ideals. The city's smaller missions, such as the First Baptist Mission, designed to reach eastern European immigrants, and the Methodist Mission, directed at Italians, prompted particularly angry responses from the city's leading Catholics who described these missionary endeavors as a "Protestant invasion."[22] They strongly resented Protestant evangelistic overtures and rejected the notion that being Protestant was the only way to become fully American. Said the *Indiana Catholic and Record,*

> Everyone who knows anything about Italians knows they are Roman Catholics. . . . If the Methodists are going to spend $15,000 on a new mission, they might well spend it on the alleged Methodists who don't go to church and who leave Protestant churches notoriously empty. . . . Let our Methodist friends take care of their own. Millions of them who don't go to church need care.[23]

Drawing on America's heritage of freedom of religion, these minority faiths directly confronted the emerging civil religion constructed by those who questioned their presence. When, for example, the cornerstone for St. John's parish was laid in the summer of 1867, thousands of the city's residents witnessed the day's events, which began with a large procession. The city's Catholics gathered at St. Mary's and from there they marched to the city's other two parishes before ending at the site for St. John's. The parishioner who led the parade held an American flag in his hand, and others holding flags representing the many countries from which Catholics had emigrated—including Ireland, England, France, Germany, and Spain—followed him. That not only the city's Catholics observed this parade was clear from the large number who stood on the streets along the parade's path. A reporter described how the streets were so crowded that people "eagerly struggled for places from which there was the faintest possibility of either seeing or hearing anything." He concluded that this was "by far the largest crowd ever assembled on a similar occasion in this city."[24]

The procession makes clear how the minority Catholic community saw its place in the larger Protestant city. Even the decision to host such a grand procession was itself significant, as it demonstrated the Catholics' belief that they should have equal access to the city's streets to express their faith. Yet the fact that they knew that many in the community believed that Catholics were not fully American likely affected the decision to have a parishioner bearing an American flag lead the procession. Combining religious and civic loyalties was especially important for new immigrant groups struggling to prove that they too were a part of the larger body politic. When the cornerstone for the Slovenian Catholic Church Holy Trinity was laid on October 21, 1906, the parishioners proudly paraded through the Haughville neighborhood, waving both American and Slovenian flags. Once gathered at the site of the new church, they listened to services given in both English and Slovene.[25] Even before the World Wars, those on the periphery knew that emphasizing the community's common "American" identity was the surest way to mitigate religious or sectarian differences.

Much like the Catholics who established St. John's, the members of Holy Trinity believed that they could maintain both their Catholic faith and their ethnic heritages without compromising their identities as Americans. For one day at least, members of St. John's and Holy Trinity merged their religious, ethnic, and civic identities. In both cases they wanted to make it clear to all that they were no less American than the native-born Protestants who dominated the city. And because the boundaries of the parish extended far into the public streets occupied in their processions and into the civic arena itself, the issue of public space was extremely important to the city's Catholics. To be Catholic was to claim all that lay within the parish's boundaries.

The public processions accompanying the founding of churches provided one way in which Catholics carved out space in the public arena, but even more important were the many civic roles Catholics assumed, including the provision of a wide array of social and educational services to "their own." In a society where Protestant leaders and city officials worked tirelessly, although often unsuccessfully, to infuse the public schools with re-

ligious messages, Catholics took seriously the mission of parochial education. Each of the city's parishes was expected to provide a primary school for
its young boys and girls. As a result, schools were an integral part of parish
life. It was not unusual that the parish school would be instituted within a
short time of the founding of the parish. Even congregational parishes
without much money, such as the heavily Slovene Holy Trinity, devoted a
portion of its resources to the education of its youth.[26] The *Indiana Catholic
and Record* put the matter plainly:

> We must have the Catholic high school where the Catholic child will not
> merely get the culture, refinement, and aesthetic conceptions of the mod-
> ern paganism known as secular education, but where his moral conception
> of his relation and duty to his creator and his fellow man will make him a
> better and more useful citizen and a much happier man.[27]

The desire of the Catholic community to protect the religious heritage of
its children, an endeavor which Catholics saw as both religious and patriotic,
also pushed the Catholic community to build one of the city's largest social
welfare networks. When Bishop Chartrand established the Catholic Charities Bureau in 1919, it comprised only a home for unwed mothers, a low-cost
cafeteria, and emergency aid for the most indigent. By the 1930s, however,
the staff of Catholic Charities had grown sixfold and had added important
services such as foster care homes for dependent children and probation
work for young offenders. Catholics recognized themselves as a minority
people that needed to protect their youth from the larger society. But instead of isolating themselves, they often engaged with the larger society on
their own terms. For example, in the 1930s Catholic Charities worked out
agreements with the public welfare department to send all Catholic children needing care outside of their own homes to Catholic Charities. Catholic leaders even laid claim to public money by arguing that they, as citizens,
were entitled to the public dollars filling the state's coffers.

The large Catholic educational and social services network makes clear
that even in those decades when the Protestant community felt confident
that its vision of the city should predominate, other groups successfully created their own social and cultural spaces within the city and understood
their right to do so in both religious and civic terms. Catholics were in
many ways marginalized from the symbolic centers of civic life, but they
responded by creating ethnic, cultural and social centers of their own. The
strength of their institutions and the coherence of this mix of religious and
civic responsibilities would have a profound effect on the whole metropolis
as the religious and civic boundaries later began to change. Traditional religious differences remained important in the neighborhoods and smaller,
more homogeneous communities; Americanism became the important
badge of identity in the wider public, the coin of common citizenship.

Meanwhile, the much smaller Jewish community also worked diligently to

Fig. 3.2. Father Petrilli and Class. Courtesy Indiana Historical Society, C1955.

care for its own. Almost as soon as Jews began settling in the city, they began offering charitable services to the less fortunate among them. As early as the 1850s, when the Jewish community numbered fewer than 200 members, Rabbi Judah Wescslen encouraged the city's Jewish women to establish the Ladies Hebrew Benevolent Society. It quickly became an integral part of Jewish life. And as the Jewish community grew in the early twentieth century, with eastern European Jews joining the German Jews who had immigrated a half century earlier, efforts to reach out to the new immigrants resulted in the founding of Nathan Morris House, a settlement house directed to Jews, and Shelter House, a home serving the needs of transient Jews. With the rapid expansion of Jewish charitable efforts, the city's rabbis began to believe that some kind of coordination was needed. In 1905 Rabbi Morris Feurlicht led the effort to create the Jewish Federation, an organization that coordinated the city's various Jewish benevolent enterprises and centralized their fund raising. Jewish leaders took pride in taking care of

Fig. 3.3. Jewish Children at Hebrew School, ca. 1950. Indianapolis Recorder Collection, C5800, courtesy Indiana Historical Society.

"their own," and they actively discouraged Jews from seeking support from other public and private sources. For most of the twentieth century, the Jewish Federation was the Jewish community's most visible public presence.

It would be unfair to suggest that Catholics or Jews were relegated to ethnic ghettos in Indianapolis or that they had no public voice. At the same time he was helping to build an independent Jewish Federation to serve the needs of Jews, Morris Feurlicht was also working with the county's juvenile justice system and serving as the president of the Children's Aid Association. He was, in fact, the first Jew appointed to the State Board of Charities and Correction. When Bishop Chartrand founded Cathedral High School in 1918, he was paving the way for increased college attendance and participation in the city's business community among Catholics. But both groups saw their activities as parallel to, but in many ways separate from, the city's establishment.

The mainline Protestant community felt confident that its vision of the city was the cultural norm during the early twentieth century. Drawing on both religious and patriotic principles, they claimed that religious people needed to speak on civic issues and that the civic body would be healthy only if it embraced the city's Protestant roots. Catholics and Jews responded by building their own communities on the city's margins without paying much attention to the Protestants at the center of public life, and by making occasional but exceptional forays into the civic public. Catholics and Jews drew on both religious and civic principles, arguing that religious freedom was an equally significant part of America's civic heritage and that they had a right and a responsibility to nurture and protect their religious communities in what was beginning to take shape as a multicentered metropolis.

ASSIMILATION AND REALIGNMENT

Well into the twentieth century, many Protestants questioned whether Catholics or Jews could fully assimilate; they questioned whether these faiths were compatible with American ideals of liberty and freedom. Said a 1908 editorial in the *Indianapolis News,* "the growth of new religious sects in Indianapolis has been so rapid that the adherents of straight and old-fashioned creeds wonder what will come next." During World War I, concerns about how best to Americanize immigrants provided the larger context within which notions of American identity and patriotic concern were articulated. But the post–World War II era represented a sea change in this thinking because discussions about religion and citizenship came under the umbrella of a much larger global context, where fears about communism rather than immigrants predominated.

The 1950s have been noted as a decade in which religion thrived, with church attendance reaching an all-time high. Of course, scholars disagree about how and why religion had such appeal. Examining the larger cultural context, where conformity and anti-communism were prized, can help us understand this religious vitality.

One of the more notable developments of post–World War II religion was the rise of ecumenical efforts among Protestant mainline denomination even as the rift between the mainline and evangelicals grew. The story of ecumenical growth is a complex one that cannot be captured by any single narrative. However, an important part of this story can be revealed by looking at the ways in which the connections between religion and citizenship were redefined within the context of a nation joined together by a strong anti-communist spirit.

The new civic ideals that mainline Protestants celebrated allowed them to embark on ambitious efforts to bring religion into the public arena, and none was more successful than the Weekday Religious Education Association. Hoping to avoid the problem of the separation of church and state which had plagued earlier efforts to bring religious instruction into the public schools, the sponsors of Indiana's 1943 Religious Education Act called for "released time" from school, time during which children could go to a local church for religious instruction. The program, which had strong support from the Church Federation and the Lilly Endowment, was quickly noted for being "the greatest interdenominational effort in Indianapolis church history."[28] Ecumenism appeared to be the answer to finding unity within diversity in the evolving city. This fit not only the religious goals of the Church Federation, but the civic, centering goals of Lilly Endowment.

The number of children enrolled climbed quickly, reaching a total of 13,500 in 1953. Even more revealing, 85 percent of all fourth and fifth graders attended, 53 percent of whom did not attend any other kind of religious services.[29] Twice a week, for sixty minutes each time, the children gathered at a local church for religious instruction.

From the beginning of the program, administrators were frank about their primary concerns with reaching the "unchurched children" and their conception of the program as a "missionary" endeavor. For example, a teaching manual distributed to teachers explained that religious education "is an important instrument of evangelism in reaching thousands of children with the Gospel message who would otherwise have had no Christian instruction."[30]

Why, in the 1950s, did the mainline churches become so concerned with bringing unchurched children into the fold? According to the director of the program, Dr. F. A. Pfeiderer, weekday religious instruction not only "buil[t] good Christian citizens" but it was the only way "we have of keeping the country from becoming a godless nation."[31] As anyone familiar with Cold War rhetoric knows, the world's most feared godless nation was the Soviet Union. Administrators of the program were open about the fact that it was the uncertainty of the larger world that underlay their fears and motivated their actions. Supporters of the weekday religious program believed strongly that the church had a responsibility to provide the children with an "understanding of this confused and changing world."[32]

The idea that weekday religious instruction promoted good citizenship was accepted by all. And increasingly this "good citizen" was defined less by his or her Protestant affiliation than by his or her commitment to America. This reflected a shift from the early twentieth century when Americanism was viewed through a Protestant lens. The WREA determined the program's impact by both secular and religious standards, although the secular standards were more important to many. For example, civic leaders commented frequently on the impact the program had had on the city's delinquency rates and on family stability. Judge Harold N. Field of the Marion County Juvenile Court was only one among many who believed that the weekday program was valuable primarily because it had a "definite effect on the reduction of the juvenile delinquency rate of the county."[33] Another one of the benefits about which religious education administrators spoke was that the children carried the religious messages back home and strengthened families that otherwise would have had no religious influences. It must be noted, however, that family stability was the goal and religion the means.

Unlike with earlier efforts to bring religion into the public schools, Catholics mounted no protests against it in the 1950s. The reluctance of Catholics to criticize the WREA might have reflected a fear of being labeled un-American or, even worse, pro-communist. They may also have felt little need to challenge the program because a large number of Catholic children attended Catholic grammar schools where they were both relatively unaffected and exposed to their own weekday religious education. Catholics in the city had worked hard to fulfill their mission to have all Catholic children educated in parish schools, an objective which became easier to achieve as the Catholic community prospered economically along with the rest of the society. This was a key to Catholicism's massive church expansion and its programs following World War II, when new parish buildings more often than not included a new parish school.

Jewish children, most of whom attended public schools, faced a different situation. Jewish groups were reluctant to build Jewish schools because they had long believed that the public school system helped unite Americans of all faiths into a common civic body. For Jews who found their dual claims to their religious identities and American citizenship challenged, participation in the public school system was one way to affirm their loyalty to a larger American ideal. Of course, Jews did not participate in the weekday religious instruction that had become a part of the regular school day for most Indianapolis children. Instead, Jewish children had access to after-school religious instruction from the Jewish Education Association (JEA). The JEA had been providing after-school instruction since 1924, and even though the proportion of Jewish children who attended the program was far lower that the proportion of Protestant children who participated in the WREA, it nonetheless addressed the need for religious education of Jewish youth.

Although both Catholics and Jews were concerned about proving the legitimacy of their claim to the body politic, Jews proved their patriotism by attending public schools, while Catholics expressed the American ideal of liberty by creating their own school systems. That Catholics and Jews developed such different attitudes toward public education demonstrates the multiple ways one could negotiate one's religious and national identities.

Even though the weekday program did not seem to upset Catholics or Jews, it should be noted that not all stood behind weekday religious education. When a state senator who belonged to Elkhart Presbyterian Church fought to repeal the Religious Education Act, he argued that it was clearly a violation of the First Amendment separation of church and state. Although his stand was not popular, reporters noted that there were several churches where parishioners strongly supported him.[34] Taking such a critical stand could be risky, however. At a time when the civil religion required good citizens to support any and all activities conducive to growing religious devotion, challenging religious instruction in the school could be viewed as proof that one was less than fully faithful, and by implication less than fully American. Worst of all, one could be accused of being a subversive, even a communist.

Fear of communism helped spur greater cooperation and conformity among mainline Protestants, but it also provided fertile ground for the nation's evolving evangelical movement. Billy Graham rose to prominence during the years when the nation was gripped by anti-communist fear, and he frequently described his evangelical message as a response to the supposed threat of "godless communism." For evangelicals strongly wedded to a premillennial vision, the rise of the Soviet Union served as proof that the world was anything but safe and secure. Evangelical ministers delivered sermons in which millennial themes predominated. Representative sermons include "One U.S. Coin Has the Emblems of the Beast of Daniel 7 and Rev. 13" and "The Crashing of the Political World. What Causes It? When Will It Be? What Follows?" Evangelicals who listened to these and other sermons could clearly identify with Billy Graham when he told a crowd of more than 12,000 at Cadle Tabernacle that Judgment Day "is almost upon us." Of course it would be naive to reduce Graham's appeal to his anti-communist message, but this does not lessen the fact that he spoke in a language that fit well into the larger culture and which no doubt drew some to him.

Although the city's Catholics had little in common with Billy Graham, they too began to understand the church within the larger context of anti-communism. As historian David J. O'Brien asserts, Catholics seeking to prove their Americanism were drawn to anti-communist rhetoric because it provided them a vehicle by which to prove that they were loyal Americans. In Indianapolis, Catholic anti-communist sentiment also reinforced the community's focus on the nuclear family as the basis for a stable, prosperous city.

Anti-communism's impact on the nation's glorification of the traditional, white, middle-class family has been well documented by historian Elaine Tyler May. May argues that in the 1950s, an atomic age when the future seemed uncertain, the family served as both a refuge from the larger world and the first line of defense against the subversive forces threatening the United States. Catholics were among those for whom the family gained grander public significance. For example, in 1950, the Indianapolis Catholic community held one of its largest public events, a Catholic family prayer rally at the War Memorial Plaza. Amidst the city's cultural and civic restructuring, Catholics now shared the same civic and patriotic religious stage once dominated by the Protestant establishment.

Concerns about preserving and strengthening the traditional male-headed nuclear family also affected Protestants and became a public issue demanding a religious response. Concern about children was especially strong and lent support to the boom in recreational activities directed to them. Both evangelicals and mainline Protestants designed new programs including a wide array of sports teams and clubs. While religious-based youth activities were intended to serve the children and help them become both good Americans and good sons and daughters, married couples turned for help in increasing numbers to pastoral counselors who believed that one of their primary goals was to help each member of the family adjust to his or her expected roles and responsibilities. That the issue of family relations was recognized to be of public significance was made clear by the Church Federation's "family life clinic," where all aspects of family life were examined, from the sources of marital discord to the relations between spouses and in-laws. The program designers believed that the city would become a better place only if and when its families had been strengthened.

The Sunday closing campaigns that occurred in the 1950s were also affected by the larger society's focus on the family. Hoping to appeal to the patriotic spirit accompanying the end of World War II, the leaders of the new Sunday closing movement decided to call it "C Day." Unlike earlier movements, when legal bans were sought, the "C Day" supporters asked the city's residents to comply voluntarily. "C Day" quickly gained support from business owners as well as churchgoers. Tellingly, they described Sunday as a day for the "family" rather than only as a day for religious observance.

Despite the excitement surrounding the "C Day" campaign, it was short-lived. By the late 1950s, most businesses acquiesced to the pressure to remain open on Sunday. The inability of the mainline Protestants to keep support strong for "C Day" suggests that the larger secular world — driven as it was by commercial interests — was having a greater impact on peoples' lives even as church membership continued to climb. And the fact that "C Day" proponents justified their campaign by pointing to the family suggest that even they were influenced by the city's rising secularism.

The failure of "C Day," however, should not suggest that pressures to conform to the dominant cultural, social, and political values were disappearing. This was something that the Church Federation learned when it came under attack from the Columbia Club because it had hosted a celebration of United Nations Day featuring Louis Dolivet as the invited speaker. Dolivet was one of many Americans charged by the U.S. House Un-American Activities Committee with having subversive associations. Fearing that its role as a leading civic organization would be compromised by hosting such a speaker, the Church Federation issued a public statement that it was "unalterably opposed to communism, its materialism, its atheism, its denial of Christian ethics, its totalitarianism, its fallacious economics."[35] The women of the Church Women United, a group which in many ways paralleled the male-dominated Church Federation, attempted to avoid such problems by issuing a "Christian Declaration of Loyalty," which stated: "No body of citizens is more alert to the threat of communist thought and conspiracy both to the Christian faith and freedom than the Christian churches."[36] After this statement was issued, however, two arch-conservative political groups, "Let Freedom Ring" and the John Birch Society, charged the Church Women United with being less than loyal because they had recommended that the U.S. Congress streamline its investigations of subversive activities.[37]

RELIGION AND THE DEMOCRATIZATION OF THE PUBLIC SQUARE

At the end of the 1950s, the city's mainline Protestant community had good reason to be confident about its future. Church attendance was higher than it had ever been, weekday religious education had reached thousands of children, most of whom had not been involved in any other religious activities, and the newly found ecumenical spirit suggested not only that mainline Protestants of various denominations could work together, but that Protestants, Catholics, and Jews could cooperate as well. Gone, at least publicly, were the overt anti-Catholic and anti-Jewish sentiments of the 1920s and 1930s. Instead, the civic ideals which mainline Protestants celebrated were rooted in a more general, open religious faith, a faith that involved equal parts Protestantism and a more abstract Americanism. The 1950s saw the city's first significant ecumenical efforts crossing the divides between the Jews, the Catholics, and the Protestants. In the post–World War II era, three different Catholics served as mayor in a city once dominated by a mainline Protestant establishment. The city's multiple religions and multiple centers existed as pluralistic parts of a cooperative whole.

There were signs in the early 1960s that this would be a decade very different from the one that had preceded it. In 1961, for the first time since its founding, the Church Federation began to revise its understanding of the city as a single geographic and cultural entity over which it held moral guardianship, acknowledging the realignment caused by decades of outward movement. As the director of the Federation was forced to admit, "the city was slipping away as one community, it is many communities."[38] Although he did not explain where these communities were, or who lived in them, he no doubt was speaking of groups like African Americans, Catholics, and Jews, who had always been in the city but had operated on the margins in their own "centered" niches. Even as mainline Protestants began to reach out to Catholics and Jews, they were saddened by the fact that they no longer could speak as the city's singular authoritative religious voice. For their part, Catholics, Jews, and African Americans appreciated that their communities were gaining greater visibility and acceptance.

Secular changes in the city during the 1960s further guaranteed that religious life would be transformed. As whites left the city for bigger homes out in the suburbs, their churches often followed. Not surprisingly, other religious activity also left the city. The Holy Week celebration, one of the city's earliest interdenominational events tied to the Easter sunrise services, offers a telling example. The celebration of Holy Week began in 1915 when downtown churches and theaters began holding daily religious services during Holy Week. The popularity of these events was made clear by the more than 7,000 people who attended religious services in 1936 at two of the city's largest theaters. However, by the mid-1950s, those attendance numbers were well below one hundred, and the services were completely canceled in the mid-1960s.[39]

The ending of the Holy Week celebration was but one of the many indications that the traditional exercises of religion which had previously taken place in the city's streets and public places no longer had the same attraction, an acknowledgment that religious worship of this sort went on out in the city's multiple communities. Many lamented this fact, including the members of Christ Church Episcopal, who in 1963 decided to celebrate their church's 125th anniversary by sponsoring a ceremony where they would honor not only their church but the seven other churches that had at some point sat on the Circle. Men and women from more than ninety-six of the city's churches participated in the service, which included a processional from the World War Memorial to the Circle, where Bishop F. Bayne spoke before a crowd reported to have numbered 5,000.[40]

The procession clearly celebrated not the future but the past, marking the end of a Protestant establishment core and the beginning of civic religious pluralism. Among scholars of religion, the 1960s is often described as a decade of crisis, a time when much of what had been taken for granted was challenged. For scholars interested in urban religion specifically, attention has usually focused on those large white mainline congregations struggling to survive in the city's changing landscape. For many religious communities, however, the 1960s inaugurated a time of hope and opportunity.

No group better demonstrates the vitality of religion in urban America than the African American ministers and laity who participated in the burgeoning civil rights movement. Having been denied full access to the promises of America, African Americans drew on the moral underpinnings of their faith to demand that the city end its practices of discrimination and segregation. One of the most visible and outspoken leaders was Andrew J. Brown, the Baptist minister whom we met in the preceding chapter and who had begun organizing the African American community even in the conservative 1950s. As the civil rights movement flourished nationally, Brown helped organize local chapters of the Southern Christian Leadership Conference and Operation Breadbasket in addition to serving as head of many Indianapolis-based ministerial alliances. Although scholars interested in the civil rights movement do not usually look at Indianapolis, it would be

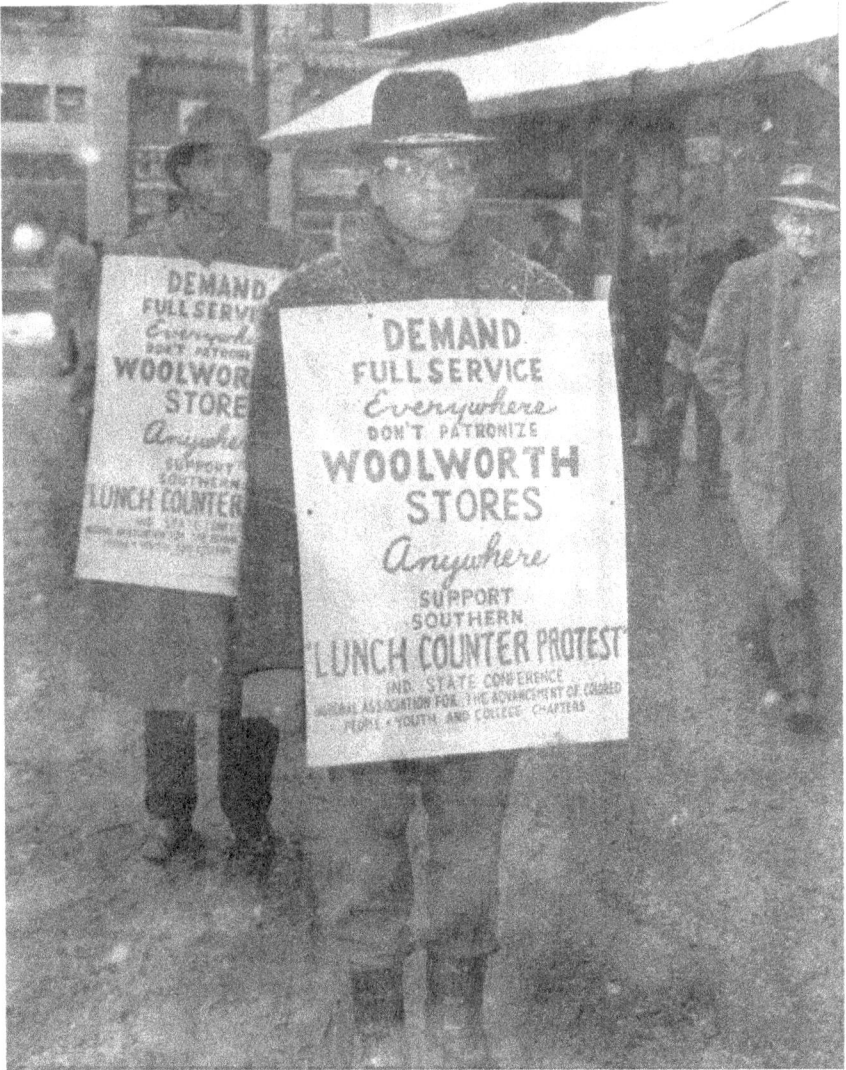

Fig. 3.4. Civil Rights Marchers, ca. 1960. Indianapolis Recorder Collection, C5772, courtesy Indiana Historical Society.

imprudent to ignore the efforts that were made and results achieved. For the first time in the city's history, African American churches played a public role visible not just to their own congregants but to the city as a whole.

The more critical view of the city held by the civil rights activists demonstrated that the political conformity of the 1950s was fast withering away. Some mainline white Protestants soon joined the fray, including the women of the Church Women United, who in 1963, the same year as the Holy Week celebration ended, began sponsoring a "Come and See Tour" as part of a larger anti-crime crusade concerned with making the streets safe for women. The tours were also intended to expose the mostly white, middle- and upper-class women to the city's poorer, neglected neighborhoods. The hope was that the women would learn about the problems people in such communities faced and propose solutions to help resolve them. As a result, the Church Women United began efforts to end illiteracy and counsel high school dropouts.[41]

Church Women United was only one of many groups that in the 1960s began to address the larger social, racial, and economic inequalities plaguing the city. In fact, greater awareness of the city's problems not only led preexisting groups to develop new strategies but also made possible the creation of new organizations, most of them ecumenical. For example, white mainline Protestants responded to the building of the city's highway system, which displaced thousands of the city's poorest residents, by establishing HOMES, Housing Opportunities Multiplied Ecumenically (later called the Inter-faith Housing Inc.). HOMES would eventually receive federal grants for its work in low-income housing ventures.[42]

The Christian Inner City Association (CICA), established in 1963 by James Pratt, was probably the most vocal critic of the city's social and economic conditions. Always concerned with the rights of the poor, CICA worked to increase the minimum wage, end racial segregation, expand voting, and protect the rights of welfare recipients. Its most famous leader, Reverend Miller Newton, sought to democratize the War on Poverty program after political authorities sought to exclude the poor from their legal right to participate in the administration of programs.

African Americans and more liberal-leaning white Protestants saw the emergence of new religious voices with different and competing visions of the city as a democratization of the religious landscape. However, this democratization had limits, something that civil rights workers and social justice activists struggled with as they sought to challenge the city's inequalities. Uncomfortable with open conflict, the city's civic leaders consistently attempted to legitimate, even to endorse, more moderate protests while marginalizing those it saw as a threat. The most vocal civil rights activists were viewed as a threat.

While African Americans celebrated the changes brought about in the 1960s, the burgeoning white evangelical movement saw the 1960s as a frightening time, when "traditional" values lost ground to civil disobedience and when hedonism ran amok. Historian William McLoughlin describes how many evangelicals "urged a return to the old ways 'that made this country great.' To do that, they say, we must wipe out all of the so called 'liberal reforms' of the twentieth century from welfare to ERA, and from labor unions to civil rights laws."[43] On the national level, fundamentalists gained a public presence they had never had. Led by Jerry Falwell, the Moral Majority received more media attention than any other religious movement of the day. Across the nation, fundamentalists became active in pockets of local politics, challenging the teaching of evolution and other practices deemed a threat to their vision of what was morally right.

Considering that evangelicals were becoming more numerous in Indianapolis, they, too, might have demanded a greater public voice in their city's affairs. For the most part, however, evangelical churches did not become especially active in public life in Indianapolis. Perhaps this was because evangelicals never saw themselves far removed from the Protestant establishment, at least not until the ecumenical movement came to be increasingly linked to political liberalism in the national and international eye. The generally conservative political culture of the city did not seem threatening to evangelicals, most of whom were concerned primarily with individual salvation rather than the institutional arrangements of the larger society. In fact, one of the criticisms leveled against Reverend Greg Dixon, the state of Indiana's Moral Majority leader and pastor of Baptist Temple, once the city's largest church, was that he focused too much time on politics and not enough on religion. The fact that Dixon spoke weekly on both radio and television and advertised the Temple extensively led some within the evangelical community to ask, "Is the sheep sacrificed for the needs of the flock?"[44] Dixon fared no better among the mainline clergy. Bishop A. James Armstrong of the Indiana Area United Methodist Church stated that what most upset him about Dixon and his followers "is the arrogance of their statements. It's as if to say if we don't agree, we are outside the pale, unchristian, unpatriotic. . . . As if God's word were only through the mind of right-wing fundamentalist ministers." Rabbi Jonathan Stein, who was concerned about Dixon's "authoritarian tendencies," voiced similar sentiments. More specifically, Stein was bothered by his attempt to force his "specific theology, ethics, and political beliefs on an entire society." When asked about what the mainline clergy as a group thought about Dixon and the Moral Majority, one unnamed mainline clergy stated that they viewed them "with contempt."[45]

Given that some clergy openly attacked Dixon, he could have directed his anger toward the establishment. But in general he reserved his ammunition for bigger foes, for "the liberals [who] thought they had America in their pocket." According to Dixon, "liberals," by which he meant political liberals, had "seized control of our educational system, our economic and political system."[46]

Many of the city's white evangelicals and fundamentalists, while no doubt sympathetic to many of Dixon's political views, did not join forces with him. The weakness of evangelicals in the public life of the city speaks to the power of the mainline Protestant community. Over time it had triumphed because it had kept broadening its inclusiveness while successfully marginalizing those who might challenge its moral authority. This applied not only to those on the far right but also to those on the left. And in the case of Dixon, the mainline marginalized him by describing his congregation as "cult-like." Even more damning, the mainline complained that Dixon's desire for political influence allowed him to ignore the spiritual needs of his flock and focus instead on building membership and raising money.

RELIGION AND THE CITY'S PUBLIC GOOD(S)

The fact that both civil rights activists and the religious right consistently drew on moral discourse to offer their competing visions of the "good society" demonstrates that there are multiple notions of the public good, many of which are grounded in religion. Recent developments surrounding social welfare — especially President George W. Bush's "faith-based initiatives" — have also made clear that there are still many different religious bodies with competing conceptions of the role religion should play in public life. For example, in 1996 the Personal Responsibility and Work Opportunity Reconciliation Act (known as the Welfare Reform Act) brought religious people of various theological and social perspectives into public debate. When the bill was first crafted, Senator Daniel Patrick Moynihan, a leading social welfare expert, described the bill as the "most brutal act of social policy since Reconstruction."[47] A large number of nationally based religious groups, including the National Conference of Catholic Bishops and the Union of American Hebrew Congregations strongly opposed the legislation. In Indianapolis, Catholic Charities and the Catholic Conference, both of whom have long-established reputations as advocates for the poor, also expressed reservations. They joined the national leaders of the Catholic Church, who argued that the bill was fraught with risk. But in Indianapolis, Mayor Stephen Goldsmith — then a prospective advisor on urban affairs to future candidate George W. Bush — was already putting the faith-based ball into play. He began by using his "bully pulpit" to organize a Faith and Families initiative, modeled on a similar program started by Gov. Kirk Fordyce in Mississippi. The goal was to enlist congregations, find needy or at-risk families, and pair them so that the religious congregations could provide a supportive community, or even surrogate family, that the family was imagined to lack. In Indianapolis, though, as in Mississippi, relatively few congregations — never more than twenty in Indianapolis — got involved. And those who did join found the going much tougher, more complicated, and more expensive than they had imagined.[48]

Undeterred, the Goldsmith administration pressed forward with more structural reforms tied directly to the prestige of the mayor's office. He developed the Front Porch Alliance, mentioned in the introduction, in the hopes that such an office would grease the skids for community-based organizations trying to find ways to improve their neighborhoods. Goldsmith hoped to focus on a few of the city's inner-city neighborhoods — his seven "target neighborhoods" — already earmarked for development. Quickly, though, the FPA became the hotline for congregations and other religious groups hoping to get more involved.

The Front Porch Alliance not only provided assistance to groups wanting to get involved, it smoothed the road for faith-based groups in other arenas. Each year, the city got federal money in the form of Community Development Block Grants. During the FPA years, faith-based groups applied for and received this money in much larger numbers than before. The same could be said for the city's Porchlight Summer Program grants, through which community groups got funds for summer youth programs. Again, faith-based groups took up a larger share than they had in the past. And this was prior to George W. Bush's call for "armies of compassion" through faith-based initiatives. Indeed, the Indianapolis experiments were happening concurrently with wrangling over the 1996 welfare reform law. Nationally, critics of the new law and its inevitable trickle-down effect were concerned about strict new time limits for receipt of aid and smaller appropriations for job training and child care. The 1996 bill abolished the federally guaranteed Aid to Families with Dependent Children program and replaced it with state-controlled Temporary Assistance to Needy Families. Under this arrangement, mothers with children would not be allowed to receive more than two consecutive years of aid, and would be limited to a total of five years of support over their lifetime. Some in the religious community feared that the potential upshot of these reforms might be the eventual end of federal government programs for the poor, leaving their care to the individual states.

Large charitable organizations such as Catholic Charities and Lutheran Family Services — affiliated with but legally separate from their denominations — have a long history of contracting with public agencies for social services. However, both the "charitable choice" provisions and the current White House initiatives represent radical new departures. For the first time, religious organizations were receiving public funds while still maintaining their essentially religious character, meaning they did not have to create a separately incorporated body. The 1996 legislation suggested that such groups would not be required to abide by federal employment nondiscrimination laws, a point President Bush seemed determined to make in his new initiatives. The purposely vague language of charitable choice says that religious organizations dispensing federal money can do so without "impairing the religious character of such organizations."[49] Of course, religious organizations cannot use federal money to evangelize. But they are legally permitted to "offer religious teaching, display symbols of their faith, and hire only those who agree with their doctrinal beliefs."[50]

The Bush administration has embraced these changes in the relationship between religious organizations and the federal government, and has made strenuous efforts to encourage smaller religious groups — especially congregations — to join traditional religious providers such as Catholic Charities in providing social services. From Henry Cisneros, secretary of HUD in 1996 during the passage of the original charitable choice clause, to President Bush today, there has been a prevailing sentiment that lasting change in social problems will come from changed hearts. Critics who see social problems as structural and institutional in nature continue to disagree.

Not surprisingly, some of the biggest questions are still about money. Recent attempts to encourage faith-based organizations to provide services have not included extra money devoted to social welfare. Instead, faith-based groups will have to compete with all other providers for the block grants the states currently receive. With less money and more providers, congregations that receive federal money might very well begin to view other congregations not as partners but as competitors in the funding game. In any event, Indianapolis is by no means the only city dealing with such issues, though it was in fact among the very first to develop a religious response to them.

Despite Indianapolis's role in the forefront of these social experiments, uptake was, and continues to be, slow. Each of these proposed partnership efforts — the FPA's summer program grants, the juvenile court, the homelessness coalition — reached out to the entire faith community. In the end, only some sixty congregations, roughly 5 percent of the total field, responded by applying to any or all of the funding competitions sponsored by their prospective public partners.[51] And these congregations were hardly a random sample. They were virtually all Protestant, primarily middle-class, and most likely to have African American members. Two-thirds of the applications in the congregational grant programs came from African American congregations.

Some of these new partners were among the biggest and best-off congregations. Eastern Star Missionary Baptist, the city's one true megachurch, submitted one of the three grant applications to which the Coalition for Homelessness Intervention and Prevention awarded a $150,000 grant. In its application, Eastern Star proposed a new partnership with city government concerning some vacant public housing near their church. The city was accommodating. This was not the first time Mayor Goldsmith had recognized the role played by the big, consumer-oriented congregations at the city's edges. In the early days of the Front Porch Alliance, he had pressured East 91st Street Christian Church to "give something back" to the downtown it had left years before. East 91st, a white church, built a new partnership with a group of African American churches in the Martindale-Brightwood neighborhood, culminating in a new recreation center, Jireh Sports, that became a showpiece for the mayor's new faith-based reforms.

But the bulk of the applications to the faith-based initiatives came from average-sized congregations of middle-class members who were hoping to make a difference in their own urban neighborhoods or, more to the point, were hoping to find additional funding for programs already underway. The typical profile of the new public partnership congregation was an African American church located in a distressed neighborhood, headed by an educated pastor, and filled with members who had historical ties to the neighborhood but who had moved further out of the city as their social class moved up the scale. The city and its congregations had come a long way from the days of prohibition, the old Community Chest, and the civil rights movement.

MOVING AHEAD

In 1971, the Indianapolis community all but ignored Mayor Richard Lugar when he suggested that the city reinstate its Easter Sunday services on the Circle.[52] Most church members were satisfied with attending service in the privacy of their own congregations and were not concerned about celebrating Holy Week in a dramatically public fashion. Equally telling, by the 1970s, few expressed opposition to the Indianapolis 500 taking place on Sunday, even though as recently as 1963 the Church Federation had still argued against it, claiming that "traffic congestion ties up the entire metropolitan area, making it impossible for people to attend the services of their church at the accustomed time."[53]

In the last three decades of the twentieth century, it became increasingly difficult for religious leaders to claim moral authority over the whole city the way some had tried to do earlier in the century. Religious leaders spoke *from* the center of their particular communities and sometimes even spoke *for* those entire communities, but they knew they no longer spoke for or to all of Indianapolis. The religious community had become too diverse to speak with one voice, and neither minority faiths nor non-churchgoers were keen to accept the leadership of the liberal Protestants who for so long occupied the lion's share of the public square. Religious diversity grew apace, out in the many communities that were pieces of the urban patchwork quilt. But that quilt was sewn together by more universally held cultural norms embodied in the patriotism of the war memorials, in the shared government that kept its administrative distance from religion, in shared commerce that was religiously neutral, and in a growing identification of the city with the very secular realm of athletics, with the city imagined as a sports capital.

Increasing ethnic and cultural pluralism changed the way religion functioned at the city's core. Indianapolis had always to look for new ways to manage differences among its residents; broadening the beliefs, values, and practices that defined good citizenship was the functional response. And in that broadening, other kinds of beliefs and practices — most notably evolving commitments to patriotism, government, sports, and commerce — took on a new public importance. It would be incorrect to say that this developing civil religion replaced the traditional faiths, because the faiths did not disappear. But it would be pointless to deny that in the context of urban realignment, the public role and location of faith was significantly realigned. What it meant to be a community, to have the sort of social capital on which the city as a whole could draw, was altered by these changes in urban structure and coextensive changes in religious culture. Even something as practical and applied as welfare reform stems from new ideas about where and how religious organizations function, preferring smaller, local groups over larger, more metropolitan ones.

Having considered large-scale cultural and structural changes in the city, including religion's shifting role in civic life, it is now time to turn our attention to religion itself and ask what happened to religious life and practice in the city's realignment. The next two chapters are concerned first with religion writ large — the denominations and faith traditions that make up the city — and second with congregations, the hundreds of smaller organizations that constitute the bulk of daily religious practice. Here we will see how urban realignment occurred not only between faiths, but also within them. It is only possible to understand what happened to religious life in the city, and to see how religious organizations have responded to the realigned city, when we understand those changes in the context of the wider urban changes already described.

4

RELIGIOUS TRADITIONS
DIVERSIFIED AND DOMESTICATED

Everyone who knows anything about Italians knows they are Roman
Catholics. . . . If the Methodists are going to spend $15,000 on a new
mission, they might well spend it on the alleged Methodists who don't
go to church and who leave Protestant churches notoriously empty. . . .
Let our Methodist friends take care of their own. Millions of them who
don't go to church need care.

— *Indiana Catholic and Record,* 1916

Urban realignment meant a change in religion's civic role, as we have just
seen, but it also meant great changes within religious traditions and organizations themselves. Indianapolis is today marked by both the enduring
strength of its mainline Protestant establishment and by a new and expansive religious pluralism. This has meant changes in the city's multiple religious subcultures and in the role each has played in the city's evolving civic
and economic core. While religious pluralism was present in Indianapolis
from the outset, its relationship to the mainline Protestant core changed in
conjunction with the loss of public religious authority.

However, the end of the Protestant establishment's hold on the city's civic
identity did not mean that other religious and cultural communities automatically gained an equal voice in the public square. If it is fair to say that
multiple religious constituencies now negotiate civic issues, then it is imper-
ative to note that the establishment Protestants continue to experience a tilt
in their favor.[1] In what follows, we will take a longer look at the changing

situations of the five dominant religious traditions in the city, considering also many of the groups that stand nearer the religious margins.

Historian of American Protestantism William Hutchison[2] points out that understanding the facts of diversity is one thing, but embracing them as pluralism is quite another. Like all large American cities, and, indeed, like America itself, Indianapolis has long been marked by religious diversity. But only recently has pluralism begun to replace the old establishment as the featured aspect of the civic religious scene. Changes in the city's religious demography underscore this change in cultural images. In the early part of the twentieth century, congregations from the Protestant establishment held the majority of religious believers. The establishment then included the many denominations and traditions that would, through a succession of mergers, become the contemporary mainline Protestant establishment: Episcopalians, Presbyterians, Methodists, Disciples of Christ, American (i.e., northern) Baptists, Lutherans, and Congregationalists (later part of the United Church of Christ).

Although the majority of Indianapolis churchgoers attended congregations from one of these traditions, it is important to remember that this did not mean that most Indianapolis residents were churchgoers. Records from the 1926 and 1936 census, along with the more recent Glenmary studies of churches and church membership, suggest that in the twentieth century Indianapolis never had a church membership rate much higher than 50 percent, though it has always hovered near that mark. But in the half of the city that was "churched," mainline Protestants held the numerical supremacy that supported their claim to the city's civic soul.

From the 1930s forward, raw membership numbers in these mainline denominations remained roughly stable and even elevated slightly. However, the city's population more than doubled in the next seventy years, so membership rates — the percentage of residents belonging to any of these groups — fell by nearly half in some cases. The establishment's share of the religious market was dropping, and it began to discover the difference between being first and foremost and being merely first among equals.

During this period of population growth, other traditions saw their memberships rise rapidly. The number of Catholics increased steadily before it also leveled off near mid-century. There was a steep increase in the number of both churches and members in the Black Methodist (AME, CME, AMEZ), Black Pentecostal, and especially the Black Baptist traditions, all tied to the arrival of African Americans from the Great Migration northward. There was corresponding growth among the evangelical traditions of white Protestantism, tied to the immigration of upland southerners to the area. Growth in the evangelical traditions continues to the present.

By the end of the twentieth century, Indianapolis exhibited a mix of *Christian* traditions that set it apart from most other midwestern cities. In Chicago, Detroit, St. Louis, Cincinnati, Louisville, and Milwaukee, Catholics

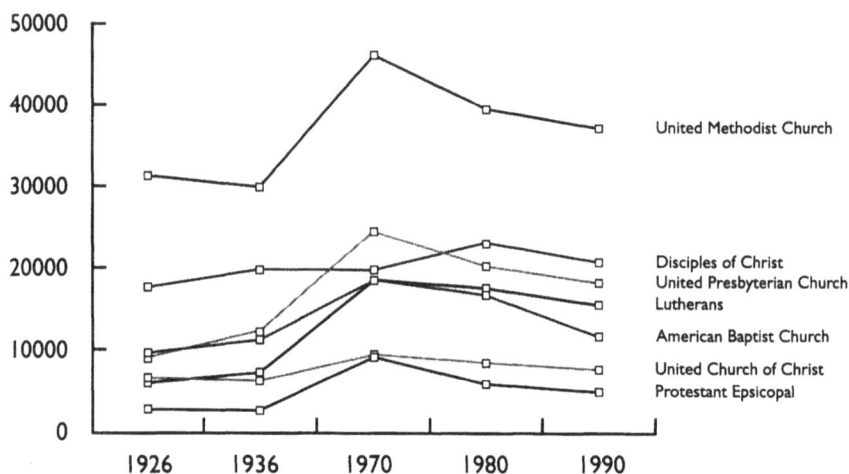

Chart 4.1. Membership in Mainline Protestant Denominations. Courtesy 1926 and 1936 U.S. religious census, and 1970, 1980, 1990 Glenmary Research Center.

account for at least half of the worshipping population. In Indianapolis, they make up just under a quarter of worshippers, or around 10 percent of the city's total population. Because American social research on religion tends to treat every Protestant denomination individually, Catholics can still be described as the largest single group. There are more Catholics than Methodists, Baptists, Lutherans, or any other denomination taken singly. But if one counts all Protestants together, there are many more Protestants than Catholics. Of all the midwestern cities named above, only Indianapolis has more mainline Protestants combined than Catholics, and more evangelicals and independents than Catholics.[3]

Similarly, in most midwestern cities, Jews and non-Western religious groups make up sizeable minority populations. Detroit and Chicago have large and growing Muslim populations. Every midwestern city mentioned here has a larger Jewish population than Indianapolis. When Indianapolis hosted the General Assembly of the Council of Jewish Federations in 1997, it was the least Jewish city ever to have done so. At that time, the entire Indianapolis metropolitan area of approximately 1.2 million people had only some 10,000 culturally Jewish residents and perhaps 6,000 synagogue members.

Indianapolis is Christian, but its Christian heritage is unusually varied. Two subsets deserve special mention. First, compared to other urban areas,

Indianapolis has a high percentage of independent Christian churches. The area has long been a hotbed for reformers seeking a return to the true, apostolic church. The influence of nineteenth-century reformers Stone and Campbell instigated a rise in independent congregations that called themselves merely "Christian," congregations that insisted on their full independence and autonomy. Many of those congregations eventually joined together into a denomination called Christian Church (Disciples of Christ), which is headquartered in Indianapolis. But a substantial number remained independent or left the denomination after joining initially. The cultural views represented by these churches — that the relationship between individuals and Christ is unmediated and that congregations are the autonomous locus of true religious community — continues to occupy a spot deep within the Hoosier psyche.

This independent Christian culture drives the conservative, evangelical wing of Indianapolis's Protestants. Many of the largest congregations are independent Christian. And although independent Christians do not speak with one political voice through any acknowledged representative, they nonetheless comprise an important body of public opinion. In the capital city of a state so thoroughly conservative in politics and in culture, the populist, conservative, independent ideas of these congregations and their members represent an important cultural, as well as religious, bloc.

A second noteworthy Christian subset involves those denominations that are not part of the mainline Protestant establishment but do not seem quite comfortable in other traditional sociological categories such as "fundamentalist," "evangelical," or "Pentecostal." Indianapolis is home to Nazarenes, Seventh Day Adventists, Friends (Quakers), and its own local denomination, the "Church of God, Anderson, Indiana," in numbers that exceed national averages. The establishment core — even when it was the city's cultural center of gravity — was always surrounded by such alternative religious centers pushing toward greater inclusion.

With this cursory introduction to the city's religious landscape in mind, we can now look more closely at changes in the metropolitan area's religious makeup in order to understand the evolving relationship among its multiple religious centers. This requires a look at not only the city proper, but also at the county that includes and surrounds it. In 1926, Marion County had a population of roughly 423,000. In the 2000 census, that population had roughly doubled to some 850,000. Keeping just those two figures in mind, it is possible to see the important changes that decreased the "market share" of mainline Protestants and their corresponding cultural influence.

There were 31,000 United Methodists in Marion County in 1926; in 1990 there were 37,000. Still, over the sixty-four-year period, the increasing raw number of United Methodists went from 7 percent to 4 percent of the population. Other mainline denominations fared much the same. The Disciples of Christ grew from 17,600 to 20,600, but experienced a considerable proportionate decline. United Presbyterians experienced greater gains, more than doubling from 1926 to 1970, before dropping back off again in the last three decades of the century. Episcopalians, always a relatively small group, went from 2,500 members in 1926 to nearly 9,000 in 1970 before dropping back off to about 4,500 by 2000.

All told, mainline Protestants dropped from about 21 percent of the population to about 13 percent of the population over the last three quarters of the twentieth century. But the area as a whole became no less "churched" during this period. In fact, allowing for some unavoidable inconsistencies in counting religious adherents, overall membership in religious groups rose from 41 percent to 46 percent of the population during that time. That means mainline Protestants declined from fully half of the church-affiliated population to just over a quarter of it, and decreased from more than a fifth of the total population to about an eighth.

Anyone familiar with American religion in the twentieth century will know which religious groups picked up the numerical slack; namely, Catholics and evangelical Protestants. Over the same historical period from 1926 to the present, the number of Catholics in Indianapolis more than doubled. Like the mainline denominations, Catholics peaked in 1970 and then declined somewhat, though Hispanic migrants in the late 1990s produced another Catholic surge. At the recent turn of the century, Indianapolis had just slightly fewer Catholics than members of all mainline Protestant denominations taken together.

However, the bulk of religious growth was paced by other religious groups. In Indianapolis as in many other cities, it is the evangelical churches, both white and black, that have flourished. In 1926, the two largest mainline denominations, United Methodists and Disciples of Christ, had between them more members than all of the non-mainline, non-Catholic religious groups put together. By the end of the century, those other groups had three times as many members as United Methodists and Disciples combined.

And yet this story of mainline Protestant declension is a little misleading. The fact that the number of United Methodists in Marion County dropped from 46,000 in 1970 to 39,000 in 1980 suggests something was up. Presbyterians went from 24,000 to 20,000, American Baptists from 18,000 to 16,000, and Episcopalians from nearly 9,000 to 5,600 in the same period. Even the Catholic Church went from 92,000 to 85,000 during that decade. All of these decreases came after periods of slow but steady increase. The "white flight" of the 1970s changed the demography of the city's white Protestants in ways that can be misleading. Those people did not all die, become irreligious, or change their affiliation. Some just moved to the suburbs.

To understand religion's presence in Indianapolis as multicentered, it is necessary to recognize the largest religious traditions and to consider the cultural role each plays in creating urban community. We begin, appropriately, with mainline Protestants.

AN ENERVATED ESTABLISHMENT

Traditionally, the tall-steeple churches of the Protestant establishment were located along Meridian Street, starting at the Circle and moving northward. By the 1970s, most of the establishment churches remained along Meridian Street, but many of their members now drove considerable distances inward from the suburbs to reach them. The Episcopalian Christ Church Cathedral still sits at the north side of the Circle, but its continuing presence is a subtle tribute to the commercial interests that dominate the downtown agenda. Eli Lilly, Indianapolis's most important business and philanthropic leader, was an active member of Christ Church. Beyond the large sums donated by the Lilly family to the Lilly Endowment, one Lilly personally bequeathed an endowment to Christ Church with the stipulation that the church stay in the city's center. In the late 1990s Christ Church's endowment passed $85 million in value, the kind of money that makes resisting the temptation to sell property with a high commercial value for a move to the suburbs less painful.

Christ Church serves as a symbolic gateway from the Circle northward onto Meridian Street. During the course of the twentieth century, the better-off, better-educated residents of Indianapolis moved farther and farther north along Meridian Street. The city's most prestigious addresses, including the eventual location of the governor's mansion, are here, as are the congregations, like Second Presbyterian, that are woven into the cultural, political, and economic networks of the city's leadership. The other Episcopalian congregations also personally endowed by the Lilly family, Trinity and St. Paul, are also on Meridian. Together with Christ Church, these three controlled far in excess of $100 million during the stock market's heyday in the late 1990s. The three most powerful United Methodist churches — North UMC, Meridian Street UMC, and St. Luke UMC — are located along the Meridian Street corridor. The current president of Lilly Endowment is a member at one of these. Not surprisingly, the city's highly visible, civic-minded, Reform Jewish congregation also has a northern Meridian Street address, as does the Catholic cathedral.

A map of these important establishment congregations shows them to be a pillar extending northward from the center of the city. A map of addresses for the members of most of these congregations looks like a river, running narrowly up Meridian Street before emptying into a broad delta across the northern suburbs. These congregations are, not surprisingly, home to many of the Indianapolis elite, so they exercise the kind of public influence associated with other elite organizations.

Christ Church, Second Presbyterian, and the other Meridian Street congregations are symbols of establishment power and influence, but the role of the Lilly Endowment, sitting in their midst, is far more than symbolic.

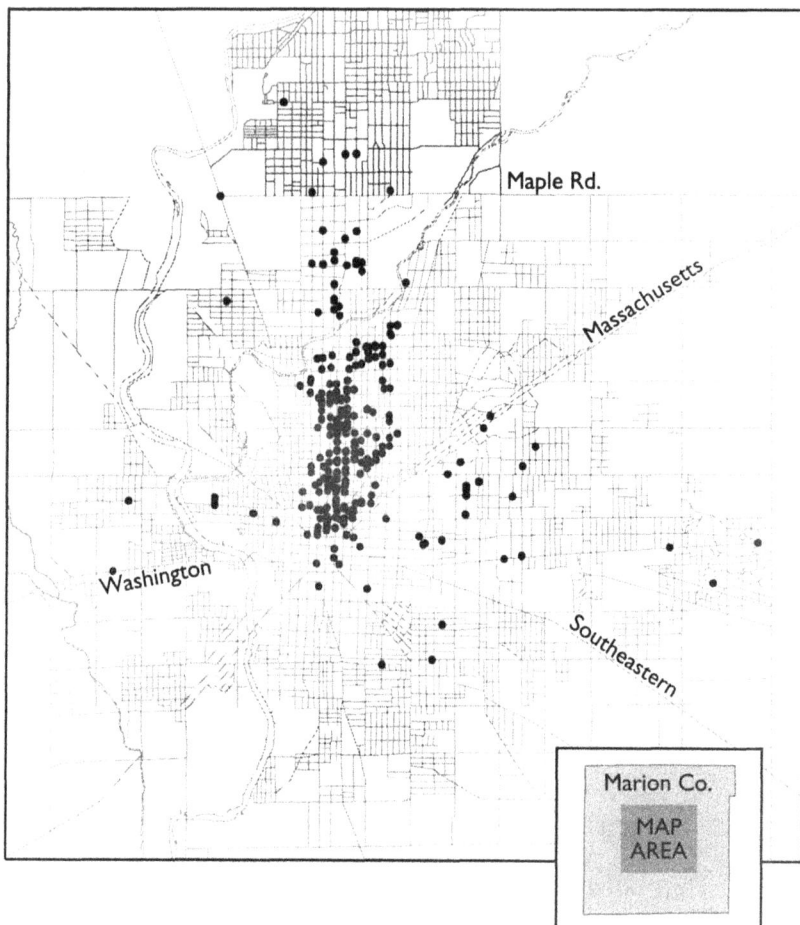

Map 4.1.(a) Second Presbyterian Church Members' Residences, 1909.
Courtesy The Polis Center.

From its own Meridian Street address, the Endowment uses its holdings —
roughly $15 billion at its peak[4] — to invest tens of millions of dollars in the
Indianapolis community each year. In addition to support for educational
institutions, the sports facilities, and a variety of community development
efforts, the Endowment makes more direct investments in the city's religious sector.[5]

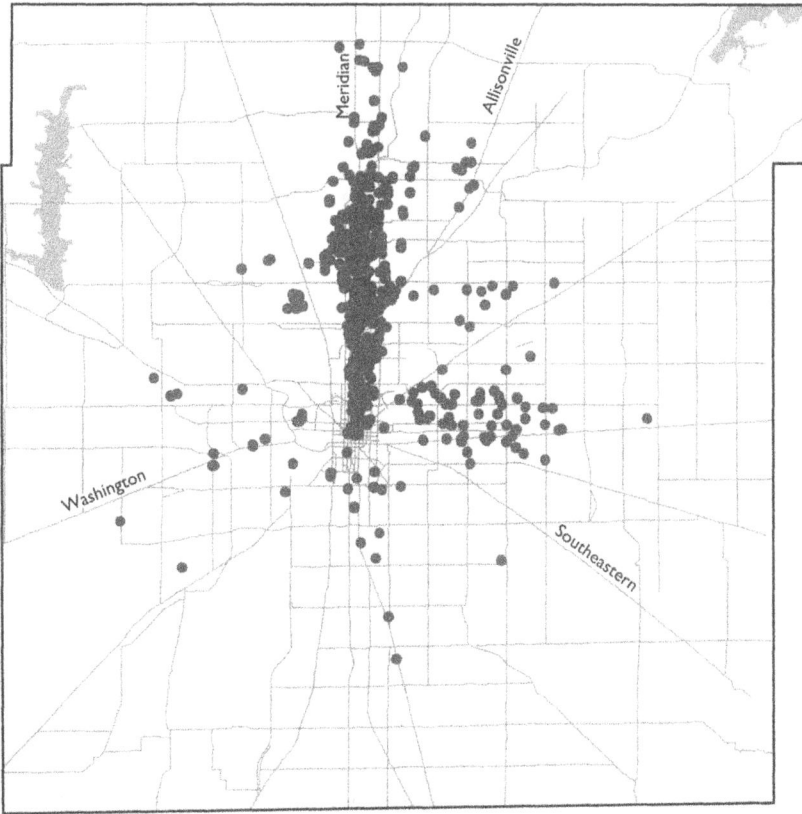

Map 4.1.(b) Second Presbyterian Church Members' Residences, 1947.
Courtesy The Polis Center.

As we saw in Chapter 2, the Endowment's largesse touches nearly everyone in the city, and its influence adds luster to the image of the mainline
churches, whose members include many officers of the Endowment. The
Endowment has a policy of not supporting the basic programs or operating
budgets of particular congregations. Still, these organizations do benefit
from programs and organizations that promote their interests. For example, in the late 1990s, Lilly invested several million dollars in the Indianapolis Center for Congregations, an affiliate of the Alban Institute, designed to provide counsel and aid to churches throughout the city.

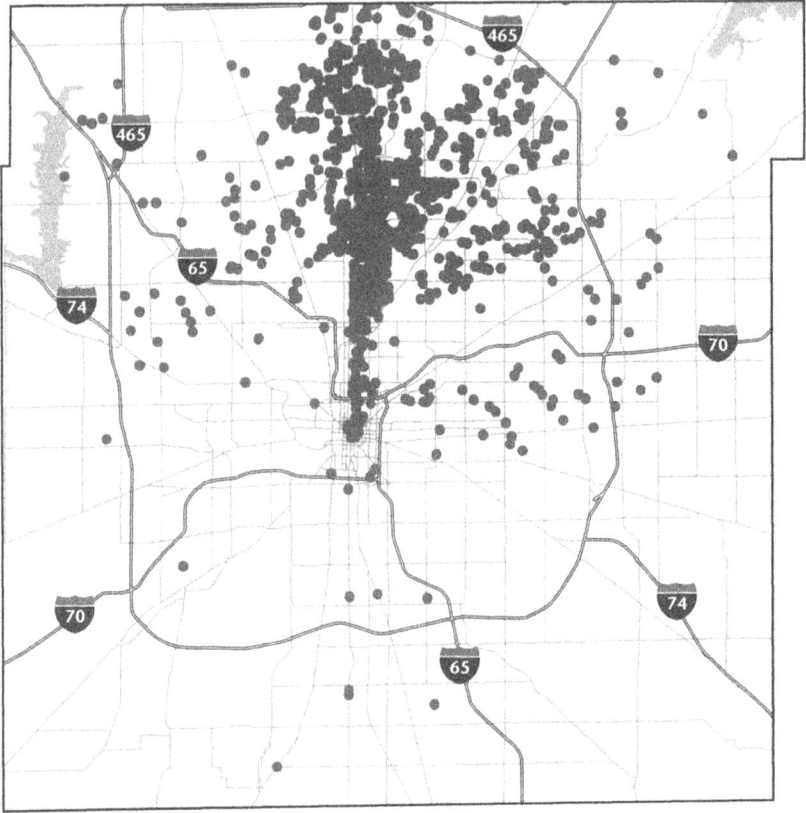

Map 4.1.(c) Second Presbyterian Church Members' Residences, 1964.
Courtesy The Polis Center.

The Instructive Saga of "Second Presbyterian"

No church's history tells the story of establishment religion in Indianapolis more clearly than Second Presbyterian Church, the "new school" Presbyterian congregation that split from the "old school" First Presbyterian because its members emphasized human initiative for salvation over the stricter, more traditional Calvinism of First. It is worth pausing to review its century-and-a-half history.

Second Presbyterian's first pastor was the young Henry Ward Beecher, later to become one of America's foremost orators of the nineteenth cen-

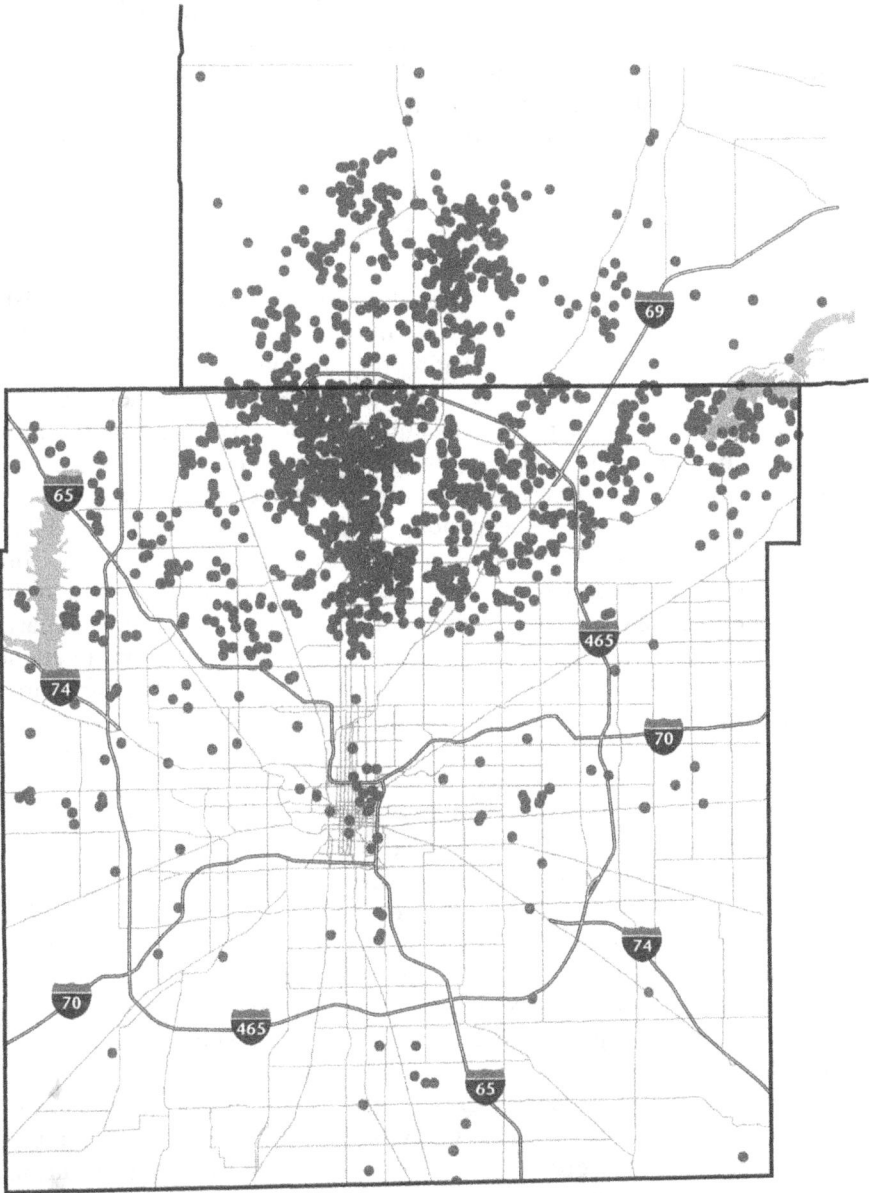

Map 4.1.(d) Second Presbyterian Church Members' Residences, 1997.
Courtesy The Polis Center.

tury. Beecher's pragmatic, informal style quickly made this the largest Presbyterian congregation in the state, and he came to symbolize the link between the religious establishment and the broader cultural elite. Not only was he an outspoken advocate of temperance and common education, but he served as editor of the *Indiana Farmer and Gardener* and as a trustee of Wabash College.

Even by the late 1800s, property on the Indianapolis Circle was more valuable to commercial interests than to churches, and Second Presbyterian moved a few blocks north, just off Meridian Street at the corner of Vermont and Pennsylvania streets. Here Second Presbyterian became the establishment's leading light, planting seven churches or missions and using the message of the Social Gospel to begin programs later termed "urban ministry." In the early part of the twentieth century, Rev. Jean Milner became a liberal, modernist leader from Second Presbyterian's pulpit in the fight against fundamentalist interpretations of evolution. His book *The Sky Is Red* took the anti-fundamentalist argument beyond the city to the nation.[6]

By the 1950s, the city was expanding its downtown War Memorial Plaza. Many buildings had been razed in the late twenties and early thirties, but now more land was needed, including the sites of two churches. Just as the Monument at the center of the Circle reflected the increasing role of patriotism in shaping the city's common bonds, so would the grassy mall and expanded World War Memorial further define Indianapolis's public character. Second Presbyterian was offered the opportunity to move northward again, this time displaced by civic-patriotic concerns rather than by civic-commercial ones.

Not everyone in the congregation wanted to move to the northern suburbs. Such a move would be expensive, and the congregation would lose touch with its urban roots. The first concern was allayed when anonymous donors provided both a parcel of prime real estate at 7700 North Meridian Street and enough money to move into a large, French Gothic church with fine stained glass and a powerful pipe organ free of any mortgage. The second concern proved more difficult. Second Presbyterian had been crucial to the city's civic life, but its urban ministries would now be conducted at a distance.

The congregation's civic influence is easily demonstrated. Second Presbyterian produced the Rev. William Hudnut, the minister-mayor who presided over major economic growth from 1976 to 1992. The long-time chairman of Lilly Endowment was a Second Presbyterian member until his death in the late 1990s. The current vice president for religion at Lilly Endowment is a member there, as is the former head of the city-county council who oversaw the merger of Indianapolis and Marion County through Unigov. The pastor of Second Presbyterian at this writing is a board member at Lilly Endowment. In 2000, Bart Peterson — both a Democrat and a Second Presbyterian member — became the city's new mayor.

The congregation is still active in urban ministry. For many years it maintained a partnership with Westminster Presbyterian on the city's struggling east side. Second provided an annual six-figure budget and many volunteers for Westminster's direct-care ministries, operating mostly out of public view.

Much more in the public eye is Celebration of Hope, an annual attempt to create intentionally interracial worship. Second Presbyterian was the original cosponsor of this event with Light of the World Christian Church, one of the city's tall-steeple, African American congregations. Light of the World's influential pastor joined with Second Presbyterian's pastor in a very public attempt to draw as many congregations as possible into a worship service in a large venue such as the old Market Square Arena or the Convention Center downtown.

In so many ways, Second Presbyterian's story is the story of the city's mainline establishment writ small. It was originally built on the Circle, intended as a bulwark of the civic-religious core of the Protestant city. It always took a "new light" view of theology, emphasizing the importance of human initiative, a foundational ideology in a city that would come to be dominated by commerce and a "can do" attitude. Like the establishment itself, Second Presbyterian was gradually displaced from its central location, first by the commercial and more broadly civic, secular interests that came to characterize the Circle and then by the civic, patriotic creation of the World War Memorial that came to represent the downtown core.

What happened to Second Presbyterian then, though, is an equally important part of the story. Although the congregation found itself in a more residential setting, surrounded by residents who shared its members' social class and status, it did not retire into a purely local role as a suburban country club. Second continued to produce, and to be the spiritual home for, important leaders in business, political, and civic life. It continued to be active in urban ministries, albeit now with partners who were truly "urban." And perhaps most importantly, it still looked for those points of intersection, most notably in the Celebration of Hope, where its own theological and moral concerns could link with those of others in the interest of improving the city's broader sense of itself as a community.

Second Presbyterian continues to be active in many important ways, but after its relocation, it acted in ways that acknowledged it was no longer itself at the center of the city, either literally or symbolically, but that it was a constituent part of one faith tradition among multiple traditions. Second Presbyterian still offers crucial leadership, but it is leadership cognizant of the fact that it speaks from the point of view of one faith community among many. Despite the congregation's wealth, despite the social influence of its members, and even despite its longstanding ties as the single congregation most intertwined with the Lilly Endowment, Second Presbyterian is today just one congregation located nearly eight miles from the Circle. Like other congregations, it is full of relatively homogeneous members who share most of the social characteristics of their immediate neighbors. It no longer sits at the city's center or imagines itself to speak for the city as a whole.

The Establishment

Of course, Second Presbyterian has not been the only home to Indianapolis's most influential citizens. A handful of other tall-steeple churches also claim important members of the city's establishment. The three endowed Episcopal congregations along Meridian Street play a role. Because of its large endowment, Christ Church could afford to stay on the Circle and offer the city's most symbolically public religious presence even as the others moved north. Christ Church also serves as the principal funding partner in a number of urban ministries. Meanwhile, three United Methodist congregations—North, Meridian Street, and St. Luke's, each progressively further north or "out" along Meridian Street—house members like the current president of Lilly Endowment and U.S. Senator Richard Lugar. When Second Presbyterian's pastor stepped aside as the white establishment partner in the Celebration of Hope in 2000, there was little surprise when St. Luke's pastor filled that role.

Away from Meridian Street, Indianapolis is home to roughly 300 churches that are members of the mainline Protestant denominations but are not so tightly linked to the city's political and economic power. These churches are scattered throughout Indianapolis and are historically tied to specific neighborhoods, even if many of their members now drive in from more distant suburbs. They tend to be larger than the average congregation in other Protestant traditions, in part because some mainline denominations are able to manage growth through closing and opening churches as needed. Together these other mainline churches help make the point that most congregations are engaged in worship, religious education, and relatively low-level mission activities, sometimes to local neighbors, but often not. Although the political, economic, and cultural interests of these congregations may be different than their counterparts in Catholic, Jewish, white evangelical, or African American traditions, in other ways they are just one more constituent part of the pluralistic congregational mix.[7]

The decline, though not the demise, of the Protestant mainline establishment was a national trend over the last four decades of the twentieth century. In 1960, of 535 members of the U.S. Senate and House of Representatives, 63 percent belonged to one of the mainline Protestant denominations. By 1997, that number was down to 249, or 47 percent. During that same period, Catholics in Congress went from 102 to 147, Jews from 12 to 32, and Mormons from 7 to 14.[8] This was not a coup of religious pluralism—the establishment was still quite established—but it did represent a gradual shift away from the old core and toward recognition of multiple cultural centers tied not only to ideas or ethnicity, but to geography as well.

In Indianapolis, other changes point not merely to the effects of urban realignment on the Protestant establishment, but also to the corresponding emergence of a new civic, economic, and political order that was more religiously pluralistic. And given the old establishment's desire to suppress division and discord, it is no surprise that public religious content grew ever more generalized, and the highly specific public rituals defined by mainline Protestant content gradually receded.

Perhaps the best example of this broadened religious base is the development of Christian Theological Seminary (CTS). Because the Christian Church (Disciples of Christ) has its administrative headquarters in Indianapolis, it makes sense that the city would have an affiliated seminary. But CTS, once Butler University's College of Religion, has quite intentionally become interdenominational, setting itself as the ecumenical learning center for all of the city's liberal Protestants and many others besides.

The CTS campus boasts architectural and artistic treasures, provided by another important central Indiana philanthropist, J. Irwin Miller of the diesel engine manufacturer Cummins, Inc. Miller was the first lay president of the National Council of Churches and one of the nation's foremost proponents of ecumenism. His home church, North Christian in Columbus, Indiana, was designed by Eero Saarinen as a modern model for interfaith worship. In many ways, CTS represents the whole metaphor: the Protestant establishment's dream of ecumenical harmony, the loss of the establishment's cultural power, and the gradual shift in religion's public role linked to its cultural pluralism.

Public religious content became more general, as the ecumenists intended, but the results were not the ones they had planned for. Establishment Protestants imagined a generalized Protestantism into which other traditions could gradually blend, a melting pot for which they forged the cauldron. But the ecumenical institutions they forged, always linked to their cultural dominance, eventually faltered.

Just next to Christian Theological Seminary sits the Interchurch Center, home to the Indianapolis Church Federation. The Federation has fallen far from its heyday in the 1950s when liberal Protestant desires for ecumenism had considerable social force.[9] As the establishment monopoly eroded, so did the taken-for-granted relationship between the core and periphery that had animated the Federation. By the late 1990s, the Church Federation was struggling to pay its bills. Most importantly, the Lilly Endowment and most of the denominational offices had stopped paying direct support, though some still give nominal sums that "passed through" for specific programs.

While Indianapolis is a more Protestant city than Chicago, Milwaukee, St. Louis, Louisville, or Cincinnati, it is now a less "mainline city" than the Indianapolis of yesteryear. The city has always nurtured alternative religious traditions that have recently become more prominent and more powerful. There are large numbers of Catholics, a small but influential Jewish community, hundreds of churches from the African American traditions, and a thriving evangelical or independent Christian community.

The interplay among and between these groups has become increasingly complex and multifocal as outward pressure raised the status of particular communities and as the city's metropolitan identity was increasingly shaped by a civic agenda ever less shaped by the Protestant establishment. These other religious traditions were never wholly defined by that establishment, they were never "sects" to its "church." But their relationship to public life in the city must be understood in the context of changes in their relationship to the establishment, all part of the larger urban realignment. It would be possible, of course, to tell much of the story of Catholics, Jews, African Americans, or white evangelicals in Indianapolis without reference to mainline Protestants. But the story of those groups as civic actors defining the city's public identity could never be told apart from their changing relationship to the elite civic core.

CATHOLICS ON THE MOVE

The decline of the Protestant establishment's local monopoly corresponded to emerging opportunities for other groups to raise their voices in the public square, and no group has done that more effectively in Indianapolis than Catholics. As we have already noted, immigration led to a rapid rise in the number of Catholics in the nineteenth century. In the twentieth century those Catholics formed strong organizations such as schools and social services that allowed them to remain separate from the Protestant majority's control.

The growth in the Catholic population did not go unnoticed or unchallenged. As described in Chapter 3, much of Indiana's Ku Klux Klan activity during the 1920s was aimed at intimidating Catholics into accepting their subordinate social status. Anti-Catholic discrimination in Indianapolis was unlike that in most midwestern cities. In many cities, Catholics were either moving toward or already held an outright political majority. Discrimination was a matter of separating Catholic places from non-Catholic ones. In Indianapolis, Catholics had to define themselves publicly vis-à-vis a much larger Protestant establishment and to survive a period of serious hostility from the Klan. This minority status helped Catholics develop an even stronger organizational infrastructure than they might otherwise have done. Strong pastoral leadership from Bishop Joseph Chartrand in the early part of the twentieth century helped both the diocese and the parishes become self-sustaining centers in response to public prejudice.[10]

In one sense, Catholics led the movement toward stronger local congregations through their commitment to parish life. Several of the parishes were clearly and unapologetically defined by ethnicity. The parishes themselves did not make any broad claim on the public symbols or the moral life of the city as a whole. But Catholics also maintained strong, overarching organizations, not least because the parishes worked cooperatively to provide their own schools and social services in contrast to the alienating public alternatives. This strong, centralized infrastructure was capable of monitoring parish boundaries and managing organizational growth. It involved the most bureaucratic, rational control of any of the institutional religious traditions. The late twentieth century saw the weakening of Protestant denominational structures throughout the country as congregations assumed greater autonomy. But Catholics have been able to maintain the importance of local parishes while still managing resources from a central organization. In that sense, then, they were especially well-equipped to countenance both the outward pressure toward particular, local communities and the need to hold the center together.

Fixed bureaucracies employing rational management techniques are not always a blessing. Administrative arrangements have histories and ecclesiastical policies sometimes assume a logic of their own that is not always adapted to changes in the surrounding society.[11] Because current diocesan boundaries were set before suburbanization hit its stride, the northern suburbs of Indianapolis are actually part of the Lafayette diocese. So, in a city where resource distribution is decidedly uneven, the wealthiest suburbs fall under the administrative control of a bishop located in a much smaller town fifty miles away in a diocese composed mostly of farmland. Still, for weal or for woe, Catholic religious life in Indianapolis is far more clearly organized than in any Protestant tradition.

There are only forty-two parishes in Indianapolis proper, and this would seem a small sample of the city's 1,200 congregations, except that they contain some 90,000 members, nearly a quarter of the city's churchgoing population. As these numbers suggest, the average parish is much bigger than the average congregation, with the average parish containing more than 2,300 members and some including upwards of 5,000. Parishes tend to have multiple staff members; many have parochial schools. The average budget is likely to surpass $1 million, making it possible to administer multiple programs for education and social services. Today Catholics enforce parish boundaries much less than they did even twenty years ago, but they still maintain clearly defined catchment areas for each. Moreover, the central Catholic bureaucracy has been willing to move resources from one parish to another, even to open or close parishes while shifting boundaries as demography dictates.[12]

But parishes are not distinguished merely by size and resources. Catholic parishes are still primarily defined by geographic boundaries. Individual Catholics are generally expected to attend the parish that serves their neighborhood. Many Catholics choose to worship outside their parish boundaries, but the fact remains that geography binds Catholic congregations more than Protestant ones, making congregational membership among people of different social classes or ethnic backgrounds more likely. Perhaps more than anything else, however, Catholic parishes are distinguished by the degree to which they are subject to centralized bureaucratic authority. It is important not to exaggerate that authority and to imagine that parishes are much more dependent on the archbishop's office than they really are. But it is equally important to recognize that centralized power gives Catholicism a centered quality that no other large religious tradition shares in quite the same measure.

If ever a church reflected both the power of metropolitan change to shape religious practice and the ability of the archdiocese to invoke central management when necessary, it is St. Francis de Sales parish, founded in 1881 near the town's center on its southeast side. With space originally carved out of St. Joseph's parish, St. Francis was a mission of St. John's and Sacred Heart churches. St. Francis was composed nearly equally of members from the two largest groups of European immigrants to settle Indianapolis, Irish and Germans.

Through the years, St. Francis's boundaries were changed to reflect shifts in population caused by new neighborhood development, increased use of automobiles, and eventual white flight. Like many urban parishes and the neighborhoods they represent, it struggled to maintain a consistent membership base. Finally, the development of the interstate highway system through downtown Indianapolis literally determined which neighborhoods would survive and which would be subdivided. When whites began leaving the downtown after the advent of forced busing, and when Unigov changed the political structure, the Catholic hierarchy was forced to respond to its changing organizational base.

A letter from the Rev. Edward O'Meara, archbishop of Indianapolis, came on the 15th of April 1983, to the 102-year-old parish. O'Meara called it "difficult to write for it is with great regret that I inform (you)" that St. Francis was to be closed. "Due to the construction of interstate Highway 70, St. Francis has lost such great numbers of parishioners that the valiant few of you remaining can no longer maintain the parish." The closing date was set for June 30, just ten weeks later. To emphasize the role played by Interstate 70 in St. Francis's demise, the archdiocese made it the new boundary for the parishes that would receive St. Francis's members. Its April 15th decree said that St. Philip Neri would begin at "Sherman and I-70, running east on I-70 to Commerce." St. Rita would run from 30th Street "all the way to I-70." St. Therese would "start at I-70 and run west to Sherman Drive."

This vignette points out three characteristics that make Catholics an important but anomalous religious center in Indianapolis. First, it illustrates just how much each parish is a center unto itself, complete with distinct boundaries and a house of worship meant to focus the geographic area's spiritual life. The centers can be moved, as they were in this case, but each area is by definition a community with definite responsibilities.

Second, it points out that Catholicism is not only steeped in a long tradition, but it is bureaucratically directed. The archbishop's office exercises a control over the whole of Catholic life for which there is no neat parallel in any other Indianapolis religious tradition of any consequence. Because Catholicism has a *center*, it is able to coordinate, or at least to influence, the trajectory of the forty-two separate Catholic parishes that make up the city.

Third, it shows just how anomalous Catholic congregations are in Indianapolis, whether measured in terms of size, membership heterogeneity, numbers of full-time staff, or central management. Unlike so many other midwestern industrial cities, Indianapolis is *not* a Catholic town. Its neighborhoods are rarely defined by parish boundaries, contemporary or historical. Extended full-time staffs are the norm for Catholics, but unusual in a city where both the mean and the median number of full-time church staff members is one. Catholic parishes are roughly *seven* times the size of the city's average Protestant congregation. Such anomalies helped Catholics merge into the city's establishment and into its cultural mainstream through the 1950s to the 1970s.

The continuing presence of parochial schools is the most visible sign of Catholics' organizational strength and the most vocal outlet for Catholic voices in the public square. In the 1970s, Indianapolis experienced busing for the purposes of desegregation. Judge Hugh Dillin intended to break yet another monopoly of the white establishment by creating equal educational opportunities throughout the city. However, he insisted only that African American children be bused out to the suburban schools of the townships, not that white, suburban children be bused inwards.

In addition to hastening a white exodus into the even more distant suburbs beyond Marion County's townships, this one-way busing left many inner-city neighborhood school districts in barren disarray. In some districts, urban parochial schools have become the de facto neighborhood schools for children of all races — and all religions. In some parishes, non-Catholics whose children attend are allowed to sit on the school councils, turning the old exclusion of Catholics from public services on its head. Catholicism has in many cases become a "public" resource.

Catholicism has gradually become a second establishment religious voice in the public square. Catholic schools and Catholic social services came to be seen as parallel, cooperative efforts with public schools and public services. Federal grants were often funneled through the city to Catholic agencies. Catholics had long taken advantage of the public educational opportunities available at Indiana University and Purdue, as well as at Notre Dame in the northern part of the state. Gradually the private colleges became more broadly based, losing most of their religious identities and abandon-

ing practices such as mandatory chapel attendance, thus making attendance by Catholics and members of other religious traditions more likely.
The Lilly Endowment began eventually to support Catholic institutions and
initiatives.

Mayor Stephen Goldsmith (1992–1999), a Jew, served as the honorary
head of the Catholic campaign to raise funds for diocesan schools. A Republican, Goldsmith mixed his enthusiasm for privatization and faith-based
solutions to civic problems with his frustration that, in Indianapolis, the may-
or's office has no authority over public schools. According to one member of
the diocesan board, Mayor Goldsmith's ardor for these private schools and
for school choice, combined with his with repeated criticisms of the beleaguered Indianapolis public schools, nearly became an embarrassment to
Catholics. The mayor toned down the comparison, though his enthusiasm
caused a diocesan official to remark that he seemed "almost Catholic."

It is not new for Catholic leaders to seek to avoid rocking the larger civic
boat while taking their turn at the helm. After World War II, Catholic political leaders began to move beyond their subcultural center to play a more
active role in the city as a whole. Since 1948 Indianapolis has had three
Catholic mayors, Albert Feeney (1948–1950), Philip Bayt (1950–1951;
1956–1959), and John Barton (1964–1967). Feeney was a Notre Dame
man, still within the Catholic circle, but Barton went to Purdue like so many
other Hoosiers of every tradition. Catholics moved into other positions of
civic power as well. Layman Michael Carroll, an IU alumnus, was deputy
mayor in the Lugar administration and later vice president for community
development at Lilly Endowment. Carroll played a major role in the downtown's revitalization and in Indianapolis's development as an amateur sports
center.

Nothing symbolizes the movement of Catholics into the mainstream
of Indianapolis culture more than the practice — begun by Archbishop
O'Meara in the 1980s — of a Catholic priest offering the opening prayer at
the famed Indianapolis 500 auto race on Memorial Day weekend. The tradition was begun and sustained by the new Catholic owners of the track. In
1999, Billy Graham, in town for his Indianapolis crusade, was selected as the
first Protestant in decades to offer the prayer, a move that was widely noted
as a popular, though hardly jarring, form of ecumenism.

Catholics have made their public voices heard without often sounding
loud or shrill. The current archbishop traditionally takes a low-key public
approach to issues such as abortion or capital punishment. He, like most
Catholics in the city, seems to recognize that gradual movement through
influence and negotiation with insiders is the key to change in Indianapolis,
not loud demands made by outsiders. The organized Catholic archdiocese,
managing forty-two centers of religious activity including schools that assumed increasing local importance in the wake of forced busing, came to
speak in tones that made the effects of religious multicentering clear. More

than any other religious tradition, Catholics have made the shift from periphery to core and have been both a cause and a beneficiary of the Protestant establishment's loosening grip.

JUDAISM AS A MINORITY WITH MUSCLE

Catholics were not the only primary beneficiaries of a more inclusive political and economic arena; Indianapolis's Jewish community is another. Although the community is relatively small, with roughly 10,000 members and five synagogues of different theological traditions, it still speaks as a community through its cooperative organizations. The individual members of the synagogues support a Jewish Federation, a Jewish Community Center, and a Hebrew Academy. Jews do not share a fully homogeneous set of political or economic interests any more than Catholics, Methodists, or Southern Baptists do. Still, ideas and practices that are important to the community as a whole are mediated through organizations that are at once religious, social, and political. Like Catholics, Jews built a self-sufficient infrastructure — a separate center — through which they negotiated organizationally with the city's political and civic organizations.[13]

As a religious subculture, Judaism has negotiated a place for itself in the emerging order. The Jewish tradition of political involvement culminated in the election of the aforementioned Stephen Goldsmith as mayor in 1992. Mayor Goldsmith's election suggests that being Jewish was not much of a handicap, though pundits continue to disagree whether Mrs. Goldsmith's status as an evangelical Christian helped his candidacy, hindered it, or indicated that religious identity just does not matter very much these days. Certainly Jewish business interests are prominent downtown. A Jewish business leader owns Emmis Communications, which features both the leading AM radio station in Indianapolis — the one with largest farm report audience — and the newest building on the Circle. Another prominent Jewish family is a leading property developer and owners of the National Basketball Association team, the Pacers.

The same social forces that eroded the Protestant monopoly and drew Jews into the Indianapolis establishment have also meant potential problems for the Jewish community. At the turn of the twenty-first century, all of the synagogues and the Jewish Community Center are located near one neighborhood, north of downtown near the city's "old money" but south of the new, expanding developments further north. As middle-class Jews, like mainline Protestants and increasing numbers of Catholics, have gradually migrated toward the far northern suburbs, the synagogues had to reconsider their location during the 1980s and 1990s. Should they invest heavily in renovating their facilities and invest jointly in rejuvenating the Community Center, or would that money be better spent building facilities farther north? The community decided, together, to stay in its current location and to invest in revitalization.

Such solidarity was hard-won. Indianapolis's Jews are now most clearly identified with one neighborhood, but they have been split before. In the late nineteenth century, most Jews lived on the south side of the city. The more prosperous German Jews — more likely to be members of the Reform traditions — gradually migrated north, leaving the eastern Europeans and the Sephardic community — more Orthodox and Conservative — on the south side. Not until the mid-twentieth century did the community coalesce in its current neighborhood. The solidarity expressed in the decision to keep the synagogues and the Community Center where they are belies the ever-present possibility of new tension among Indianapolis's Jews.

As a minority religious presence, Jews have managed their own internal affairs in the face of metropolitan changes over which they have had little control and vis-à-vis an evolving economic and political realm that has been largely indifferent. Like Catholics, many members of the Jewish community have held high public profiles in business and media, but they tend to minimize political stridency, as is the Indianapolis way. Even during the Klan years of the 1920s, the *Indiana Jewish Chronicle* recommended "silent contempt" as a response to rabid xenophobia. Today, when rabbis write columns for the "Faith and Values" section of *Indianapolis Star,* they are more likely to use stories and parables to illuminate broad principles about moral life than to challenge established political practice. It is not farfetched to say that in Indianapolis, change is gradual. People go along and get along.

Indianapolis's Jews have become part of the city's political and economic order, with key business leaders and a two-term mayor. Unlike Catholic interests, Jewish interests are not high on the agenda of the Lilly Endowment. But like Catholics, Jewish civic leaders tend to downplay religious difference or dissent in ways that allow this distinctly minority community to participate fully in the city's evolving, yet culturally Christian, civic life.

The handful of Jewish congregations in Indianapolis are easy to discuss as a group, but it would be wrong to miss the different congregational identities within the group or to infer too much social homogeneity. Indianapolis Hebrew Congregation is a liberal congregation in the Reform tradition. It is Indianapolis's oldest synagogue, founded in 1856. Sitting along Meridian Street in the most upscale section of town, it remains virtually the "tall-steeple church" among synagogues. Several prominent business leaders attend this congregation and it hosts regular public lectures on topics of broad concern.

Three of the other synagogues are tightly clustered around the Jewish Community Center in one relatively small inner suburb. Beth-El Zedeck, a Conservative-Reconstructionist synagogue, is the largest of these three. Its husband-and-wife rabbi team are celebrities in Indianapolis, at least compared to most other clergy. Their fiftieth birthdays — celebrated the same year — merited a mention, with photographs, in *Indianapolis* magazine.

The other two synagogues in the neighborhood represent two other important wings of American Judaism. The larger of these is B'nai Torah, the city's Orthodox synagogue. Although this congregation does not have a prominent public presence in Indianapolis life, it also counts influential business leaders among its members. The other synagogue, Etz Chaim, is part of the Sephardic tradition. Etz Chaim keeps an even lower profile and is, indeed, largely unknown to those outside the Jewish community.

The fifth synagogue, Shaarey Tefilla, is today Conservative, but in 1963 it was a United Orthodox congregation formed by three groups emigrating northward from the south side. In 1992, Chavurah Shalom, a new Conservative group composed mostly of baby-boom newcomers to the city, approached the United Orthodox congregation about the possibility of renting space to worship since the synagogue already had a kosher kitchen and four scrolls of the Torah.

The members of Chavurah Shalom displayed entrepreneurial fervor from the outset. To announce their first Shabbat service, they invited everyone on the Jewish Federation's mailing list, promising that theirs would be the normative standard for Conservative worship. Not surprisingly, the leaders of Beth-El Zedeck, the city's established Conservative synagogue affiliated with the Reconstructionist movement, took offense. As a Conservative-Reconstructionist congregation, they had coexisted with the Orthodox, Reform, and Sephardic congregations in support of broadly cooperative efforts like the Hebrew Academy and the Jewish Community Center. In general, everyone knew the differences that separated the groups, and the lines were relatively neat and distinct. But a new Conservative group, especially a group willing to question whether a "Conservative-Reconstructionist" synagogue was really Conservative, blurred those lines.

After those first services, Chavurah Shalom and the United Orthodox group moved from a space-sharing partnership toward an actual merger. Despite compromises and safeguards built to respect the theological opinions of all concerned and to protect the role of the older Orthodox group, unavoidable changes took their toll. The aging Orthodox group became smaller and weaker as members died or naturally became less active. The younger members from the Conservative group became more and more dominant.

Shaarey Tefilla is the merged congregation that is now essentially a group of younger Indianapolis newcomers reaching out to inactive Jews. But it has escaped no one's attention that many of those inactive Jews have moved to Carmel and the surrounding northern suburbs, having already accepted the distance between themselves and the other synagogues. Shaarey Tefilla was not bound by the earlier decision to stay in the current neighborhood and was farthest from its center. The congregation's greater flexibility should it decide to move northward toward Carmel provides an interesting tension.[14]

The synagogues of Indianapolis are the axis around which Judaism revolves as an identifiable social force. The "Jewish community," represented by the Community Center, the Federation, and other institutions, not only reflects the synagogues but serves the interests of a wider group of "cultural" — as opposed to "religious" — Jews in the area. To date, the various organizations that make up this small community have cooperated to such an extent that one can reliably describe Judaism as a religious tradition that constitutes a social center for about 10,000 Indianapolis residents. But the fact that this center involves very different subgroups and diverse individuals indicates that even this stereotypically homogeneous religious minority is itself multicentered just beneath its surface.

CHANGE AND CHANGELESSNESS IN THE BLACK CHURCH

As mainline Protestant influence has receded and members of other religious traditions have moved into the civic circle, religion has become a decreasingly important public badge, regardless of its salience for individuals personally or in their smaller communities. Most city residents are probably unaware of the religious affiliations of many of the city's key political or business leaders. But not every subcultural center of religious identity has seen its elite move into roles of civic leadership in a manner parallel to the Catholics and Jews. The African American denominations that together constitute the Black Church continue to occupy a distant position on the margins, though their relationship to political and economic power has changed gradually through the twentieth century.[15] It is no coincidence that the civil rights movement in the 1950s and 1960s overlaps the waning of the Protestant establishment monopoly.

Indianapolis has had a significant African American population for more than a century. In 1900 there were roughly 16,000 African Americans, about 10 percent of the total population. By 1960 there were 98,000 African Americans, then about 21 percent of the city. The advent of Unigov lowered the percentage of black population within the newly expanded city limits, but by 1990 African Americans, then numbering some 170,000, again made up about 21 percent of a much larger Indianapolis. The 2000 U.S. census showed African Americans making up 25 percent of Marion County's population.[16]

Like the Catholic Church, the Black Church has long constituted a separate but substantial portion of the religious periphery. Unlike the Catholic Church, however, and even unlike the much smaller Jewish community, the

Black Church has never established the institutional infrastructure to negotiate firmly for greater political power or better access to public funds and social services. Catholics constitute a single organization whose leaders speak with authority for the whole. Jews have separate traditions but well-established cooperative ventures with leaders authorized to represent their interests in specific matters. The churches of the mainline Protestant establishment have enjoyed considerable ecumenical cooperation, plus they act in concert with the help of institutions like the Lilly Endowment. But the "Black Church" is really only nomenclature for a myriad of congregations that share several key demographic characteristics and interests but lack organizations that speak with overarching authority.

African American religious groups cover a wide range of theological traditions. Indianapolis is home to the Methodist denominations such as African Methodist Episcopal (AME), AME Zion, and the Christian Methodist Episcopal (CME), plus a large selection of Baptist and Pentecostal churches. Given the strength of Methodism in Indianapolis, it is not surprising that the African Methodist traditions are also strong. As is true elsewhere, the African Methodist congregations tend, on average, to draw better-off, better-educated members. However, a number of African Americans in Indianapolis also belong to the United Methodist denomination; indeed, as the twenty-first century began, the local United Methodist bishop is African American. These churches of the "black mainline" grew along with the population throughout the twentieth century, but, like the churches of the white establishment, their numbers leveled off.

The Black Baptist and Pentecostal churches, along with independent churches, experienced rapid growth in the second half of the twentieth century and came to dominate the religious practice of African Americans in both the North and the South. Strong pastors from these churches pressed the claims of their community on the wider city. In Indianapolis as in most cities, a disproportionate share of the civil rights movement's leadership has been drawn from such pastors. Andrew J. Brown, the city's foremost civil rights leader, was pastor of St. John's Baptist Church. Today, groups like Concerned Clergy and the Baptist Alliance continue to stage occasional protests and to lobby the mayor's office on behalf of their neighborhoods and constituents.

But these are coalitions, not institutions. These pastors may speak with some moral authority and may exert political power in proportion to their standing in the community and the size of their congregations. They do not, however, have the organizational authority to represent the wider African American community because that can only be conferred by the kind of overarching institutions—fund-raising federations, social service boards, community schools—the Black Church lacks. Individual Catholics may disagree with the archbishop, but there is no question that he speaks for the

Catholic Church as an institution. The head of the Jewish Federation could never represent the disparate opinions of all Jews in the city, yet the Federation does its best to act on the Jewish community's behalf.

Because this authority does not exist in the Black Church, power is established through continual jockeying for position.[17] When the mayor's office or the Lilly Endowment wishes to speak with leaders from the "black community," they must make *ad hoc* choices based on their perceptions of which churches are largest, which pastors the best connected to the right networks, and who is likely to be most cooperative. They are likely to choose different leaders in different circumstances. For instance, when the Lilly Endowment and the Alban Institute decided to start the Indianapolis Center for Congregations, they sought the imprimatur of pastors from the city's largest, wealthiest congregations. But a conversation about social services is likely to turn to the congregations in the most distressed neighborhoods, which are seldom the largest or wealthiest virtually by definition. In the absence of authority, and without a voice that speaks for the whole, both de facto power and perceptions of power are the determining factors.

Black Church leaders therefore often negotiate from a position of institutional weakness, and this is especially true within the city's broader arena. African Americans make up a quarter of the city proper, but they are only about 10 percent of the wider metropolitan area. Black Baptists make up about 15 percent of churchgoers in Indianapolis, but they do not equal even 1 percent of religious adherents in the eight surrounding counties. In a city where all the economic and political power rested in the immediate downtown, such a population concentration might be an advantage. In a multicentered city with multiple political, economic, and subcultural centers bound by Unigov, it is not. Without cooperative organizations, African Americans find that their geographic concentration is a liability, making them appear to be a localized minority. It is easy for residents in eight of the nine counties that make up the metropolitan area to associate African Americans and their political or economic interests with "downtown."

No generalization fits all African Americans, but there are clear patterns that separate their religious beliefs from those of whites as a whole. In Indianapolis, African Americans are 40 percent more likely than whites to describe themselves as "very religious or spiritual." They are more than *twice* as likely — 63 percent to 30 percent — to say that the Bible should be taken literally as the word of God. This higher degree of religiosity translates directly into beliefs about religion's role in secular affairs. On any question about economic or political decisions, from general influence on public policy to specific influence on the minimum wage, between 75 percent and 85 percent of African Americans say that religion should be involved. On the same battery of questions, whites answer affirmatively 45 percent to 55 percent of the time.[18]

African Americans are more likely to believe that churches should represent the interests of all the community and more likely to see churches as necessarily active in politics and economics. Because African American residents *expect* churches to speak for them, those churches assume an important role in the community. But they do not guarantee African Americans a seat at the civic table and they do not bridge the enduring gap between African American conceptions of what is publicly sacred and the commercial, patriotic vision at the heart of the city's businesses on the Circle or the war memorials. African Americans are not as tightly tied to the city's public sense of itself as a sacred community or to the civic emphasis on the sacredness of commerce and patriotism. One study of worship services on the Fourth of July found that African American churches were much less likely than white churches to play martial music or wave the flag.[19] Black pastors made few references to patriotic ideals or to individual liberty in their sermons. Similarly, African Americans are typically disconnected from the commercial growth of the city and are unlikely to see their interests directly tied to those of downtown businesses.

Indianapolis is home to roughly 350 African American congregations of every size and description. As in the mainline and evangelical Protestant traditions, the Black Church is often represented by a few very large, very powerful congregations. But beyond these enormous congregations are hundreds of congregations with memberships running from a dozen or fewer to several hundred. Martindale-Brightwood, a downtown neighborhood in which 95 percent of the residents are African American, has roughly one hundred churches for approximately 11,000 residents.

No religious tradition represents the twin concepts of disestablishment and religious pluralism more than the Black Church, where new groups appear as quickly as old ones fade away. Because so many churches open in distressed neighborhoods where property is inexpensive, one of the few barriers to the entry of new organizations into the religious marketplace is lowered.

Many African American congregations have fewer than 100 members and very limited education or mission programs. Of the ninety-odd congregations in the Martindale-Brightwood neighborhood mentioned above, few have large memberships or budgets. Many African American congregations are truly "local" in the sense that they serve as small, elective communities for people who share particular histories, often through family ties or very specific beliefs.

This is not to say that these churches are more tied to the neighborhoods where their facilities are located. While it is true that Black Churches are in African American neighborhoods, our data show that they are no more likely than white churches to draw their members from those neighborhoods. They are "local" in the sense most widely used in this book: they are composed of people who have formed an elective, voluntary community based on closely shared interests. They are personal and particular.

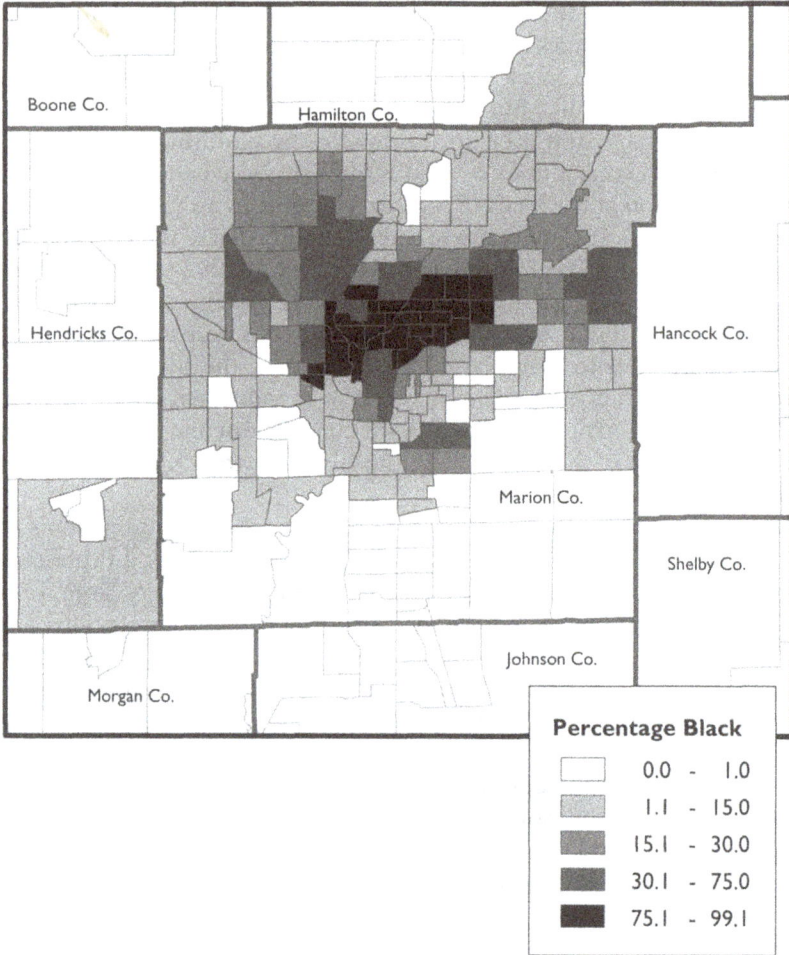

Map 4.2. African American Population Density by Census Tract, 2000.
Courtesy The Polis Center.

There has certainly been a Black Church establishment that has, in some ways, paralleled the tall-steeple churches of the mostly white, mainline Protestant establishment. And despite openings and closings in the field of African American churches a whole, many of these churches are historical pillars of the community, with histories of a hundred years or more. For nearly a century, Light of the World Christian Church has been the pre-

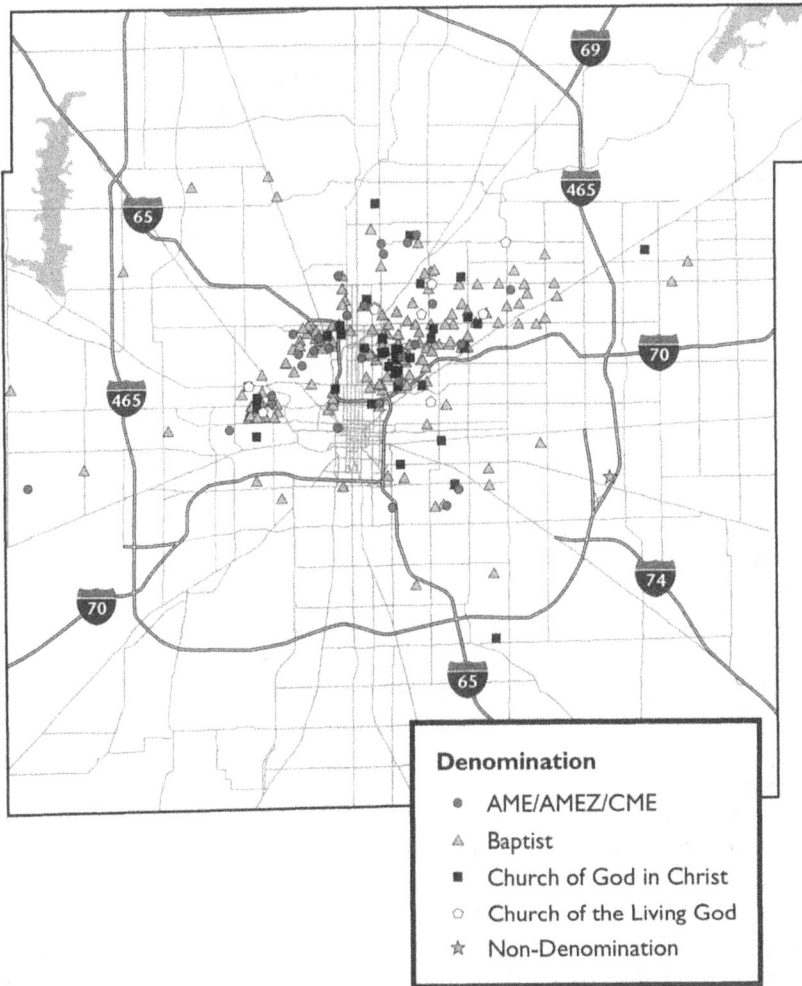

Denomination

- AME/AMEZ/CME
△ Baptist
■ Church of God in Christ
○ Church of the Living God
☆ Non-Denomination

Map 4.3. Congregations with Predominantly African American Members, 1997. Courtesy The Polis Center.

eminent establishment African American congregation in the city. It was founded in 1866 as Second Christian, a mission church of the Disciples of Christ denomination and so a minority wing of the mainline establishment.

The highly charismatic pastor of Light of the World continues to be seen by members of the white establishment as a spokesperson for African American interests in the city. But he recognizes that his civic authority comes only from the political power he can muster as pastor of a congregation filled with influential members or as a spokesperson perceived to have credibility in the wider African American community. Indeed, at one point he conferred additional authority on himself by having young men who had gone on from his congregation to become pastors proclaim him their "bishop," a role synonymous with authority in some traditions but not formally recognized by his own denomination.

Because racial toleration and great social inclusion are goals most residents associate with the agenda of the churches, it is significant that the bishop and his congregation partnered with Second Presbyterian in the city's most visible display of racial unity. Although the two churches are essentially uniracial internally, they cosponsored a joint worship service — Celebration of Hope — that has drawn dozens of other congregations to a joint annual worship service. Supported by the establishment, the celebration drew considerable attention from the *Indianapolis Star* in its early years. The *Star*'s printed attendance estimates were double the highest estimates offered by half a dozen of our researchers, suggesting the paper's desire to lend credibility and public interest to an endeavor it regarded as worthwhile.

While involvement in Celebration of Hope cements the civil authority assumed by these two large congregations, it makes a larger point about religious life in the city. Just a few decades earlier, interracial religious cooperation would have been seen as the prerogative of the Church Federation or the Indiana Commission of Human Equality or some other ecumenical body. But by the mid-1990s, it was clear that these efforts fell to the individual congregations that had both the interest and the resources to mount such a campaign. Here, as elsewhere, the religious circus had left the big tent in favor of a much more variegated midway and a multi-ring presentation in which its multiple traditions performed simultaneously while only overlapping in the eyes of the beholder.

Light of the World was the foremost congregation of the African American establishment for much of the twentieth century, but the 1990s saw the rise of Eastern Star Missionary Baptist Church. Claiming a membership of 12,000, virtually all African American with a high concentration of young adults, Eastern Star is the largest Protestant congregation of any kind in the city and the only true megachurch. A few of the largest Catholic parishes have memberships in the thousands, but no church has Eastern Star's number of regular worshippers and attenders.

Led by their young and charismatic pastor, Rev. Jeffrey Johnson, Eastern Star has gradually become the premier congregation for a younger generation of African Americans. Rather than the Celebration of Hope's attempt at interracial worship, Rev. Johnson is involved in Promise Keepers, the evangelical crusade for men to be more responsible husbands and fathers. His televised sermons are about marriage, child rearing, family finances, and responsible relationships. His church is also involved in local faith-based welfare reforms, having accepted a contract from the Coalition for Homelessness Intervention and Prevention to manage transitional housing.

Eastern Star exudes a spirit of youth and independence, but more importantly it focuses on the domestic, personal concerns of young families. It is the church of a suburbanizing, rising middle class. Light of the World, long the critical minority voice recognized by the city's establishment, represents an older organizational arrangement. The gradual shift in status between these churches marks an important change in Indianapolis's institutional religious landscape. The family-focused Eastern Star is gradually eclipsing the black establishment church that has always served as the loyal opposition to the city's white Protestant establishment. This shift is a subtle acknowledgment of the triumph of personal over public concerns in the realm of religious practice.

But, of course, Light of the World and Eastern Star are only the most visible African American congregations and do not represent the whole. African American religion in Indianapolis, as in most cities, is defined by hundreds of organizations all acting more or less independently. In a time of crisis, a prominent individual may come forward to speak for "the black community" and the other churches fall in line as circumstances require. This happened during the civil rights movement, when the aforementioned Andrew J. Brown of St. John's Missionary Baptist Church became Indianapolis's link to the Southern Christian Leadership Conference and the wider national movement. It happened again during the Michael Taylor incident in 1987, when the Indianapolis police reported that the sixteen-year-old African American had used a hidden pistol to kill himself while sitting handcuffed in the back of a patrol car. Bishop Benjamin was a leader in the Human Relations Task Force set up to investigate community relations during the resulting civil tension.

It is easy to think of the Black Church as an institution engaged in the struggle for civil rights and trying to provide services for members of the African American community. But the very use of the word "institution" is suspect here, because it is difficult to point toward any broader institutionalization of religious cooperation serving the community. There are, to be sure, several bible colleges and Martin University, a nominally Catholic educational institution with roots in the African American community. There are also several ministerial alliances within denominations or neighborhoods. But the fact that there are *several* such alliances suggests that they, like the churches themselves, are relatively parochial and self-contained. Because the tradition of congregational autonomy is even stronger here than in the other traditions discussed so far, there is no archdiocese, no community center, no Jewish Federation, no Christian Theological Seminary, and no Lilly Endowment.

The point is not that African Americans do not participate in any of these organizations—the current president of CTS and the current president of the Church Federation are both African American. But these organizations do not exist to promote the interests of the African American religious community as a social force, nor do they serve to center it as one among multiple centers, each representing a set of particular interests. In Indianapolis, African Americans must choose either to work within the existing institutions or work separately, church by church and small coalition by small coalition, from the margins.

This tradition of independence works against much coordinated political or civic effort. The good news is that there are many openings for leaders, but that is also the bad news. Despite this lack of coordination, it still makes sense to think of the Black Church as a religious tradition and one of the city's multiple and alternative religious centers. Its inability to move African Americans into the city's wider establishment is hardly the primary fault of either the Black Church or the African American community, given the long history of distance and discrimination in the city and the nation.

WHITE EVANGELICALS COMING IN FROM THE HEAT

If there is a line between those who are "in" and those who are "out" of the evolving Indianapolis establishment, white evangelical Protestants stand astride it, with one foot stepping gingerly toward a new, more pluralistic city, but the other planted more firmly on the periphery. White evangelicals do not occupy the considerable public space in Indianapolis that they do in the true Bible Belt. There has not been a strongly evangelical mayor since the rise of Moral Majority politics—in fact, Stephen Goldsmith oddly comes the closest—nor are there serious disputes about textbook censorship as might be found in other cities. Anti-abortion politics get little play in Indianapolis. Still, there has been an increase in home schooling, here as elsewhere, and a 2000 test case about posting the Ten Commandments at the statehouse probed the reach of conservative cultural values before it was quashed by the courts.

Although there are white conservative Protestants in virtually every sector of Indianapolis, they are mostly concentrated in the city's southern half. The north-south corridor of Meridian Street may be the city's establishment pillar, but the dividing line for white culture in Indianapolis is between north and south as marked by Washington Street, also known as east-west

U.S. Highway 40. South of Washington Street, Indianapolis is almost entirely white, ranging from working poor to middle-class to some upper-middle-class suburbs. North of Washington Street, African Americans live in the greatest concentrations up to about 42nd Street, although this concentration is not nearly as solid as it is in other cities. Above 42nd Street lives the professional white middle class, the considerable African American middle class, and the upper classes of Indianapolis white society.

That conservative Protestants would dominate the landscape south of Washington Street is therefore not surprising. And the further north or south one goes, the wider the religio-cultural divide becomes. It is true that fifteen miles either north or south of the Circle live white suburbanites who have many similar economic and political interests, but the religious culture is still very different. In Hamilton County, the metropolitan area's wealthiest suburban area that sits due north of the city, there are twelve times as many Catholics as Southern Baptists and seven times as many Methodists as Southern Baptists. In Morgan County, the farthest south region of the Indianapolis metropolitan area, there are more Southern Baptists than Catholics or Methodists.

As in the Black Church, the congregations and denominations of conservative white Protestants defy simple description. There are several very large churches with more than 1,000 members, but also hundreds of congregations with fewer than 100 adherents. Some of the denominations, especially the Pentecostal ones, exercise considerable centralized authority over the churches in their jurisdiction. In other denominations there is little centralized administration and for the independent congregations there is none.

As with the Black Church, no institutions speak with authority for the city's many white evangelicals. There is no Thomas Road Baptist Church of Lynchburg with a charismatic Jerry Falwell and a university, no First Baptist of Atlanta with a televised Charles Stanley. Indianapolis has an evangelical newspaper and many bookstores that serve the born-again community, but the city's power brokers, whether in the mayor's office or at the Endowment, cannot easily put a face on the evangelical community.

White evangelicals represent a large and growing sector of the religious population, but they are even less unified than the Black Church because there is no identifying marker or set of interests so obviously held in common. Although many white evangelicals are well enough off, as a group they are still drawn from the middle and lower classes. But this does not promote common interests because they do not attribute their status to race and because their conservative ideology prevents them from defining themselves in economic terms.

In the early twentieth century, Indianapolis Protestantism had a strong, public, conservative streak. At the same time churches like Second Presbyterian were pressing the notions of modernism and the Social Gospel, the city had both a large Klan presence and a very successful, very charismatic conservative evangelical movement—though it would be unfair to link the two too closely. An earlier evangelical tradition boasted preachers like Charles Grandison Finney of Oberlin College who championed the integration of African Americans into American society. But the story of Indianapolis's religion must acknowledge how much of it was bound up in tight connections to particular communities.

In a city run so tightly and for so long by a "liberal" Protestant establishment, conservative Protestants found it futile to organize politically and therefore have never exerted the same political pressure in Indianapolis that they do in some other cities. Indianapolis has experienced no concerted, well-organized effort to overtake school boards, to limit access to abortion, or even to forward the interests of right-wing political candidates. The Indianapolis suburbs have produced a very conservative congressman, Rep. Dan Burton, but in downtown Indianapolis, Rep. Julia Carson, an African American widely regarded as liberal, has handily defeated conservative, often staunchly pro-life, Republican candidates.

In many ways, white evangelicals do just fine in Indianapolis. Because they have not seen themselves as so separate from the mainline establishment and the establishment has not defined them as outsiders, evangelicals never needed to develop an institutional infrastructure of their own. Indianapolis has some Christian academies linked to white flight and busing, but not as many as some other places. It has no strong, white, fundamentalist bible colleges. So evangelical leaders do not thrust themselves to the fore, but rather join the civic choir in singing the city's upbeat hymns.

Nothing demonstrates this quiet spirit of cooperation better than the 1999 Billy Graham Crusade. Graham's meetings promised to be a rallying point for the evangelicals, but instead became an exercise in establishment nostalgia where Presbyterians, Baptists, and Disciples of Christ church members also reflected on their shared experiences, with the Lilly Endowment underwriting half a million dollars of the Crusade's expenses. Differences among Protestants, and even differences between Protestants and others, were downplayed in the interest of citywide Christian harmony.

The range of white evangelical congregations is nearly as great as among African American churches. Indianapolis is home to dozens of independent Christian churches, all distant conservative cousins to the liberal, mainline Christian Church, Disciples of Christ. There is a growing number of Southern Baptist churches, especially on the south side. It is also home to many Pentecostal and Holiness groups representing the Assemblies of God, the Church of God, Cleveland, Tennessee, and Indiana's homegrown Church of God, Anderson, Indiana.

City residents have historically associated conservative, evangelical congregations with the city's white, working-class south side, and they've been right to do so. But recently, congregational growth in virtually every region of the city has been led by such churches. Even the city's northern suburbs are not exclusively liberal Protestant, Catholic, or Jewish. Evangelical groups are growing quickly in every suburb, every surrounding county, and every region of the greater Indianapolis metropolis.

Public attention has often focused on the most vocal, and often most conservative, representatives of the evangelical churches. In the 1920s, while the Ku Klux Klan played a leading role in state politics, evangelist Howard Cadle became a potent religious force in the city. He constructed a tabernacle capable of holding 11,500 worshippers and of bringing fundamentalist and Pentecostal evangelists of note — including Billy Sunday and Aimee Semple McPherson — to the city.

As the tabernacle began to wane after Cadle's death, a new church, Indianapolis Baptist Temple, assumed the mantle for itself. The Temple was a magnet for conservative Protestants. It, too, constructed a large campus with a considerable auditorium on Indianapolis's south side. But as the city developed new suburbs through the latter part of the twentieth century, and as money and political power gravitated toward the north side, the Temple's stance became more and more defensive. God was still using its south side position, said its pastor, "to confound the worldly ways of the wise," but few now paid attention long enough to be confounded. Temple membership gradually receded through the late twentieth century and the organization became ever more closely aligned with a rising Christian militia movement. Baptist Temple ceased to use its Zip code or to withhold federal tax from its employees.

By the mid-1990s, the Temple's story was winding down. A federal judge found them guilty of tax evasion and ordered the property seized to pay outstanding debts. The issue wound its way through the courts and the Clinton administration for several years. In late 2000, Baptist Temple became a rallying point for a militia movement that had dwindled since the Oklahoma City bombing. National leaders like Bo Gritz camped out at the church, though such interest inevitably waned as the weeks turned into months. In early 2001, the federal marshals who had waited patiently seized the building and all of its assets quickly and quietly.

The Temple's end was front-page news, but the real story is just how far evangelical religion in Indianapolis is now removed from such separatism. The Indianapolis suburbs, north and south, are full of the sprawling complexes that surround every city in America. Most of the large, conservative churches keep a relatively low profile on issues such as school board decisions and abortion. Again, it is not as if the decline of the old Protestant establishment opened the floodgates to a host of challengers mounting vigorous countercultural attacks. Evangelicalism has become arguably even less strident, adopting the same go-along, get-along tone that characterizes the synagogues, the Catholic parishes, and even the African American churches to a considerable degree. The politics of religious contention is considered bad form and avails little in a city bound by patriotism and commerce.

Meanwhile, beyond the mainline Protestants, Catholics, Jews, African American churches, and the white evangelicals, there are many smaller religious subcultures that speak from the periphery, yet not always as the opposition. Adventists, Quakers, Nazarenes, and similar groups are even smaller islands in the metropolitan sea. They are not easily placed in any of the categories above, yet the space they may occupy is defined by the larger groups that surround them. Some churches and meetings within these groups are active and vocal, but the impression is always that they speak for separate minorities, not that they are centers of organized interests. Public decisions in Indianapolis rarely account for those who might celebrate the Sabbath on Saturday or for pacifists, especially given the linkage between patriotism, military service, and good citizenship.

The various world religions, Western and non-Western, that are gradually migrating toward Indianapolis also act only on the furthest margins. The city has relatively few Muslims, Sikhs, Buddhists, or Hindus, but there is a concentration of each, usually tied to specific ethnic identities. Religion often serves as the cultural glue that holds these small communities together. As often as not, religious organizations are places where these communities can maintain some level of separate, unique identity, but where their interests can be mediated against, and gradually worked into, the social, political, and economic life of the city.

CONTEXT AND CONCLUSION

Seen in the context of the city's ongoing religious realignment, these changes in religious life make better sense. The trajectory of the city's many faith communities was inseparable from their relationship to the old Protestant establishment. The degree to which their members and their ideas gradually entered the new, evolving establishment is tied, at least in part, to the strength of their own institutions.

Chapters 3 and 4 demonstrate that there are many different ways to think about the nature of community and religion's role in it. There are the local communities equated with neighborhoods, which are what many people mean when they use the word "community." But there are also the "faith communities" that organize the ideas and activities of people with similar worldviews from many locales. Both of these are molded by the outward forces that make the metropolis a mosaic of many different, sometimes overlapping, constituencies. And there is also the larger community, the common enterprise, of the city imagined as a whole, always being molded by the inward, centralizing tendencies.

When we think about religious and cultural pluralism, it is important to think not only about the "many," but also about the "one," to see individuals who live in small communities defined by particular values — living usually in more than one kind of community at once — but who also live in larger communities defined by more general values. When we look for evidence of social capital and its supposed demise, we need to think critically about which level of experience we mean. Activities that build social capital at the local level may not do so at the metropolitan one. For instance, a neighborhood or a faith community might build internal bonds by jealously guarding its borders, but this would be counterproductive from the standpoint of the city or the larger community as a whole.

Following the same logic, when we think about civil religion, we should not begin by assuming it has replaced traditional faith commitments. In Indianapolis, we have seen the evolution of a civic faith based on broad, generalized values that has not weakened the particular faiths practiced by hundreds of thousands in their own churches, synagogues, and mosques. The fact that the ideas and practices that fund the city center seem more secular because they are less identifiably Protestant, or even Christian, does not mean that the culture as a whole has become more secularized. It means, instead, that when we think about secularization or about the evolution of civil religion, we need to be very careful to identify the institutions we are talking about and to acknowledge important differences among different levels of analysis. Whole societies can exhibit religious tendencies though the individuals within them are not very spiritual; individuals can remain religiously musical even as religion loses public authority.

So far, our analysis here has focused primarily on religion and community at the broadest levels, thinking first about the city as a whole and about religion's role in civic life, then switching to an analysis of faith traditions writ large. But the outward pressure toward smaller, local communities goes far beyond the separation of community life into regions of the city or distinct denominational or theological traditions. To a large extent religion is lived, and personal identity is shaped, at the level of very small communities like congregations and neighborhoods.

We have argued that traditional religious faith gradually lost most of its public, civic authority for a variety of reasons linked to the growth in religious pluralism, the development of shadow civic institutions among minority faiths, and the evolution of a more general, non-sectarian civil religion that made patriotism, sports, government, and commerce the badges of good citizenship. But we have also argued that religion did not go away, that it remains vital in the lives of individuals, families, and smaller organizations. Moreover, all of these exert public influence as lives of faith are lived in shared civic institutions.

The city is composed of multiple layers of community. To this point, we have been especially interested in the broadest layers defined by the macro processes of suburbanization and centralization, by changes in civic culture, or by the broad differences among theological traditions. To understand religion's role more accurately, though, we must now focus our attention on the smaller layers of community. Common sense tells us that when most people talk about their local community, they mean the neighborhood. And when they talk about their faith community, they mean their congregations. It is time to consider how each of these in turn has been affected by religion's changing role in a realigned city.

5

TYPES AND TENSIONS OF
CONGREGATIONAL LIFE

We are looking at two things: what is driving folks out and what is
bringing them back, and how do we put the two together.
What drives folks out of the city is taxes, race, education, and crime.
The one element bringing folks back into those neighborhoods is the
church. Now how do we marry the church and neighborhood to
address these issues?
— a member of former Mayor Stephen Goldsmith's
Front Porch Alliance

The breakdown of the taken-for-granted linkage between establishment
Protestantism and civil authority and the corresponding decline in religion's public prominence could appropriately be described as secularization. When some observers commonsensically note that society seems somehow less religious than it did in the mid-twentieth century, it is not as if they
have been subtly deceived. Indianapolis, imagined as a unified metropolis
with one civic identity centered on the downtown mile square, *is* less religious. There are many fewer churches downtown than was true a century,
or even fifty years, ago. Overtly Christian rituals no longer receive the civic,
political imprimatur. Members of clergy are not accorded the same public
stature. New, more secular, symbols and rituals define common citizenship.

But if it is fair to say that civic life has therefore become more secular in
this one broad sense, it is dangerously wrong to think that this change
has translated automatically into individuals and families who are also less

religious, that it has resulted in a general decline among religious traditions or organizations, or that communities of faith have been evicted from the public square. Particular faith traditions and some congregations within them have declined, to be sure. In a mainline Protestant city, the statistical decline among liberal Protestants and the relative decline in their cultural authority cannot help but look to some like a general waning of religion. But religion considered more broadly, religion conceived as the full range of beliefs and practices inherent in the multiple communities of many specific traditions, is alive and well.

Traditional religion's changing role in the realigned city does not ultimately amount to a privatization of religion, though that interpretation is frequently offered. The fact that we do not share a single, common religious culture does not mean that we are reduced to isolated individuals or families. Religion is practiced in community. It is practiced in the large communities defined by a common faith tradition — liberal Protestants, Catholics, Jews, the Black Church, and evangelicals — and it is embodied in the institutions these traditions create, such as schools, hospitals, and service organizations. But each of these larger manifestations of community rests atop the true building blocks of religious community, the congregations.

INDIANAPOLIS CONGREGATIONS IN BRIEF OVERVIEW

Anyone wishing a closer look at these building blocks of the faith traditions will quickly learn that they are not hard to find. In this city of some 850,000 people, there are approximately 1,200 congregations, or one for about every 700 residents. In virtually every neighborhood there is a Catholic parish, a representative sample of congregations from mainline denominations, and several evangelical churches. In some urban neighborhoods, especially African American neighborhoods, the churches are the defining features of the non-residential landscape. The Martindale-Brightwood neighborhood mentioned earlier has nearly 100 churches for its 11,000 residents, a ratio approaching one church for every 100 residents.

Religion's practitioners understand the congregations' central role. When asked to distill the city's religious life to its essence, one pastor said,

> I can best describe religion in Indianapolis as being "church." To people in Indianapolis, the size of church and the name of the minister are all-important. To "have religion" is to participate in or identify with a congregation.

Said another,

> My personal experience in Indianapolis is defined best as congregationally based. I'm very aware of overarching institutions and some attempts to "network," but I still sense that "local churches doing their own thing" summarizes the religious scene.

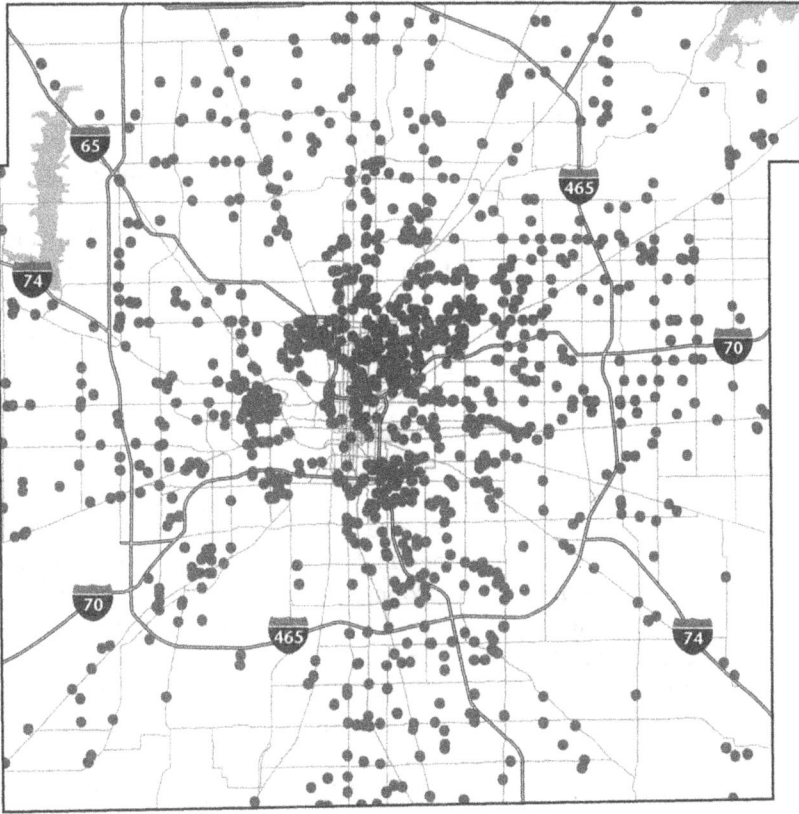

Map 5.1. Congregational Locations in Marion County, 1997.
Courtesy The Polis Center.

Most congregations, considered as distinct, individual units, are homogeneous by comparison to the general population. Their members share ethnicity, race, and social class. Indianapolis's racial makeup is roughly 70 percent white, 25 percent black, 4 percent Hispanic, and 1 percent other. Yet in nine out of ten congregations, at least 90 percent of the members are of one race, and most congregations are considerably more racially homogeneous than that.

Indianapolis's congregations have, on average, some 400 members and a budget of roughly $270,000. In real life, most congregations are nowhere near as big as those averages suggest. A small percentage of very large congregations with substantial budgets inflate the average. At least half of the congregations in Indianapolis have fewer than 150 members, so the majority of congregations are relatively small groups where no more than 100 people gather on the Sabbath to worship. The median budget for congregations is closer to $150,000 than to the $270,000 average, and this leaves little after paying a pastor's salary and benefits and the bills for facilities and their upkeep.[1]

Congregations, by their own report, draw fewer than half of their members from the neighborhoods surrounding their houses of worship. Even Catholic parishes, which are arranged as geographic catchment areas, draw substantial numbers from outside their parish boundaries. Clergy, sometimes assumed to live next door to the house of worship, usually commute. Nearly 60 percent of clergy say, by their own definition, that they live outside the neighborhood where their congregation is located.[2]

How, then, do congregations function as the de facto centers of religious life, the building blocks of religious community? Congregations are centers of concurrent interests that overlap with shared race and social class. Members usually share a common history, including family ties. They often have intertwined interests in schools, property values, and public safety. Once again the sociological truism about "birds of a feather" holds firm. Congregations are, above all, places where people of similar social characteristics gather to worship, to learn, to teach their children, and to socialize. Congregations often function as extended families or as the small villages of an earlier epoch. Even larger churches that are complex organizations run by sophisticated management techniques are held together by bonds that are both highly personal and interpersonal. Even in an enormous suburban Catholic parish, the family metaphor predominates. Said one staff member:

> We have six masses on the weekends now, so we're just bursting at the seams. Since we are so large now — and our philosophy is we want to reach people from womb to tomb — we have over 55 organizations with different types of leadership in each. We try to hit every age group. Now we are a large family, and it's not as intimate as it used to be, but that's the price you pay for growth. I hate saying that large churches are big businesses, but they must be run like one if you're going to make money count and pay your bills. Still, my family made our church a home away from home and my kids all feel the same way. Although my eldest son moved away, he says "I can't see my kids playing in sports against St. Ignatius, you know." He said it just does not feel right. So that's why they all come here.

The idea of congregations as many smaller, relatively self-contained religious organizations fits very well within contemporary notions of religious pluralism grounded in a uniquely American sense of religious *disestablishment*.[3] Because America has no state church, no official religious institution, there are few barriers to the entry of new religious groups and each is free to compete for religious "market share."[4] It is relatively easy to start a congregation that addresses an unmet need, and organizations enter and leave the field more or less continuously. Some individual congregations are, of course, remarkably stable over time, especially when compared to the rapid changes in business or politics. But there is considerable flux and turnover among the field of congregations as a whole. In fact, clergy careers depend on it. In contrast to the stable managerial priests of Catholicism, many Protestant clergy are more entrepreneurial. Especially among evangelicals, there is a well-known saga in which a small storefront congregation winds up a suburban, prosperous, tall-steeple — or now more accurately, red brick — church.

Considering religious practice at the congregational level, it is easy to see how people can choose the group that is most convenient for them and most identified with their particular interests. Or, alternatively, they can choose the group that best fits their personal beliefs or desires for worship, education, or group activity. Congregations are well suited to a market model of religion in which potential members are the consumers and larger groupings, such as denominations or even whole religious traditions, are the name brands.[5]

The profile of congregations as public actors has risen proportionately as the profile of other forms of religious organization has declined. Changes in denominations and in ecumenical groups, linked to the changing role of the city's Protestant establishment, make clear just how much responsibility for public life congregations now bear. Fifty, even twenty-five, years ago, urban racial reconciliation would have been the work of an ecumenical council. Today two congregations — originally Second Presbyterian and Light of the World Christian, then St. Luke's Methodist and First Baptist Church North — carry the load through the annual Celebration of Hope. Once, Lilly Endowment would have focused its attention on ecumenical coalitions like the Church Federation, hoping to unite common interests in a common institution. Now the Endowment puts millions of dollars into the Indianapolis Center for Congregations, a consulting organization with the specific goal of empowering congregations of all kinds. Time after time, the "big tent" strategy has given way to an acknowledgment of multiple communities and multiple cultures, and the emphasis on civic cooperation has switched to finding important points of overlap in the ongoing negotiations rather than seeking total integration or creating some hypothetical common center. Congregations have gained strength as the increasingly independent centers of individuals' religious activity.

Congregations' raised profile as public actors has marked them as potential "community-building" organizations for the wider community as well. African American churches have long histories of service to their communities. Catholic parishes usually serve their geographically defined areas in multiple ways. Protestant establishment churches driven by the message of the Social Gospel took up the cause of downtown missions, later captured under the rubric "urban ministry." But new pressures, some embedded in legal changes, ask even more of congregations.

During the last two decades of the twentieth century, many civic leaders and social reformers came to see congregations as the community organizations of choice. Churches and synagogues were increasingly deemed capable of delivering social services, revitalizing distressed neighborhoods, and even building the social capital urban America was deemed to have lost. Scholars turned increasing attention to congregations.[6] Foundations, especially the Lilly Endowment, directed more funding toward national studies of—and resources for—congregations. Eventually even government turned toward partnership with congregations in the "charitable choice" provisions of the 1996 Federal Welfare Reform Act and the more recent White House push for "faith-based initiatives."

Congregations are now hailed as potential solutions for many urban problems, even though most are relatively small organizations and many are not as tightly tied to their neighbors as some reformers hope.[7] Congregations are carrying the load once carried by ecumenical associations and denominations on public issues such as race relations. Congregations are the new focus of public funding from government and foundations. And congregations are the constituent elements of the faith community, the organizations in which religious culture thrives despite changes in the overarching culture wrought by pluralism and urban realignment.

For all those reasons, we must now move below the broad discussion of faith traditions and civic life to ask how congregations are shaped by, and are shaping, urban realignment. Changing congregational roles have been forged by the outward pressure that creates multiple neighborhoods and communities—the many centers of urban life—bound together by race, class, socioeconomic status, and geography. But those roles are also shaped by the inward pressure toward one center with a common civic identity: congregations constantly negotiate their missions in their local environment and in the city. We understand how religion really operates on the ground when we understand congregations in relationship to their social circumstances and see their activities in the context of broader urban change.

TWO AXES OF CONGREGATIONAL ALIGNMENT

Anyone who attempts to define congregations primarily by their relationship to their external environment runs a great risk. Congregations are, first and foremost, centers of worship, education, and character development. They are producers of culture.[8] They are elective communities, neither as intensely personal and rigidly ascribed as families, nor as impersonal and rational as the polity or the market. Congregations, like other small groups, offer a communal space between the large institutions that shape our lives and the most intimate and tightly textured places where we live day to day.[9] In these ways, congregations today function much as they have for centuries.

But congregations do not exist in a vacuum. To say that they create a space between the isolated individual and the larger institutions of polity and marketplace is to claim that they are connected to both. Recent attempts to involve congregations more actively in roles like social service delivery or neighborhood development assume that congregations can serve as "mediating institutions," as the conservatives often have it,[10] or as "institutions of civil society," as the liberals are more apt to say.[11] But such well-intentioned models must take into account the many different ways that congregations experience and address the realigned city. Therefore, we can acknowledge some important similarities among congregations, but we must also explore the principal axes along which congregations differ as they seek their balance in a shifting urban landscape. Before asking how congregations address a changing city, it is useful to consider briefly how different congregations frame religious change in theological terms. Understanding something about how a group thinks theologically about itself in relation to its social environment helps analyze what role it may or may not play as a community organization.

Religious understandings of change differ both on the questions of what must be changed and how change occurs. Some theological worldviews focus on change in *individuals,* while others focus on changes to *society.* To be sure, enough changed individuals will eventually alter society, and a changed society will ultimately affect the individuals within it, but the question of where the congregation's missions should begin could hardly be more crucial. On the question of "how" change occurs, some worldviews emphasize change that is *revolutionary,* while other worldviews picture change as *developmental* and incremental.

Entire books can be written just about these different religious worldviews, but theological analysis is not this book's goal. Understanding the variety of theological views helps us to consider how congregations think about what they do, but, ultimately, our goal is to describe how they act. These different theological visions provide a tool which we will use to analyze congregational activity, but in the end we must let the activities — the real-life responses of congregations to their urban environment — speak for themselves.

Toward that end, it is important to note at the outset that no congregation, no community of faith composed of complex human beings, can be adequately defined using only one combination of these theological worldviews. These conceptualizations are, after all, ideal types, meant to represent the logically and theologically consistent endpoints on a broad spectrum.

Actual people and their groups pick and choose among these, creating patterns of ideas and practices that combine many different elements at once. Just as the fundamental tendencies noted in a Myers-Briggs personality inventory help us to understand — but do not wholly define — differences among complex human personalities, so do these ideal-typical worldviews help us to understand variation among complex groups.

With those different theological visions in hand, it is possible to consider two different axes of congregational activity.[12] All congregations serve the needs of the community. But there is a crucial difference between congregations whose activities focus on the *internal* needs of the congregation itself and those whose activities focus on the needs of their *external* environment. Used in this manner, the designations "internal" and "external" are clearly ideal types, because virtually every congregation serves both an internal and an external community, though in widely varying proportions. Every congregation must look to the spiritual and material needs of its own members — must act internally — or it will find itself out of members and out of business. Moreover, virtually every congregation looks beyond itself toward mission to some external audience. But it is still important to ask which has the highest priority as a congregation defines its role in the community of faith and in the wider community around it.

Just as all congregations serve a community, so do all congregations work toward the ideal represented by the kingdom of God. But there is a second, crucial distinction between congregations who focus their activities on the *horizontal*, day-to-day relationships of this world, and those whose activities are oriented toward the *vertical* relationship between God and humanity. Again, the question is not a pure "either/or." Faith communities that emphasize the needs of the everyday world do so because of their beliefs about God's will and about their relationship to God; they may even emphasize spiritual growth as the key to their activities. On the other side, groups that begin with the unique relationship between God and humans regularly engage the mundane world. But a real difference in priority surfaces in congregational activity. Every congregation *believes* that its mission is guided by needs that are both vertical and horizontal. The question is: What do they do?

These two axes provide four ideal types of congregational missions, each of which suggests a different way that congregations use their theological presuppositions to confront a changing environment. No congregation can be successfully pigeonholed by the four boxes these axes create, because every congregation draws, to differing degrees, from different theological worldviews. But by looking at congregational archetypes, by thinking of groups that come closest to fitting the categories we are creating, we get a better feel not only for the ways congregations act to address their environment, but for which type of responses make sense to particular groups in particular circumstances.

Table 5.1. Congregational Missions and Response to Change

	Horizontal	Vertical
External	Community Outreach	Conversion
Internal	Customer Service	Cloister

We believe that this new classification of congregational mission is called for, not because it supplants earlier work, but because it allows us to link congregations' mission activities not only to their theological worldviews, but also to the manner in which their conceptions of "place" and "community" shape their missions in the realigned city. Congregational responses must be fluid in an environment that permits, or even requires, individuals and their organizations to create their own social and cultural centers. Therefore, we offer a brief description of congregations that lean toward our archetypes not because we want to stereotype these groups, but because they illuminate important tendencies that help us make better sense of religion's role in urban environmental change.

Because our first responsibility is to treat fairly the many groups who trusted us as observers and analysts, we have chosen not to use these congregations' real names or to identify their neighborhoods. The issue is not really confidentiality; although no one has the individual permission from every member of any group, we had blanket permission from the leaders of all the groups we studied and usually spoke to a fair range of laypeople. But we are not journalists whose story depends on having everyone "on the record," so even the smallest risk that we might cause any group harm is not worth taking. We are analysts seeking to describe relevant trends and changes by placing specific organizations in their larger social context. So the congregations described below are pseudonymous, but they are not composites. Every quote or description came only from the congregation in question, not from another congregation somewhat like it. We offer these as miniature case studies of particular groups in the hope that the congregational types they illustrate will lead to more constructive thinking about religion's relationship to its urban environment.

Community Outreach Congregations

To find their balance in the fast-changing city, *community outreach* congregations understand their mission in the context of society's needs. They begin with the question, "Where are we?" in order to answer the questions, "Who are we?" and "What ought we to do?"[13] In our ideal-typical description, these are congregations that act externally and focus on the vertical, moving toward God's kingdom by meeting worldly needs.

In seeking to serve a population outside their congregation's walls, community outreach congregations are living up to the expectations of their neighbors. In our broadest survey of Indianapolis residents, 52 percent said that "serving others" should be a congregation's highest priority, rather than items such as sharing their faith or attempting to change social or political structures. When church and synagogue members are removed from the sample, a full 68 percent of non-members said that social service should be congregation's highest priority.[14] This is what the "general public" thinks congregations should do.

There are, of course, many kinds of community outreach. The most obvious forms include the traditional mission tasks of providing food, shelter, or clothing. But because community outreach congregations usually view their mission in developmental terms, the desire to build strong, interpersonal connections is at least as important. Community outreach congregations are seldom revolutionary, looking to make fundamental changes to the structure of society. Rather, they are congregations that see themselves as part of the neighborhood community network, who hold membership in ministerial alliances and service coalitions, and who seek to work as partners in either traditional service provision or in civic or political activities. The crucial element is that the congregation's identity is shaped primarily by its place in a web of social relationships, where it is constantly reaching out to build external connections. Progress toward God's kingdom is incremental, but these congregations move in that direction by trying to meet the daily needs of an external population. Consider the following congregation as an example.

"Trying to find its tradition": St. James' UMC

St. James' United Methodist Church (UMC) is in an exclusive outer suburban neighborhood. In the early 1970s the suburban population began to grow at such a pace that new institutions of all kinds were needed to bolster the community's infrastructure. It was clear that the established United Methodist Church in the middle of town could not serve all the prospective Methodists in the expanding area. When the denomination conducted a survey, 161 people expressed interest in a new Methodist church for the area. In the late 1970s, the first pastoral team was assigned to start the new congregation. Twenty families signed on immediately and 187 people — more than the median size of all Indianapolis congregations — attended the first worship service. St. James' began with 110 charter members, 18 of whom are still with them at this writing.

St. James' began as, and remains, a center of worship and community for people whose lives are radically affected by urban recentering. Attractive suburbs with high reputations for good schools tend to draw the wealthier, and more transient, business executives who move in to head the Indianapolis office of whatever business they pursue and then move on toward the corporate headquarters, which is likely based somewhere else. St. James' pastor estimated that about 25 percent of his congregation relocates year to year, a figure he thinks is probably consistent for their suburb as a whole. And he is under no misimpression about why they find themselves on the city's suburban edge, so far from the center. "A lot of people move to our suburb," he says, "because they are frightened of the city."

St. James' has roughly 800 members. Fully 98 percent of them are white, and, unlike the majority of mainline Protestant congregations, young families predominate. Nearly two-thirds live somewhere in the surrounding suburban area, but the remaining third drive in from other communities around the rim of the city. The pastor knows why they come. The church's goal, he says, is to "provide a stable worship environment with more of a traditional service." But, he said, a corresponding goal is to "be very conscious of the whole Indianapolis metropolitan area in which we live — not losing sight of the larger context."

Both the pastor's portfolio and the church's mission bear out this contextual interest. He is a member of the Indianapolis Foreign Relations Committee, the Indiana Historical Society, the Urban League, the Methodist Church's Metro Ministries, the NAACP, the ACLU, and the local ministerial alliance. The church's interests are similarly broad. St. James' first mission activity was to house three Vietnamese refugees who could not speak English. At one point, the church had fourteen Vietnamese in regular attendance. The congregation is also active in the Brightwood Community Center, located in an inner-city black neighborhood, as well as Fletcher Place Community Center, located in an inner-city white neighborhood. St. James' participates in the Interfaith Hospitality Network, where a group of congregations take turns hosting a newly homeless family while helping them to regain stable employment and accommodation. It has been a partner with Vida Nueva, the city's Spanish-speaking Methodist congregation, as well as with the Shalom Wellness Center, a partnership with the Indiana University School of Nursing run out of an urban United Methodist congregation. Moreover, St. James' participates in an international educational mission known as Operation Classroom, providing school supplies and health kits to parts of Africa and Asia.

St. James' makes it a point to serve both its own members and the larger community. The pastor wonders aloud "how congregations cope with the grief of so many people coming into the church and leaving the church in a short amount of time." "A lot of good-byes," he notes, "get said in this community." Yet St. James' seems to embrace its role as a stabilizing force for traditional worship for very mobile families. It simultaneously and unselfconsciously promotes the slogan "where mission is a way of life," attempting to tie transients who have deliberately chosen *not* to live in the urban center with a variety of missions meant to increase understanding and integration across the metropolis as a whole.

"Not just a place where people show up on Sunday":
St. Stephen Catholic Church

St. Stephen is a Catholic parish nearly coextensive with its inner suburban neighborhood. The neighborhood prides itself on being an integrated community with a strong neighborhood association, but it is, in fact, very nearly three neighborhoods. Its northern end is largely upper-middle-class and white. Its southern end is racially mixed, though predominantly black and generally working-class or below. Only the middle section of the neighborhood might be said to be truly integrated and is, predictably, middle- to lower-middle-class. This neighborhood was radically changed by the "white flight" former Mayor Goldsmith identified earlier. In 1950, the neighborhood was 90 percent white. By 1960, it was 69 percent white, and by 1970 it was 57 percent white. It has been roughly 60-40, white to black, ever since.

St. Stephen parish virtually shares the neighborhood's boundaries. The congregation deals daily with issues of integration both in the parish and in the neighborhood. About 85 percent of the congregation's members are white, compared to 62 percent of whites living in the neighborhood. Still, in a city where fewer than 10 percent of the churches are integrated, the fact that 15 percent of St. Stephen's members are non-white is noteworthy.[15] During the 1960s and 1970s, St. Stephen was a relatively radical congregation by Indianapolis standards. It announced its commitment to racial diversity and inclusion. It worked hard to be a true post–Vatican II parish, with substantial lay participation in worship. Its priest was seen as a leader in Catholic and civic reform.

Over the years, however, St. Stephen grew gradually less radical, more a part of the liberal mainstream. Today it has about 1,500 parishioners, a relatively modest size for a Catholic parish. Its priest is still committed to racial integration, but integration is not the congregation's signature. Instead, it strives for a moderate approach that will not alienate mainstream Catholics. For instance, when some more liberal members recommended that the parish support a movement to declare the neighborhood gun-free, other members — and the parish priest — resisted because they did not want the church involved in what some saw as a divisive, yet essentially peripheral, political issue.

By any standard, St. Stephen is a neighborhood institution. Its school provides a strong local presence, with about 30 percent of its students coming from outside the faith. But even this very close relationship between parish and neighborhood can be overstated, as it often is in contemporary discussions of the congregation's role in urban life. The optimism, the anxieties, and the radicalism of the 1960s are over. Today, both the neighborhood and the parish are struggling to find the right mix of social activism, tradition, and everyday community life.

Only about 40 percent of parish members come from the neighborhood proper. This is normal for most congregations, but a little surprising for a Catholic parish so tied to the neighborhood. Clearly, many members choose St. Stephen over their own geographic parishes, for some reason. Many come because they like the history of activism and the less formal liturgy. Not surprisingly, the most politically active among these are rankled by the congregation's evolving centrist approach, as is true in any congregation trying to balance the needs of its activists with the needs of other members.

As for integration, both parish members and local residents say that there is little animosity but not enough genuine friendships among people of different races. As in Indianapolis as a whole, people get along but they do not generally engage in deep personal relationships or ongoing communication. The neighborhood association has, as one member put it, "grayed a little." Volunteer time and donations for local activities have gradually decreased. But if the congregation has a less activist approach, it is still "not just a place where people show up for church on Sunday," as the priest put it. The parish hosts an active Dignity chapter, a prominent gay and lesbian movement within American Catholicism. It subsidizes education for a number of neighborhood children, both black and white, having assumed as much of the local educational burden as it could when the public grade school closed. Parishioners are involved in the worship process itself and some remain involved in the local neighborhood association. But for some who elect to drive in to attend St. Stephen because of its activist history, the more settled community outreach is less satisfying than direct activism.

Despite their differences — one is Catholic, the other Protestant; one is urban, the other suburban — each of these congregations focuses much of its activity on the community outside its doors. Their approach is developmental; God's kingdom is ushered in through an incremental change whose instrument they strive to be. Changes in individuals occur in interaction with social change: a just world spawns just people. Both places are about spiritual growth and both work to meet the needs of their members, but they define their role as a community of faith by their responsibility to meet the daily needs of the people around them. By emphasizing these congregations' community outreach, we choose to move away from categories that define such groups by their proximity to the older "civic" establishment, highlighting instead their access to resources and their self-defined commitment to a community beyond their doors.

Community Outreach and Public Partnerships

Some community outreach manifests itself in direct service provision, and changes in the contemporary city have been met by changes in the relationship between government, the non-profit sector, and congregations that provide those services. The mid-1990s and later saw an enormous upswing in the public profile of inner-city congregations. Henry Cisneros, then Secretary of Housing and Urban Development (HUD), wrote the tract "Higher Ground: Faith Communities and Community Building," in which he asserted that congregations alone had what it took to revitalize crumbling downtown neighborhoods.[16] In 1996, Congress passed welfare reform legislation that contained the so-called "charitable choice" clause, allowing religious organizations to claim government funds for their social services without forming separate non-profit groups or abandoning their religious character. HUD opened a new office, originally headed by a Jesuit priest, to manage faith-based involvement in urban affairs. Then the George W. Bush administration pushed the envelope further still, looking for ways to enact "charitable choice"–style reforms in the relationship between "faith-based institutions" and other government activities.

These new reforms were different from the longstanding partnerships between government and religious charities such as Salvation Army or Lutheran Child and Family Services. Drawing on increasing interest both in the devolution of services to lower levels of administration and in expanding the "social capital" available to urban neighborhoods, faith-based welfare reform was aimed at enhancing social service and community development capacity at the most local level. What was needed, reformers believed, was not further involvement by large-scale bureaucracies, whether secular or religious, but increased and enhanced participation by local organizations. Congregations felt the glare of the spotlight as civic leaders like Cisneros praised them both as the most stable and enduring neighborhood organizations and as those most likely to transform the lives of the poor by transforming their values. As we have already seen, Indianapolis pioneered new public partnerships with congregations. Mayor Stephen Goldsmith created the Front Porch Alliance as an organizational bridge between city government and neighborhood-based groups, especially congregations.

African American congregations have responded most vigorously to new public partnerships in their ongoing community outreach. This signals real cultural differences between blacks and whites on the degree to which religion and politics mix. In response to a direct survey question, African Americans were 50 percent more likely than whites to say they favored churches receiving public funding. More than 60 percent of applications to these new partnerships have come from the Black Church, though African American congregations make up only about 30 percent of those in the city.[17]

African Americans have never made the acute separation between church and state that is common among white Protestants. African Americans recognize the historic role and attendant responsibilities of churches and synagogues in the civil rights movement. More prosaically, they are likely to have members with historic ties to the distressed neighborhood, which is in some cases why they return there to worship. The simultaneous waxing of multiple religious centers and the waning of religion's establishment at the center of metropolitan life elevated the role of these congregations and made these new partnerships possible. The same forces that discounted denominations and the Church Federation in favor of individual churches and synagogues prompted the eventual shift from large-scale religious charities to particular religious organizations. These new public partnerships are intimately intertwined with the other changes in the multicentered city. Said a member of the mayor's Front Porch Alliance,

> We are looking at two things: what is driving folks out and what is bringing them back, and how do we put the two together. What drives folks out of the city is taxes, race, education, and crime. The one element bringing folks back into those neighborhoods is the church. Now how do we marry the church and neighborhood to address these issues?

Cloister Congregations

At the other end of the spectrum from community outreach are congregations that begin by looking internally, focusing on the vertical relationship between themselves and God. Not everyone who inhabits the new city has an equal ability to choose or to try to alter her environment. Surrounded by a political and economic environment that seems increasingly hostile, or at least savagely indifferent, congregations with a cloistered view of their mission respond by battening down the hatches. They draw ever-tighter circles that define their neighborhood, their ethnicity, their community, and those who can be fellow members of their local collectives.

The classic example of a *cloister congregation* is the fundamentalist Christian group that stands steadfast against what it sees as the relativizing tendencies in social pluralism, and indeed in urban realignment. "A lot of people have the 'form' of God in their church," said one such preacher, "but they deny making the personal change. A lot of people in our town, in our city, are not saved. Just because a man tells me he is a United Methodist does not mean he is saved." Consider two Indianapolis congregations that highlight the cloistering tendency.

"People are not interested in salvation here": Few Are Chosen Missionary Baptist Church

In the mid-1990s, when we first visited Few Are Chosen MBC, it had nine regular members, eight of whom were women. They were all members of an extended family, including their pastor. Because Few Are Chosen is in a primarily African American, inner-city neighborhood and because all of its members are African American, most observers would judge that it was truly a neighborhood-based institution. But in 1996, not a single one of the nine members lived in the surrounding neighborhood. They all lived in a more suburban neighborhood on the northeast side of the city. In fact, they had no roots in the neighborhood and no desire to be connected to it.

Make no mistake. The members of Few Are Chosen were aware that their neighborhood was home to the city's most successful coalition of urban churches, that the city's most prominent inner-city, church-sponsored recreation program took place directly across the street, and that other small, African American churches just around the corner were engaged in a Ten Point Coalition, a clerical alliance modeled on the one in Boston, to try to keep the streets safe from crime and drugs. They just wanted no part of this.

In 1999, the pastor died and was replaced by another. The congregation — now numbering ten members — experienced a wholesale shift from the first pastor's family to the next pastor's family. The new members all lived within walking distance of the church building. Only the original pastor's brother came in from the northeastern suburbs to continue serving as deacon, treasurer, and administrator. He says he "likes smaller churches because he can be more involved."

Critics might ask whether this really constitutes a congregation at all. Yet in 1999 they proudly burned the mortgage on a $60,000 church building, thanks to one substantial gift intended to keep them going. A church founded by people from a different neighborhood who simply got a good deal on a building when another church moved out had now come to be populated — indeed owned — by people who lived just up the block.

The changeover from non-residents to residents did not, however, change the congregation's outlook toward the neighborhood. Few Are Chosen maintains a small food pantry, but mostly they refer people to the surrounding mainline churches with "urban ministries." Few Are Chosen's pastor is succinct in describing the neighborhood where he both lives and ministers: "It is a battleground between home and church." He sees the battleground dominated by youth with all their problems:

> 9500 youth from surrounding neighborhoods participate in sports at the Presbyterian church right across the street, but most of them don't attend there. We have all kinds of problems with shootings, gangs, and drugs. The Presbyterian church lost members because they were afraid to come to church, to walk through the neighborhood to church.
>
> I won't walk outside myself. One time I walked through a gang fight and didn't even realize it. After that, I stopped walking to church from home. Some kids asked me for money one time and I said that I didn't have any, so they started throwing rocks at me. People are not interested in salvation here. They run away from me because they know I'm gonna preach Jesus to them. They just ain't interested.

There is a misconception, especially among whites, that because an inner-city, African American, "storefront" church is in an African American neighborhood, the members of the church must be from the same neighborhood. In this case, though, residents in a completely different area of the city simply bought a building when the opportunity arose. The fact that it came to be owned by "locals" did not make it any more of a local organization.

There is a similar misconception that these black churches must function as pillars of the community, the front line in the ongoing struggle against the effects of poverty and deprivation. Some do struggle in just that way, of course, but even when Few Are Chosen became a "neighborhood organization," with its membership going from 100 percent living outside the neighborhood to 90 percent living inside, it still wanted nothing to do with a neighborhood that was already way beyond its powers to redeem.

It would be wrong to infer too much from one congregation of ten people, but Few Are Chosen makes the point dramatically that many romantic notions about urban congregations as indigenous community organizations are misguided. Most congregations in Indianapolis are larger than Few Are Chosen, but it is important to remember that fully half have fewer than 150 members and see fewer than 100 on any given weekend. A substantial number have fewer than 50 members and no full-time paid staff. The point is not to belittle these congregations. That they continue to persevere and to serve the spiritual needs for worship and religious education of their members is a phenomenal achievement. But when we think about the amazing diversity of religion and its role in shaping multiple cultural and social centers, we must be careful not to slip into the trap of too quickly identifying congregations as the moral and spiritual centers of needy urban neighborhoods, or of ethnic or racial solidarity. Sometimes congregations embody the spiritual quest of a few relatively homogeneous, possibly related, people forming a small community. We must take that for what it is.

"Remember where God has brought you from": Calvary Evangelical Church

Calvary Evangelical Church has sixty members. Of these, thirty-six are women and twenty-four are men. More than forty of the members, about 70 percent, are well over the age of fifty-five. The congregation runs on a $20,000 annual budget. The people are friendly and warm, greeting our young researchers with genuine enthusiasm even on the second and third visits, when it was clear the researchers were not likely candidates for membership. Calvary comes so close to the stereotype of the small congregation that readers might be forgiven for wondering if it is a fiction, or at least a composite. But Calvary is quite real, and there are a number of congregations in its urban, white, working-class neighborhood that are very much like it.

As the pastor's wife explained to our researcher, "most of the folks here are from the South." She was from Tennessee and her husband was from Kentucky. "I moved here when I was sixteen," she said, "but I've worked hard to speak the same because I'd hate to lose my southern accent." The music at Calvary maintains a high standard, though it would be out of place in many other congregations because it is played on a bass guitar, a piano, an organ, and a fiddle.

Calvary has some of the trappings of a *conversion* congregation. Across the front of the church, between the stained glass windows, a banner reads "Untold Millions Dying Untold." On either side stand the Christian and American flags. The preacher's sermons are hellfire and brimstone, urging the congregation to repentance. "I have a problem with people who say they are Christians but love the world," he said. "We have been given names like far-right and fanatic, but sin is sin." "The Lord is returning," he said another time, "and he is taking us to heaven. It is important to remember where God has brought you from."

But Calvary does not proselytize because it has limited contact with either its neighborhood or the rest of the city. Once a year, at Thanksgiving, it collects a truck bed full of goods for the local community center. Otherwise, it keeps to itself. Its members fit comfortably and quietly into this small, semi-urban neighborhood made up of poor and working-class whites.

Perhaps the most remarkable thing about Calvary Evangelical is how unremarkable it is. It is a church of older members, with a majority of women, who share a common culture. It emphasizes that culture through worship. It constantly reminds itself of its distinction from a fallen world. It advocates *mission* as the correct Christian posture, but has little opportunity to engage in missions itself.

Neighborhood context is an integral part of the decision to remain cloistered, as we will see in Chapter 6. Few Are Chosen sits in an African American neighborhood awash in religiously based community activism. The congregation must make a conscious, intentional decision to remain cloistered, because it is not possible for a congregation to sit in such a neighborhood and not consider its role in the community. But in Calvary's white, working-class neighborhood, a decision to engage the community actively would be bold. Calvary is neither out of place nor out of step with its neighbors.

Cloister congregations often define away some of the complexities involved in urban realignment by homing their mission in on the unique importance of a personal relationship to God and by emphasizing their community's own special relationship. Most of their activities point inward, with the goal of creating respite from the secular world's temptations, always keeping one eye on the kingdom yet to come. When their mission turns, less frequently, to the outside world, they frame their efforts in terms of their circumscribed environment. The key is not the level of activity—some might be quite active and others much less—but that the religious sheep are separated from the secular goats by prior definition. Increasing pluralism in politics, business, or religious culture is proportionately discounted across the board in favor of the one, ideal thing that matters and the true community that knows it. Cloister congregations usually think in revolutionary rather than developmental terms about salvation, seeing it as a one-time event. They describe it in terms of the individual rather than in terms of society: good people constitute a good society.

It is a mistake, and one frequently repeated, to assume that these cloister congregations do not understand the stance they are taking vis-à-vis a changing environment. Some within these groups have made a scholarly attempt to defend their position in an arena defined by contrasting opinions. But even those who are less erudite understand that by staking out a position of certainty and drawing fixed boundaries in a fluid, negotiated environment, they are anchoring against the tide. Competing sacred ideologies are not to be tolerated or engaged, but defeated. "Away with the idols," said one testimony. "Away with the tree hugging."

Cloister congregations sometimes represent a brand of sectarianism almost totally defined by ideology. If that ideology can be blended with characteristics of race or class, then the circle is drawn tighter still. For instance, Indianapolis has only one congregation tied to the Nation of Islam, but its definitions of who is in and who is out, of "us" and "them," are well-known. But hyper-parochialism can also be rooted in more subtle cultural ideas and even in specific neighborhoods. This is not the "choice" behavior of the cultural consumer, but a kind of ascribed identity that attempts to hold fast against encroaching pluralism. When a pastor in a poor, white neighborhood of the city screamed, "This church is on the corner in *this* neighborhood so that humanity can commune with Jesus Christ," he was doing more than announcing their mission, he was identifying that mission with their given place. The testimony of a parishioner in the same neighborhood was notable not for its intention to exclude, but for its ability to circumscribe just who was included: "Our church is like the Ancient Israelites. They was no different. My family is just common people like everyone else here. I have a knife collection and like to go turkey hunting, just like many of you. We are the people. We are the world."

Anyone looking at these cloister congregations would say that they fit under the loose rubric of "evangelical" as it is widely used, primarily because their actions are based on personal conversion. But if these are "evangelicals," then they are very different from the groups who are out to save the world by converting strangers or by welcoming more and more spiritual seekers into the fold.[18] Cloister congregations seek fundamental, revolutionary change in individual lives and focus their attention on the lives of those in their community or others immediately surrounding it.

Conversion Congregations

A third type of congregational mission takes the message of God's unique relationship to humanity to the world outside their doors. Every congregation thinks about itself in terms of God's relationship to the world, but conversion congregations want to create social change by changing individuals' relationships to God. If cloister congregations huddle together against the world while awaiting the kingdom yet to come, conversion congregations reach out in an attempt to bring the rest of the world, or at least the part they feel responsible for, in with them.

Conversion congregations come closest to what most people mean by the term "evangelical," but we have consciously eschewed evangelical as our sole descriptor because its loose usage can apply to congregations within any of the categories we are suggesting. Caution is required when considering whether evangelical churches are flourishing while others languish, as some assert. The truth of that assertion depends on the size of one's evangelical umbrella.

We have chosen "conversion" as the label for this third kind of congregational archetype because we mean to specify those congregations whose primary interest is in bringing new members into the fold, causing outsiders to become insiders through conversion to correct belief and practice as defined by God's special relationship to humanity. Our conversion congregations seek to change the world by changing the individuals within it. Like cloistered congregations, they put the vertical relationship between God and the world first, but unlike cloistered congregations, they focus their energies on the world outside. Having learned the truth, their mission is to tell it to others while sustaining an internal community of disciples. Consider these examples.

"People are too involved in religion instead of Christ": Widow's Mite Christian Fellowship Church

Widow's Mite Christian Fellowship Church meets in an old paint store and warehouse in an inner suburban neighborhood that is slowly decaying on its borders and main thoroughfares. The pastor comes from Arizona but is of combined Navajo, German, and Spanish descent. After joining Widow's Mite in Arizona where the group is headquartered, he decided to return to his wife's hometown of Indianapolis and open a mission congregation, one of nearly 1,000 such missions now spawned by the original vision of the group's founder.

Neither the pastor nor his flock know much about the inner suburban neighborhood, nor do they live there. They chose this location because it has a mixture of young people, urban social problems like prostitution and drugs, and a growing Mexican presence. Their vision is straightforward and single-minded: they lead people to a personal relationship with Jesus Christ without concern for distinctions in class, race, or ethnic origin.

Our researchers learned firsthand about Widow's Mite's inclusive attitude toward evangelization. Both our college-aged researcher — a Muslim woman of Turkish origin — and our senior researcher — a white, male, American Baptist minister in his early forties (now working toward his Ph.D. at an Ivy League university) — were actively pursued. During a visit together, they watched "A Distant Thunder" — from the genre of "real life" apocalyptic movies popular in the 1970s and early 1980s — at an evening revival meeting. The young woman was struck by the intensity with which the possibility of conversion and the reality of the world's end were raised; the Baptist minister was amazed to see a film he had first seen more than twenty years earlier still being shown to youthful audiences. When the twelve-year-old drummer at Widow's Mite asked the Baptist minister if he was going forward during the altar call, our researcher responded, "Well, I did that about twenty years ago." Countered the twelve-year-old, "In my experience, a lot of people fool themselves into thinking they are believers in Jesus Christ. Anybody can say they're a Christian."

Although Widow's Mite actively canvasses the neighborhood on Saturday mornings, they are not looking to become engaged with it in any civic way. They are hoping to lead their neighbors to Jesus. "Drugs and prostitution are the most visible problems," says the pastor. "But another serious problem is that people are too involved in religion instead of Christ." Accordingly, he makes no effort to meet other ministers or to become involved in ecumenical alliances or programs. Most clergy, he said, "mix up every kind of belief and do not go to the Bible."

Both the pastor and the members at Widow's Mite view the outside world very warily. The pastor preaches about the coming Beast, linking the end times to the growth of the European Union and the use of computers to identify and control the movement and choices of individuals. He follows in a long line of fundamentalist leaders who are concerned that political globalization of any kind is a move toward ungodliness and distant, and therefore potentially more satanic, control. None of this is new for students of evangelical fundamentalism in the U.S., but it is quite uncharacteristic for this inner suburban enclave. Among other things, it shows just how different a church located on a major thoroughfare can look from the rest of the neighborhood, because most of the young professionals living in this former artist's colony are likely to view Widow's Mite with bemused detachment.

As Widow's Mite centers itself in a complex world, it takes a decidedly vertical, even other-worldly, approach to human affairs. One's relationship to Christ and understanding of eschatology takes priority over all temporal concerns. But its concerns are nonetheless external. Widow's Mite knows that its members are saved. Its sense of urgency is driven by the state of all the non-members whose destiny is less certain. Given that stance, Widow's Mite actively and aggressively engages the world on those terms, seeking to lead people to a saving knowledge of Christ. Widow's Mite conducts its mission within its given neighborhood, but it is not neighborhood-oriented in any civic sense. Its focus is on heaven.

"Ease of location": Church of Jesus Christ of Latter-day Saints

A passerby from the neighborhood might notice that the simple, brick structure on the outskirts of town is a Latter-day Saints church because the plain sign out front says so. But that is as far as the relationship is likely to go.

The sign contains no phone number, no times for worship, no names of leaders, no clever quips. Those who need to know already do.

This LDS congregation is in a growing edge city that is demographically similar to those on the east, west, and south sides of Indianapolis (the northern suburbs are wealthier). Like other small towns that became suburbs, this community is a mix of in-town homes and sprawling developments, of mom-and-pop stores in the center and Wal-Marts on the fringes. It is primarily white and middle-class, but there are trailer parks and lower-class housing, as well as some upper-middle-class suburbs.

It would be tempting to assume that this LDS church, like many in more urbanized areas, just happens to be here for historical reasons and that its members have no direct connection to the neighborhood. But fully two-thirds of its members live within this edge city's limits, with the other third living in nearby suburbs. The church was, in fact, built intentionally on this spot because of its ease of location. Although this ward started as a branch in a nearby town, its growth led the central offices in Salt Lake City to shift the primary church here because it was "most convenient for members to reach, and most of the members live here." The church structure itself was built by architects and contractors chosen in Salt Lake City; it reflects the "high degree of standardization" one expects of Latter-day Saints buildings, as one of the members put it.

Knowing that the members live nearby, the anonymity of the congregation's plain sign in the front might suggest a hostile, or at least indifferent, attitude toward its local environment. But in fact the members of the Latter-day Saints church like living here. The current bishop — an unpaid leader who works roughly forty hours a week as a volunteer — grew up in California and then moved to Utah when he was fourteen, going on to graduate from Brigham Young University. Yet when his family was driving through this suburban edge city, the spirit told them to stop, that this was the place for them. Even when they moved to Korea for two years as part of his job at Lilly Pharmaceuticals, he always intended to come back here. It is, he says, "a good feeling community with strong values, education, and good neighbor relations."

The bishop acknowledges that the congregation is not very involved in local community life, but says this is not an intentional disengagement. They have sponsored a booth at the town fair and their scout troop has done more than 500 hours of local park beautification. Also, the church contributes to the local food pantry. But without paid, professional leaders, it is difficult for the church to have a visible presence in local politics. The bishop already donates virtually a full working week to the church in addition to his full-time, paid employment at Lilly.

In this particular community, however, the disengagement is palpable. The town has a Values Committee that sponsors a value of the month that is taught in Sunday school classes across town and is posted and discussed in the local schools. There are several cooperative religious activities including the food pantry. The Latter-day Saints church posted the monthly values and discussed them for the first year of the program, but then gradually drifted away. The congregation makes no conscious effort to avoid community issues, especially since the town's emphasis on nuclear families, hard work, honesty, and sobriety fits very nicely with LDS theology, but it has found it difficult to stay regularly involved.

This gap between town and church is no accident. This LDS church is far more allied with Salt Lake City than with its edge city home. In virtually all of its affairs, direction comes from the central office and most of the energy and effort is directed back there. It would be hard to overestimate the degree to which Salt Lake City serves as a center for this congregation's activities. Not only are the educational materials and the hymnals produced in Utah, but the congregation's leaders are also chosen there. Missionaries from Utah are frequently sent to Indianapolis, with some of them coming under the care of this ward. The size and location of the congregation is determined at the home office. Within the last decade, the ward has been carved up several times, both to keep it a standard size and to serve the interests of other nearby wards or branches to which certain members of this group were directed. The church went from 300 members down to 200 in one such carving, and then down to 120 in a second redistricting, but is now back up to 180 members.

This kind of reorganization makes clear that building a strong sense of internal community within any particular congregation is not the goal. The loyalty and sense of community is to Mormonism as a faith, not to particular local branches that are just outward manifestations. The extraordinary level of commitment shown by members proves that such a bifocal understanding of community works, at least for certain people in certain environments. Members routinely give twenty to forty hours a week as volunteer leaders and pay an official tithe on income statements they freely make available to the church, even though the money all goes to Salt Lake City.

For those within the worshipping community at any given time, the level of interpersonal interaction is very high. More active members are each assigned a less active one whom they see several times during the week other than Sunday. Not only does this build social capital and encourage less active members to become more so, but it provides a discreet opportunity for those who might need help of any kind to ask for it.

The members of this Latter-day Saints church are aggressive converters, just as in any similar LDS congregation across the country. Their children go off for two-year missions. Missionaries from elsewhere come here. Although the content of the mission work differs from that at Widow's Mite and the socioeconomic status of the members is much different, in many ways they are the same. Both have their eyes turned toward heaven and toward a mission defined elsewhere. Both regard their present community as their mission field, and define themselves thereby, but neither feels any special connection to it because their ultimate goals are determined neither here nor now.

With all the talk these days about the success of evangelical congregations, it is worth noting that within our ideal types, fewer congregations fall into this conversion cell than any other. This alone demonstrates the importance of seeking new ways to categorize congregational activity that describes new urban realities. Most congregations are publicly proactive in some way. Many have conservative theologies. Many encourage others to join them. Therefore, it makes sense to move beyond older ideas about what constitutes evangelism or activism to look at how congregations and their members imagine their missions in a realigned city.

Conversion congregations view religious change as individual and revolutionary, just as cloister congregations do. But they more aggressively pursue the social consequences of their theological beliefs. Cloister congregations may hope that the world is redeemed through their good example, but most have insulated themselves from a world that is lost in ways that are beyond their control. Conversion congregations, by contrast, have an obligation to tell the world about the unique relationship between God and humans. They can be widely more or less optimistic about the ultimate success of their efforts in changing society, but in the end what happens to society will not matter because it ultimately gives way to God's radically different, coming kingdom.

Customer Service Congregations

In a city defined by strong outward pressures creating multiple social and cultural centers, there is a very real sense in which many individuals and their families must construct their own communities out of the various instruments available in their cultural tool kit. In this sense, even as congregations seek to balance themselves in a fluid environment, so their members seek their own identities and their own communities within a matrix formed not only by congregations, but also by other, very different institutions. In this context, some congregations try to meet their members' needs for identity and community by addressing virtually all their everyday needs and their spiritual needs as part of one complete package. These customer service congregations strive to give their members the opportunities for the intellectual, spiritual, social, and even physical development they require. They marry the worldview of personal conversion to much broader notions of spiritual, personal development that take in virtually every aspect of everyday experience.

As noted above, the concept of "consumer choice" applies to some kinds of people more than to others. Virtually no one gets full, unfettered choice about what career she will have or how much money he will make, or where she will live, much less who makes up his family. Still, consumer choice remains a useful concept despite its limitations. Many people regularly move in and out of Indianapolis. Moreover, they move frequently from neighborhood to neighborhood within the metropolitan area. Those who can afford to do so make choices based on the quality of schools, on housing options, on the convenience and quality of shopping or entertainment, and on proximity to their places of work, though many have shown themselves willing to travel long distances for work if it improves their other choices. They construct a mental map of their community that includes the schools, the workplace, the shopping and entertainment venues, and possibly a congregation, but this map need not, and usually does not, correspond to anyone else's definition of "neighborhood." Such maps, stacked one on top of the other, help to define the true complexity of conceptualizing community in a city that has both one center and multiple centers.

People who live in these multiplex areas, especially suburbanites, are creating new forms of metropolitan community. Said one observer, "There's a part of me that feels like the whole idea of neighborhood or of being a neighbor is so devastated, so far from our reality. In our highly mobile state, we're still redefining it." Another ex-suburbanite who returned downtown was more succinct: "Maybe you can recreate a neighborhood on a cul-de-sac, but I think you can't."

An evolving type of congregation is addressing this complexity by seeking to build communities of worship that are geared toward customer service, seeking to meet the demands of those who are constantly redefining their communities through consumer choice. They respond to the horizontal needs of the here and now, focusing their attention on the needs of the group's members. As one of our respondents put it, "Consumerism defines religion in the suburbs. It's about church shoppers looking for institutions with non-institutional flavor, places that suit their individual tastes and provide opportunities for growth and development."

"You are free to go, but if you have anything you would like us to pray with you about, please stay": Paradigm Fellowship

Paradigm Fellowship is in a growing suburban community much like other "new paradigm" congregations across America, all of which have been made more familiar by Donald Miller's *Reinventing American Protestantism*.[19] The congregation meets in an office park, its fourth location in just a few years. Although it professes to have no "members," the congregation totals 450 to 600 every Sunday.

Everything about the congregation is casual. There are no coats and ties, no "Sunday best" dresses. Visitors are made to feel welcome and are told clearly that they are under no obligation. When the offering plate is passed around, visitors are reminded to "just relax and not worry. But if you've been here a while, you know what to do." The music is rock-oriented, with live acoustic guitar, electric guitar, electric bass, drums, and tambourine. When the live concert stops, taped music fills any gaps in the service.

Sermon topics, especially on Sundays, emphasize individual freedom. "Too often we approach God like a religion," intoned the pastor. "Maybe some of you are not experiencing joy. Maybe it is from religion and rules and regulations that drift from freedom." Congregants are encouraged to let go of those things that stifle joy, especially selfishness, resentment, and fear. Topics and motifs are drawn from popular culture, from the physical office space to the music to the self-help nature of the sermon. On Wednesdays, the inner core of members are more likely to emphasize spiritual discipline and to focus more on Scripture. But on Sundays, the emphasis is on finding your own spiritual way. This could not be more intentional. Brochures promise to deliver on topics that discuss "real life," with teachings "that really apply." Even at the end of the service, in place of an altar call there is an invitation to stay for extra prayer as needed. "You are free to go, but if you have anything you'd like us to pray with you about, please stay."

The members at Paradigm, many of whom are young, tend to live outside of I-465, the circular interstate that marks the city's perimeter. They know the reputation of their white, middle-class suburb and define themselves thereby. When one of our young researchers suggested she had heard that "everyone here goes bowling," they replied, "We're too cheap for that," before adding, "There's nothing to do here."

As with any such group that is "seeker sensitive," as Donald Miller put it in his research on these new Protestants, there is considerable movement in and out. The members related the story of a charismatic leader who left to start a new group nearby. The new congregation looked like another Paradigm Fellowship, but was in fact associated with Willow Creek, the Chicago-area megachurch known nationally as a model for growing, consumer-oriented congregations. Another member had come to Paradigm from the nearby Community Church, the local parallel to Willow Creek. He came because Paradigm, with its forty-eight-channel soundboard, had "something that moved."

"I love this place — not the location, but the experience of meeting the Lord": Christian Independent Church

Every community of neat suburban houses and densely packed strip malls is likely to have some variation of Paradigm Fellowship and some congregation much like Christian Independent Church. The independent church we offer here meets not in vacant office space, but in a huge structure with a covered drive-through entrance, a sanctuary that holds well more than 1,000, and dozens of classrooms. One of the many pastors on staff estimated that in an average week, as many as 5,000 people pass through the doors, though Sunday worship is not anywhere near that large.

Membership and attendance are difficult to quantify for a place like this. The church does not seek to grow ever larger as a single congregation, but instead "plants" new congregations across the region. At the time of our research, there were six such plantings, mostly in nearby Indiana, but some as far away as Lexington, Kentucky. These new start-ups are usually headed by a younger pastor who has served as an assistant at the mother church and has been mentored by the senior pastor and founder. The mother church usually lends a few of its elders to these new congregations for a few years. All of these congregations take a relatively casual approach to worship and use popular music played with live instruments, though dress is not as casual nor the music as loud as at Paradigm. There is didactic preaching, with points clearly numbered for the many who are taking notes. The services do not include many unplanned, spontaneous testimonies, but those called on to speak, as at the congregation's twentieth anniversary celebration, know what makes the community special. "I love this place," said one. "Not the location, but the experience of meeting the Lord."

At this point in the story, those familiar with emerging congregational trends may be nodding knowingly. Our independent church fits well their stereotype of the big church with charismatic leader, multiple satellite off-shoots, and an enormous range of programs for members and their children in all age ranges. There are such churches on all four sides of Indianapolis, as there are in the suburbs of every large city. Christian Independent Church not only has staff members dedicated to adolescent youth and to children's needs, it has a pastor with an MBA to help consider the management issues in such a far-flung enterprise. When we were visiting the congregation in the late 1990s, it was considering adding a substantial recreation and family life center. It would not be fully open to the public, because the congregation made it a point not to offer use of its facilities to programs it did not directly support. But another of the pastors made the bottom line of the proposed center clear: "if there is no ministry tied to this center, if it is not done in conjunction with a ministry outreach to the community, it will not be built."

That mission focus — that service to external customers — cannot be separated from Christian Independent Church's service to its own members. CIC begins with its members and their needs, and always keeps one eye focused there, but its other eye is always looking out to those in need of community. In addition to the local start-ups under the umbrella of the mother church, CIC has also planted new congregations in Latin America, particularly in Brazil. They send their own missionaries, upwards of 100 per year, for various lengths of time to places such as El Salvador, Mexico, Hungary, and Kenya.

The simplest way to define the degree to which "mission" motivates this community is to look at the budget numbers. Christian Independent keeps two separate budgets—one for its internal needs and one dedicated to missions, both local and abroad. At the time of our initial visits, each of these was in the low $500,000s. By the time of this writing, the mission budget had surpassed $1 million.

So any who were nodding at the description of Christian Independent Church must be careful not to assume that customer service congregations cater only to their members and turn their backs to the rest of the world. These congregations do provide for their members in a multitude of ways, creating a kind of alternative community that devotees of small, local, grassroots community are likely to find too corporate and expansionist. But the creation of new community can be based every bit as much on missions as on exalting individual freedom. A customer service congregation begins with the need to build an alternative community for its members, but it does not end there, in a closed circle. It goes on to build other communities for others with the same need.

Christian Independent Church, like Paradigm Fellowship, attempts to fill a perceived void, as the many forms of social decentering have made it less likely that extended families, governments, companies, schools, or neighborhoods can provide a mobile population with the sense of community that so many desire. These congregations have become social centers themselves, functioning as extended families and offering the full range of mundane activities that members might once have sought from a geographically defined neighborhood. They are, as one resident put it, "recreating a neighborhood for their members," and they are doing it on their own theological terms. CIC even sponsors its own alternative Halloween so that youngsters can still get treats without exposure to anything tinged by the occult.

Customer service congregations often take the form of large campuses, with facilities for recreation and sport as well as for education. Except for one African American church with more than 10,000 members, Indianapolis does not have any 5,000-plus-member Protestant congregations known as megachurches, but it has several large congregations that are well on their way. Moreover, some of those large congregations have even larger memberships than first appearances would suggest, if one counts the many satellite congregations started by each of these mother churches.

Much recent attention has been paid to these growing, consumer-oriented congregations and with very good reason. Increasing numbers of young and middle-aged professionals are less embedded in traditional, ascriptive social networks and more comfortable with creating personal communities tailored to their particular needs. It was no surprise when a Paradigm Fellowship pastor said that his young congregants referred frequently to the movie *The Matrix,* in which traditional assumptions about places or actions give way to individual constructions of parallel realities. As in any population, some are more motivated by a desire for tight interpersonal and emotional bonds, but virtually all are seeking deeper, more transcendent meaning. However, unlike many other populations, these seekers have fewer ascribed traditions and meanings to fall back on. One of our respondents went so far as to call them "self-absorbed," a backhanded version of Miller's "seeker sensitive." But these congregations are more than just successful experiments in religious entrepreneurialism. They constitute a logical, and evidently quite successful, response to urban realignment. They are meeting needs largely created by changes in the city and in the nature of community within it.

Leaders in the Christian community have been paying close attention to these large and growing congregations for years. But if we see these consumer-oriented churches not as random successes in religious innovation, but as a form of organizational evolution inextricably tied to changes in urban social life, then it becomes clear that other civic leaders must learn to pay close attention as well. These large congregations are not simply aberrations, a skewed sample of evangelical churches that were "successful" by marketing measurements. They represent a real change in congregational response to a changed urban environment, as an ever-larger percentage of churchgoers attend an ever-smaller number of congregations. The large Catholic churches are already powerful organizations, though their potential growth is limited by the diocesan prerogative to rearrange parish boundaries and limit growth managerially. But the large Protestant churches such as Christian Independent appear poised to assume an ever-greater market share. There is a strong link between their success and the changing definitions both of place and community caused by urban change, a link that is likely to matter even more to leaders throughout the civic community — from politics to business to non-profit groups — in generations to come.

SIGNIFICANT RELIGIOUS CHANGE
IN MULTICENTERING CONTEXT

This congregational typology helps identify trends, but it cannot, as we have frequently repeated, shoehorn the majority of congregations into neat pigeonholes. Many congregations have adopted customer service tactics, offering a range of mundane activities alongside spiritual development, but do not fit the type in many other respects. A number of congregations are involved in community outreach. Most congregations, like most communities, have at least a little parochialism in them, even if they are not truly cloistered. There must be, after all, some way to say who is "us" and who is "them" even if that delineation is wholly non-judgmental and the goal is to expand the concept of community.

As the urban environment changes, congregations are engaged in negotiation with the evolving city, sometimes deliberate and intentional, other times not. Many congregational members and their leaders see — even if only dimly at points — the evolution of multiple religious centers, as well as changes in politics, business, and secular culture. Sometimes they regard the most aggressively innovative attempts to adapt to realignment as a kind of cultural capitulation. They are wary of approaches that seem too linked to the management culture of the marketplace. But they also recognize the futility of denying or trying to escape the multicentered city, especially to the degree that their members participate and succeed in it. Sectarian cloistering is not a genuine option for those who have, or hope to have, influence in political or economic spheres.

The congregations involved in these ongoing negotiations need not embrace the new urban pluralism wholeheartedly in order to realize that attempting to turn back the tide is a waste of energy. Instead, they try to make sure that their traditions and values inform the new institutional arrangements as much as possible or, when that cannot be fully achieved, that the new urban order protects their values and traditions within the emerging diversity.

Having set the urban context and described different congregational roles therein, it might be possible to analyze a wide variety of trends in the hopes of understanding how religion's role in the metropolis has changed. We have opted to focus on two important religious changes — changes to the Protestant establishment and changes in the role of clergy — that best demonstrate how a shifting urban context, and the related realignment of congregational missions, affects religious practice.

Renegotiating the Role of the Protestant Establishment

One inarguable effect of congregational realignment is that congregations wishing to grow — and by no means is this a goal for all of them — are experimenting with new forms of customer service. The "Faith and Values" section included in each Saturday's *Indianapolis Star* is now liberally sprinkled with advertisements for alternative worship services, usually held in congregations that still offer traditional services too. A number of other congregations have experimented with two different worship services, one containing traditional music and a sermon and one oriented toward more contemporary music and less formal, more conversational, teaching. Even Second Presbyterian, the bulwark of the mainline establishment, now holds a service called "Second at Six," a significant concession to consumer choice. The church advertises on popular radio stations that this service is held at 6:oo P.M. on Sundays for younger adults who might like to sleep in and / or brunch out. It is promoted as open, contemporary, and discussion-based; sometimes a jazz trio performs. Second has hardly joined the ranks of the megachurches meeting the needs of a newly suburban middle class, but even it is acknowledging changes in its target audience.

Second is not the only mainline establishment congregation that is navigating new waters in a city defined by a disestablished metropolitan center and multiple religious centers. The tall-steeple congregations must look for ways to exercise leadership while at the same time acknowledging the legitimacy, indeed the inevitability, of cultural pluralism. We have already seen the changes at work as mainline congregations form partnerships with inner-city churches and offer contemporary evening worship. But no congregation, indeed no organization, in Indianapolis defines the process of ongoing negotiation — or understands the need for negotiations — better than the Lilly Endowment. And no other city has a philanthropic foundation with the resources and the mission commitment to use those resources to move the dialogue forward. The Endowment still supports some ecumenical activities, though not as strongly as it has in the past. Moreover, it has been the country's most generous and influential funder of basic research about religious life in America, including the present volume. But the Endowment's interest in ecumenism or research is really driven by its primary focus on sustaining religion's public role, especially the role of the historic mainline denominations. As the 2000 annual report says,

> Lilly Endowment in its religion grantmaking seeks to enhance the quality and depth of the religious lives of American Christians. *Attention is focused primarily on the one religious institution in which virtually every active Christian is most deeply involved — the local congregation — and on the leader of that institution — the pastor.* (emphasis added)

Leaders at the Endowment are keenly aware of the limitations of universal strategies designed to pull together disparate religious and ethnic cultures into one common enterprise. They know that the cultural arena, like the political and economic one, is now negotiated by people who come from a variety of different starting points, with assumptions and practices centered in different cultural and geographical centers of the metropolis. But rather than throw their hands up in dismay, the Endowment tries to strengthen religious ties at the local level and to help congregations negotiate more successfully in a complex and plural environment. Beyond that, they look for pastors and civic leaders capable of recognizing the important points of overlap among the multiple cultural centers and leveraging them into cooperative action. In the absence of a common religious center, with the myth of overarching religious organizations shattered, those points of overlap represent the best hope for creating an urban community that appreciates religion's contribution both to important shared values but also to a genuine pluralism of ideas and social goals.

The Endowment's support of the Indianapolis Center for Congregations crystallizes its commitment to strengthening religious practice at the local level, letting cooperation among the multiple centers work upward from that rather than being imposed downward. The Center provides many practical resources for dealing with budgets, staff changes, and the like, but it is also well aware of the constant give and take of a decentered religious environment. Its first major conference topic was "Faith, Families, and Congregations" and its second, even more tellingly, was "Meaningful Worship in a Changing Culture." Although the Center's first director admitted that they were "building an airplane while flying it," there can be no question that the Center hoped, and hopes, to fill a gap caused by denominational decline tied to other changes in the social structure as well as the religious culture.

> A kind of diagnosis took place recognizing that within the changing landscape of American religion, the roles of denominations and their relationship to individual churches had changed over several decades. Then, too, within the whole ecology of church life there have been many changes — generational differences, theological differences, and less established pathways for congregations to get resources and help. (From Indianapolis Center for Congregations newsletter)

The Lilly Endowment does not, of course, limit its involvement in urban life to the religious realm. To whatever degree the inward pressures have succeeded in creating a metropolitan Indianapolis identity rooted in commerce, patriotism, government, and sport, the Endowment was actively involved. Without Endowment backing, Indianapolis might not have the domed stadium that brought a National Football League team. Its new downtown mall, Circle Center, would not have a performance venue — the eye-catching, all-glass, Artsgarden — suspended above the street. The NCAA headquarters would probably still be in Kansas City. Some version of the zoo, the fine arts, and the Children's Museum might exist, but undoubtedly in more modest proportions.

Beyond these activities of the Lilly Endowment as an institution are the many individual acts of Endowment insiders. Had a senior member of the Lilly family not been a member of Christ Church Cathedral, for instance, and had he not bequeathed a personal endowment there that now totals tens of millions of dollars, there might not be any churches remaining on Monument Circle.

One story from late 2002 brings the many elements involved in the establishment's ongoing negotiations into perspective. Thomas Lake spent a long career at pharmaceutical giant Lilly, the city's largest employer and highest-profile corporate taxpayer. He then spent twenty-two years at Lilly Endowment, first as president, then as board chairman, then as honorary board chairman. After his death, his children used $5 million to establish the Lake Family Institute on Faith and Giving to honor their parents. The new center is based at the IU Center on Philanthropy; its mission is to teach and learn about the relationship between faith and giving, always with an eye toward community outreach and mentoring in Indianapolis.

Retired Endowment vice president Robert Lynn was tapped to launch the new initiative. William Enright, twenty-one-year pastor of Second Presbyterian Church and board member of the Lilly Endowment, would begin his retirement from the pulpit as the Center's first "senior fellow and executive." Said Enright at the Center's unveiling, "My task will be to help the community — its *Jewish, Christian, and Muslim congregations* and its civic leaders — in conversations about service and giving from a religious perspective" (emphasis added).[20]

A city as large and diverse as Indianapolis cannot be contained within a nutshell, but the announcement of the Lake Center was more than a little symbolic. The family of a civic leader who had spent a lifetime with Lilly the company and then Lilly the foundation creates a new institution. The Center looks for leadership to the most "inner" of the city's inner circle of elites. It joins a downtown Center already built upon Endowment support. And its first proclamation announces its intention to embrace Indianapolis's plural faiths by engaging its congregations.

At first blush, it may seem odd to place an extended discussion of Lilly Endowment — a foundation — within a chapter on congregations. But the Endowment's commitment to congregations, and its understanding of these as the primary components of the faith community, helps to define the relationship between religion and public life in Indianapolis. The many congregations of the old establishment are seeking their new role in the realigned city — some through different approaches to customer service, most through new forms of community outreach. But we cannot understand these churches' response to urban realignment without understanding the Endowment's role in negotiating the growth of religious pluralism and the disestablishment of religion at the city's center.

The Changing Role of Clergy

New forms of congregational response to a changing urban environment have called forth new kinds of pastors, as the Lilly Endowment's mission statement suggests. Some have the charisma, the public speaking talent, and the managerial acuity to lead the new customer service congregations. Others have the desire and ability to lead their congregations into public partnership, always stepping gingerly along the line that separates their internal duty to create a worship experience and counsel parishioners from a visible role in the broader public.

The role of clergy has been altered by both the inward and outward pressures that shaped the city. Just as steeples are less prominent in the mile square, so are clergy voices much softer on the civic stage. Christian Theological Seminary's president put it best when he said, "My fear is that the mainliners will think, if we could just do this and just do that, we can get back to the early 1900s. Ain't going to happen. We are not going to be at the center of the show."[21]

The inward pressures that have democratized the public square by making it less traditionally religious have undercut the public authority of the city's foremost pastors. A variety of religious leaders — evangelical, African American, Jewish, Catholic, and mainline — take turns writing columns for the *Indianapolis Star*'s Faith and Values section, but the days of sermons printed in the paper are long past. Columnists speak to the whole community from the perspective of their one community, just as activist conservative or African American pastors represent their groups' "special interests" to the whole. Congregations often become communal havens from a world now dominated by the impersonal, individuating forces of the polity and the marketplace. They attempt to create a new kind of community in an environment where older kinds of community have broken down. Unlike the entrepreneurial pastors trying to create new forms of religious life to meet new community needs, some pastors can only name a force apparently beyond their control. One such pastor said he mourned "the loss of many of the congregation's elders and the difficulty in finding younger people who shared their leadership and loyalty." "The newer members," he worried, "have an unhealthy attachment to transience and constant movement. They do not really understand community because of their 'ludicrous hustle and bustle.'"

A suburban housewife expressed a similar sentiment when asked about problems facing her community. She cited the fast pace of life, the "go-go" mentality, and the attitude that you always had to be a winner. She recounted a female friend recently on her doorstep in tears because she could not handle the pressure, even though she "only had two small children." "The pressures of suburban life need to be put second to one's relationship to God," said our informant. "That's why our church stresses spending time each day with God."

It might be a stretch to describe the pastors as the "fathers" or "grandfathers" (and only occasionally, in Indianapolis, "mothers") of these extended families, but the graying of the city's pastors makes this metaphor seem apt. The average Indianapolis pastor is a fifty-two-year-old male. The average age of students at Christian Theological Seminary is now over forty. By way of comparison, the average public school teacher is forty-four years old and the average lawyer is forty-two.

The congregations these pastors serve are supporters, even creators, of strong, healthy families, even as the congregations themselves function as extended families in just the way that the Center for Congregations' first conference made plain. Members expect their pastors to be counselors or strict authority figures, depending on the mission stance of the congregation. But public expectations are different. Those outside the churches and synagogues expect clergy to be involved in issues of public morality and even of public policy. As one Methodist pastor put it, "The congregation is likely saying to the pastor: 'Your role here is the spiritual nurturing of your congregation.' There is a larger public audience that seems to be saying, 'Your role is to have more influence in public life.' "

Within their congregations, some pastors speak on matters of public concern, but they tend to appeal more for personal, moral transformation than for any structural social change. More than 70 percent of pastors reported that they had preached on problems associated with crime, poverty, and discrimination against racial and ethnic minorities. Fewer than 25 percent, however, had addressed sociostructural elements such as business development or the minimum wage. Sociostructural issues are not necessarily natural sermon topics, but the activities of clergy suggest that they steer clear of such issues outside the pulpit as well. Only 21 percent reported ever having tried to influence public policy regarding business development; only 12 percent reported the same regarding the minimum wage. Considerably more, from 45 percent to 70 percent, said they had tried to influence policies concerning crime, poverty, and discrimination.[22]

These numbers suggest that many clergy see themselves trying to make a difference in public affairs — certainly at a higher rate than one would expect to find in the general public. But the numbers also suggest that clergy activities have been circumscribed by changes in religion's social role. Pastors are expected to exhort their members not to kill or steal and to advocate racial tolerance and help for the poor. They are not, however, expected to interfere with structural decisions that are now made within the economic and political realms. Once again, religion matters deeply in the multiple, smaller centers of urban life, but it exerts little force at the city's structural center.

Indianapolis residents see this distinction in everyday life. When asked how much various groups were doing to make Indianapolis a better place to live, 81 percent of Indianapolis residents said that business leaders were doing a lot or a moderate amount, and 73 percent said the same about government officials and leaders of social service or non-profit organizations. Only 67 percent said the same about religious leaders.

To see just how much most pastors are locked in to the multiple, particular communities they serve, one need only look at how they say they spend their time. Pastors spend from twelve to twenty hours per week on administration and another ten to twelve hours leading worship. They spend six or more hours in Bible study, another six providing counseling, and six more making home and hospital visits. By contrast, they spend about three hours per week — by their own account — on social outreach.

Some will read that division of labor as an indictment of clergy, but that judgment requires a prior opinion about what clergy *ought* to do. Without assigning moral value, though, it is plain to see that the role of clergy fits the description of religious life, as practiced in congregations, offered throughout this book. Religion builds social capital, it creates community for particular, elective groups in specific places. As one pastor said, "It's the consumer mentality that controls the way pastors see the church. That is what is expected of you."

THE RISE OF CONGREGATIONS IN THE MULTICENTERED CITY

Congregations are voluntary organizations. They tend to be full of similar people. They are, in short, extremely well-suited to creating and sustaining community in the multiple, local centers of the city. More than that, they can manage, even mediate, the relationship between those smaller communities and the larger metropolitan community.

Recent attempts to involve religion more vigorously in public life — most notably the faith-based reforms of the Bush administration following on the so-called "charitable choice" legislation of the late 1990s — have enhanced the public turn from denominations and large religious bureaucracies to particular congregations. Because congregations are perceived to be local, voluntary, and flexible, they are driven by specific religious values generally shared by most of the members in ways that denominations cannot always claim. The whole point of religious welfare reform is to give these smaller, more particular organizations the freedom, and even the funds, to act without external administrative constraint, using their specific religious and moral values to bring change to specific groups in need. This voluntary and local conception of religion fits well not only with Indianapolis's perception of itself, but also with the national trend toward reform through organizational devolution.

But from a different point of view, admitting that religion operates primarily at the local, particular level is insidious, if inevitable. If religion is about relatively small, homogeneous groups with particular interests, then it can have only small, localized effects in a world shaped primarily by economic and political institutional interests. Put in the terms offered by this book, religion has power, sometimes considerable power, out in the multiple centers of urban life, but it has gradually ceded power in the shared, common center. Even religion's values and moral teachings are considered specific to particular target groups who find them hospitable. A religious sphere that once had broader public authority — albeit in the guise of only one of its constituent parts — is now confined to small groups that may act publicly, but with limited institutional effect.

In a city where establishment congregations are displaced from the Circle by commercial interests and then displaced again from the mile square by the war memorials, it is easy to see establishment Protestantism becoming as local and particular as other religious movements already were. But it is also important to see that religious life has adapted precisely by emphasizing the ability of congregations to influence society in smaller, more specific ways.

This is why we have attempted to define contemporary congregational mission orientations with the ideal types of *community outreach, cloister, conversion,* and *customer service.* These summarize the many ways that congregations, as groups of worshippers with much in common, seek to address a metropolis with one and many centers. Rather than bemoaning the loss of religion's institutional influence in a fit of establishment nostalgia, we must look at the 1,200 congregations and the roughly 400,000 people of faith and ask what effects their actions have on everyday life. We must ask what new ways they find to create centered communities that build a sense of self and other that need not be theologically or philosophically airtight, but must allow them to respond day to day in a complex world.

The changes to which congregations respond are global, national, and, for our purposes, metropolitan in nature. But the effects on people's daily lives are local, so it is important to seek them out in neighborhood settings. Accordingly, the neighborhood is the next and last step as we examine the changing role of religion in the context of urban change.

6

BACK HOME AGAIN: RELIGION
IN THE NEIGHBORHOODS

Maybe you can recreate a neighborhood on a cul-de-sac,
but I think you can't.

— ex-suburbanite resident who moved downtown

In the late 1990s, then Secretary of Housing and Urban Development
Henry Cisneros highlighted one Indianapolis neighborhood as a national
model of successful urban ministry.[1] He used the Mid-North Church Council of the Mapleton–Fall Creek neighborhood to show what urban congregations could accomplish. Three urban congregations had banded together to
provide needed social services; they later welcomed other neighborhood
churches. The impressive range of services eventually included neighborhood economic development, a health center run jointly with Indiana University's School of Nursing, legal advice, recreation programs, and food
delivery.

Little wonder that Cisneros saw this neighborhood coalition as a model of
best practice. But how relevant is this model? Mapleton–Fall Creek's residents were primarily poor and black. The congregations involved in the
Mid-North Church Council had members who were white and middle-class,
or even upper-middle-class. This unusual combination resulted from a specific set of historical circumstances. Mapleton–Fall Creek was the city's first
affluent suburb, located directly on Meridian Street. It was full of large,
beautiful homes that had deteriorated through the years. Mapleton–Fall
Creek had been home to the city's grandest high school, Shortridge, whose

alumni include Senator Richard Lugar and author Kurt Vonnegut. The congregations built there in the early twentieth century were large, imposing structures.

When white flight hit Indianapolis in the 1960s and 1970s, the affluent residents who moved northward did not abandon their grand church buildings. Rather, they commuted back to the neighborhood, which still housed other important institutions like the Lilly Endowment and the Indianapolis Children's Museum along its western border on Meridian Street. It was these congregations, full of members who now lived elsewhere, who were providing services to neighborhood residents of a different race, different social class, and different church memberships.

On Mapleton–Fall Creek's eastern border lies the Martindale-Brightwood neighborhood. Martindale and Brightwood were once separate neighborhoods, one white, the other black. Both have always been working-class. White flight drove most of the white residents out of the area. When these residents left, however, they left their old, plainer church buildings behind and sought new church homes elsewhere.

In the late 1990s, anyone looking at the kind of demographic statistics favored by urban planners would have thought these neighborhoods were very similar. More than 90 percent of the residents in each were African American, high percentages lived in poverty, high percentages of the households were headed by single mothers.[2] But to anyone driving through, the neighborhoods did not *look* the same. Martindale-Brightwood had small homes and small churches — nearly 100 congregations in all. Mapleton–Fall Creek had big homes and big churches — fewer than twenty congregations, though the neighborhood was 50 percent larger by population. The average congregation in Mapleton–Fall Creek had more than 500 members; in Martindale-Brightwood, the average was fewer than 100 members. There were other differences too. Residents of Martindale-Brightwood were, for instance, much more likely to attend worship in their own neighborhood. In many ways, the area was *more* stable, containing within it a census tract with one of the lowest homeowner turnover rates in Indianapolis between 1990 and 2000. The community outreach congregations of Mapleton–Fall Creek were *for* the neighborhood, but not really *of* it.[3] Not surprisingly, in the last several years the big homes of Mapleton–Fall Creek have been gradually revitalized as gentrification slowly changes the neighborhood's demographic structure yet again.

The Mid-North Church Council may well have been, and may still be, a "model" urban ministry, but it is a model suited only to a specific set of social circumstances. The work of the churches there could not be duplicated even in the neighborhood next door, even though the two places seem statistically similar. Just as different congregations have different mission emphases, each keyed to different elements in the multicentered city, so are different neighborhoods, districts, and regions within the city affected differently by urban restructuring. Distinctions among congregations are even more apparent when seen in the context of distinctions among the urban places they inhabit.

Twenty-First-Century Neighborhoods and Districts as Multiple Centers

It is a truism to say that lives are not led in the abstract, but in *specific* places. Modern downtown landscapes and contemporary suburbs have become increasingly standardized, less distinguishable than they were fifty years ago. Yet Americans continue to yearn for an authentic sense of place.[4] Changes in Indianapolis over the past century tell us these places are not always the neighborhoods of an occasionally mythologized past characterized by tight personal bonds among residents and identities rich in history. Indianapolis was in recent memory a big small town, but today it is a metropolis loosely connected by suburbs and highways spreading in every direction. Overall, Indianapolis now seems new, clean, and plain — all qualities that bespeak prosperity and orderliness, typical American urban values that historian Richard Hofstadter first associated with American towns and cities.[5] But these values do not necessarily promote "community" in that older sense.

Nor is neighborliness itself enjoyed equally in all parts of the city. The 200-odd neighborhoods and districts of Indianapolis involve various combinations of social bonds that make up the urban community; they also involve diverse and multiple centers of activity and allegiance, not all of which overlap. These urban centers reflect important differences in race and social class, with marked contrast between urban and suburban environments. And as religious congregations act out their missions in any given social environment, they both contribute to those differences and resist the forces that bring them about.

The great University of Chicago sociologist Robert E. Park first defined the field of urban community studies in 1915 as consisting "in its physical organization, its occupations, and its cultures."[6] He further suggested that such study requires close views of the groups who live in urban settings, particularly their modes of conflict and control, network and segregation, vocation and lifestyle. Park is a helpful guide for those seeking to map the landscapes of neighborhoods and to identify the place of religious institutions within them. Taking his cue, we ask how congregations participate in creating different kinds of neighborhoods and how they, as religious organizations, are created by them through the networks they form, the lifestyles they support, and the resources they employ.

Traditional neighborhoods consist of relatively bounded and distinct areas defined by the characteristics of the people who live there. Some live there by choice, others because that was the only place where they were welcome or that they could afford. Neighborhoods have historically been identified by race or ethnicity, by occupation or commerce, or by religion. Park defined a neighborhood as a "locality with sentiments, traditions, and a history of its own."[7] For example, in the earlier part of the twentieth century, Indianapolis had, among others, a black neighborhood along Indiana Avenue, artist colonies in Broad Ripple and Irvington, a Quaker dairy farming enclave on the southwest corner of Mars Hill, university districts in Butler-Tarkington and Garfield Park, and a working-class industrial neighborhood in Brightwood. Today the neighborhood around Butler University is still thriving, and Broad Ripple and Irvington have become viable middle-class communities mostly without the artists, although Broad Ripple's commercial district has become the city's most lively club and restaurant scene. Otherwise, these neighborhoods are no longer distinct in the way they once were.

As noted in Chapter 2, Indianapolis has few ethnically defined neighborhoods, in large part because so few immigrants came to Indianapolis in the early twentieth century when the large-scale migration from Europe to the U.S. took place. As a result, large chunks of Indianapolis do not fit typical notions of neighborhoods. While there are important ethnic, racial, and class distinctions between the northern, central, and southern sectors of the city, there are few markers to announce changing territories, to warn outsiders that they do not belong, or to define "defended neighborhoods" as systems of social control and sources of residential cohesion, security, and identity — often in mutual opposition to adjacent neighborhoods with different "primordial" identities such as race, ethnicity, or religion.[8]

Of course, Indianapolis has had "defended areas" in the past. A prime example on the near east side is the 80-acre Woodruff Place, incorporated in 1876 as a separate town within the city. Its layout involved three north-south boulevards with artful concrete walls at each end and statuary on the esplanades, plus an east-west cross street in the middle whose intersections featured majestic fountains. One resident recalled joining with other neighborhood children to put on theatrical events in her large basement with bottle caps for admission in 1920. She also recalls a morning after such an occasion when she discovered that her younger brother had put a sign on the lawn announcing "No Colored Allowed" because, he explained, "every proper theatre has one." Such "defenses" have since crumbled. In 1962 the city annexed Woodruff Place, though it continues to be on the National Register of Historic Places.

Contemporary neighborhoods, especially those characterized by suburban housing developments, seek a similar security, but they rely on different defenses to attain it. They rely less on their own internal networks and ethnic solidarity and more on a shared sense of class, although usually unspoken. Defended neighborhoods enforced exclusion on the basis of racism and perceptions of crime associated with excluded groups, particularly minorities. Today's neighborhoods are characterized by more porous boundaries and weaker communal bonds than in the past. In fact, some areas would not even be labeled "neighborhoods" at all by traditional definitions, but are more accurately described as "districts." They share certain characteristics that make them identifiable, even unique, urban places where residents share common bonds, but they are not the residential blocs or enclaves many imagine when they think of "neighborhoods."

Because Indianapolis grew so quickly from town to metropolis and because it staunchly resisted most federal housing programs, it skipped much of the intensive neighborhood development stage that other cities experienced. It also has less of the conventional urban infrastructure such as high-density housing, extensive street illumination, subterranean public transit, large parks, and small residential lots. The identity of many of its residents is tied to one of its "sides" — for example, the "east side" or "south side" — or in an outlying suburb where, as elsewhere in the United States, the largest recent growth has occurred. New immigrants are following the same patterns of dispersal. Asian immigrants prefer to locate in one of the outlying suburbs, and Hispanic immigrants have spread into all parts of Indianapolis, including some of the suburbs. There is no Chinatown or barrio in Indianapolis.

Indianapolis's neighborhoods and districts have political dimensions as well as these social and spatial ones. The city's official neighborhoods are carved into semi-juridical political units overseen by the city's Department of Metropolitan Development. These units include community development corporations (CDCs) and neighborhood associations. This political devolution to the local level creates an administrative system for passing through federal funds, among others, but the decentralization, especially with its overlapping and multiple boundaries, has reduced the coherence of neighborhood systems. It has become more difficult to define any particular place.

Marion County's nine township divisions represent a larger unit of governance, yet they further heighten the fragmented nature of Indianapolis's municipal governance. The township boundaries determine responsibility and control of essential public services. Perhaps most importantly, they define the de facto class-based and race-based division between the Indianapolis public schools (city) and township schools (suburbs). Center city schools are widely characterized as inadequate except for a small number of magnet programs; by contrast, the township schools are well-funded and well-respected. Township authorities are also responsible for additional basic services — fire department services and some emergency social welfare assistance in each separate township, and a sheriff's departments that controls the townships as a whole.

In sum, Indianapolis neighborhoods are sometimes hard to distinguish as specific places, though they often follow broad race and class lines. They are politically weak and underrepresented in municipal contexts, and the institutions within them, including the churches, tend not to collaborate for area-wide goals. Taken together, they bear witness to the city's social and cultural multicenteredness, to the fact that religion, the polity, and the marketplace create many overlapping centers. Geography certainly matters, and the city must be understood as both spatially and culturally multi-centered, but not in the ways traditionally associated with strong neighborhoods containing layers of concurrent interests that contribute to strong local communities. Many of Indianapolis's neighborhoods have an "open" quality with relatively unbounded territory that supports loose rather than tight ties among residents.

In all of this, one might see Indianapolis lagging behind other large American cities, but it is possible to argue that Indianapolis is leading rather than lagging. Neighborhood change and the blurring of once clear boundaries is an oft-told story in every one of the nation's metropolitan areas. In contrasting Indianapolis's open neighborhoods with neighborhoods elsewhere that are more sharply defined and defended, we may be comparing a twenty-first-century urban scene with its twentieth-century predecessors.

Despite their relatively loose boundaries, there remains considerable variety among the neighborhoods, districts, and regions of Indianapolis. The city's multiple centers are less well defined, and more overlapping, than neighborhoods are sometimes characterized in other times or places, but they still create social and cultural boundaries for their residents. Not surprisingly, then, religious organizations within them have different mission emphases as they seek to create "community" for their members and to serve others within their local reach.

PARLOR, KITCHEN, PORCH, AND GARAGE:
A TYPOLOGY OF URBAN PLACES

In all the profusion and confusion of variety among urban places, two basic distinctions rose to the fore as we considered the roughly 200 neighborhoods and districts in the Indianapolis metropolis, including the eighteen that we sampled for special examination. Just as with our typology of congregations, these dichotomies are intended to be more conceptually suggestive than empirically ironclad. The types created here represent tendencies, but each points to an important difference among the places that constitute the multicentered city of the twenty-first century.

The first distinction is between neighborhoods that are *in demand* versus neighborhoods settled *by default*. Of course, the difference here revolves importantly around factors of social status and the related issues of material capital and social capital. Neighborhoods of high social standing — whether due to economic class, race, ethnicity, or religion — tend to be in demand, with properties and property values that reflect it. On the other hand, neighborhoods of low social standing — for example, those dominated by racial or ethnic minorities, recent immigrants, low occupational status and/ or high unemployment — tend to be occupied by default. These are often residential areas of nearly last resort, places whose major appeal lies not only in their relatively low cost but in the stigmatized character of the residents already present. *Demand* and *default* are the ideal endpoints on an axis that runs from high levels of material capital to low levels of such capital, with most places falling somewhere along the line.

The second distinction involves the extent to which a neighborhood imprints and involves its residents' lives. On the one hand, some neighborhoods are *centered*, by which we mean that they tend to dominate at least the non-working day through their institutions and associations, and they have a primary impact on their residents' sense of self and collective identity. Importantly, the community's institutions are crucial to the collective sense of self. On the other hand, there are also neighborhoods that are more *decentered* in that they serve more as collections of houses that share a common locale. The institutions within these communities are less central to residents' lives because they fail to create a common collective identity, or, at least, create a much weaker one. In contemporary parlance, this axis runs from high social capital to low social capital. Once again, most places fall somewhere between the ideal endpoints. Consider now the four cells that result from combining the two distinctions as depicted in the accompanying table.

Table 6.1. Urban Neighborhoods and Districts

	Centered	Decentered
In Demand	Parlor	Garage
By Default	Porch	Kitchen

Parlor neighborhoods are in demand; they are centered communities conferring primary social imprints on their members. They have high levels of both material capital and social capital. These are basically elite areas that many city residents envy but few reach. Here the lifestyles and overall status achievements are envied as much as the residential properties. People living in such settings rarely make a secret of it; they tend to wear their neighborhood addresses on their well-tailored sleeves. We have called these areas parlors because they not only reflect the residents' own proud and somewhat formal presentations of self but they represent the city's own living room where private entertainment is often enacted as public display. It is tempting for outsiders to slip into a cynical mode and castigate these areas as instances of what Thorstein Veblen once characterized as "conspicuous consumption," but that is not our intent. These are the lairs of many metropolitan leaders, and it would be surprising indeed if they did not share the characteristics described.

In sharp contrast are neighborhoods sharing the opposite combination: they are lived in by default and their institutions do not create a shared sense of common identity. These areas suffer from a lack of both physical and social capital. Lives here are more hunkered down than socially expansive, and since there are few parts of a residence more appropriate for hunkering than a *kitchen*, we have used this as the shorthand designation. Many of these neighborhoods have known better days, and some very much better. Such neighborhoods tend to host the sort of pathologies that are both cause and consequence of their default standing, including crime, drugs, poor schools, a battered economic infrastructure, and little sense of political vision or leadership.

Of course, the difference between the parlors and kitchens largely (but not exclusively) reflect the stock difference between upper-class areas on the hilltops and lower-class areas near the landfill, on the other side of the proverbial tracks. The other two neighborhood types are less stereotypical but no less common. As a case in point, consider those neighborhoods we have associated with the *porch*. These areas are inhabited more by default than demand, but they are also relatively well-centered by their shared cultural, political, economic, and racial-ethnic qualities. They lack material capital, but have a substantial stock of social capital, not least because the residents' patterns of interaction make a virtue out of their shared liabilities, as the porch reference suggests. It is true that their shared social fate and identity often represents as much multigenerational discrimination as transgenerational pride. But the pride is nonetheless present as a mobilizing device. These are neighborhoods that often — but not always — speak and act forcefully on their own behalf despite a shortage of material resources.

Finally, our *garage* neighborhoods are in relative demand, but are nonetheless characterized by decentered and decentering institutional life. Often pricey suburban communities that were once small towns on the city's periphery, these places frequently comprise a series of small quasi-neighborhoods linked to each other to surround one or more malls that serve as their commercial centers. It is true that the housing values continue to rise, and there are even small nests of true trophy homes. But while these sprawling tracts all convey the message that their residents have made it into the middle mass, they signal few deeper meanings and have identities and institutions that are seldom deep-seated. The material capital available in these areas cannot always be used to purchase social capital. One common constant is the dependence on the automobile, as parents and children seem frequently on the move to explore a considerable expanse of life-style options and opportunities. It is, of course, the centrality of the car in an otherwise multicentered existence that leads to the term *garage* neighborhoods.

These four types describe ideal-typical centers—both cultural and so-cial—in the realigned city. These ideal types now must be tested against actual settings. We originally chose urban areas to study because they repre-sented certain basic characteristics. We wanted samples from the inner city, the inner ring of early suburbs, and the outer ring of newer suburbs. We wanted places that had high, low, and middle incomes. We wanted places whose residents were predominantly white, predominantly black, or clearly mixed. As we began to analyze our chosen neighborhoods, we realized that the analytical categories suggested here—high to low levels of material and social capital—corresponded better to congregational missions than did our original selection criteria. In the end, we studied *garage* neighborhoods on three sides of the city. We studied the city's two premier *parlor* areas. Although we studied the full variety of inner-city and inner-suburban neigh-borhoods, we wound up with several more *porch* neighborhoods than *kitchen* ones. This is perhaps not surprising as research tends to gravitate toward venues where the action is, so we found ourselves in more places full of active, outward-oriented congregations and urban social programs. None-theless, we were in multiple areas of each type and saw the full range of variation in congregational mission there.

In what follows, we present accounts of four Indianapolis neighborhoods that were originally selected for research because they met some combina-tion of our original criteria, but which we subsequently singled out because they illustrated what we came to understand as the most important differ-ences among urban places. We then discuss the congregations within each neighborhood in order to describe the obvious affinity between types of congregations and types of neighborhoods or urban districts. The linkage between types of urban centers and types of congregational mission helps us understand religion's multicentered role.

In Chapter 5 we chose not to identify congregations or their neighbor-hoods because, as we said there, our primary interest is *not* to build a jour-nalistic argument in which everyone must be "on the record" by name, but rather to describe trends and movements affecting all of society. Specific names add nothing to that analysis; therefore, even the slightest chance of harm or embarrassment to those who generously allowed us to study them is not worth the risk. In this chapter, however, it makes sense to identify the specific urban places because Indianapolis readers will already know where they are and other readers will not care. The congregations are named as well, when appropriate, because the people who live there will easily identify them and no one else will care. We have therefore been especially careful not to identify any individuals who shared their ideas with us or to identify details about the congregations that would not be apparent to any casual observers if they chose to look.

THE UPPER MERIDIAN "PARLOR"

As we have seen earlier, the Meridian Street corridor is the city's main north-south axis. Moving from Monument Circle toward the Hamilton County line, it is a seven-mile stretch of valuable real estate holding several major businesses, twelve elite congregations, and a series of neighborhoods whose succession of prestige over time reflect the history of high-status Indianapolis as it shifted northward during the twentieth century. Williams Creek and Meridian Hills, Marion County's two priciest subdivisions, are located along this axis, as upper Meridian Street blends into Hamilton County and its town of Carmel, Indiana's wealthiest suburb with its separate and superior school system. Given the city's northward expansion over the years, this is the place where the city, which is coextensive with Marion County, is so closely pinched by the Hamilton County line that the transition is barely noticeable.

Hamilton County's median family income is the highest of any county in Indiana and ranks in the top twenty counties nationally. In 1998, Hamilton County's figure stood at $72,330 compared to $58,323 for the next highest — another Indianapolis suburban county, Hendricks — and to $39,719 for the state as a whole. Put oppositely, only 3.2 percent of Hamilton County residents live below the poverty line, less than half the percentage of the city's other affluent county neighbors such as Hendricks or Boone. Clearly Upper Meridian Street, as it blends into Carmel, represents Indianapolis's most presentable parlor by far.

But in many respects, the upper Meridian Street corridor and its churches are part of an urban religious district[9] that still includes lower Meridian Street and the urban congregations that have been part of the Indianapolis establishment for nearly a century. If Meridian Street from downtown to the Carmel suburbs is not really a "neighborhood," it is nonetheless an identifiable urban place and one of the city's most important centers.[10] Even on the lower end of Meridian Street, where the inner-city neighborhoods along the corridor show signs of wear, Meridian itself is flanked by museums, insurance companies, and the Lilly Endowment office building. Some of the city's finest homes sit along Meridian, even in neighborhoods that are otherwise less affluent. Maps showing where the city's elite have lived, and continue to live, show the progression of wealth running straight northward for more than a century, before emptying like an urban river into the Hamilton County delta.

Religion and *Noblesse Oblige*

"I'm tired of hearing about Meridian Street," remarked a downtown pastor, clearly a bit annoyed at all the attention given to Indianapolis's mainline churches and their tall-steeple representatives on "the main stem." Indeed, what is the influence of these elite congregations, especially the dozen or so older congregation within Marion County, compared to the hundreds of other religious institutions that connect people across the larger metropolitan region? These congregations exert influence through personal and organizational networks and by the use of financial capital, but, as we have seen, they no longer speak for the city as a whole.

There is danger in characterizing the well-heeled congregations of Meridian Street as a united front. These groups are principally members of mainline Protestant denominations, with highly educated, above-average-income members, but they differ spatially, politically, and culturally. Two Catholic parishes, one being the archdiocesan cathedral, plus a Reform synagogue are also part of the Meridian Street corridor in Marion County. Further north, Carmel is home to two strong Catholic parishes.

These congregations have changed with the times, just as the plainest church in any ordinary neighborhood. The cultural and political power associated with prestigious churches does not shield them from the larger social changes experienced in other quarters of American society. Admittedly, the troubles of having money and prestige are hardly the same as the troubles of not having either. But their distinctiveness does not always give them the advantages usually imagined. These elite religious organizations engage in the same kinds of social, spiritual, and organizational negotiations as other congregations throughout the city.

Five distinct areas along Meridian Street help tell the story of how Indianapolis religion changed over the last century. Nearest the downtown metropolitan core, the city's two cathedrals, Christ Church Episcopal and Sts. Peter and Paul Catholic, remain diocesan and citywide symbols of an earlier centralization of authority and prestige. Both cathedrals are pressed by commercial buildings on all sides, but stand defiantly against any suggestion they are out of place. The first phase of congregational movement out of the mile square downtown extended to Mapleton–Fall Creek, the second distinct Meridian Street area. A typical urban, mixed residential and commercial neighborhood, Mapleton–Fall Creek was once wealthy, has recently been quite poor, and is now again the scene of rapid gentrification. The important congregations of Trinity Episcopal, Tabernacle Presbyterian, and North United Methodist are located here. Each developed an "urban ministry" identity as a result of the choice to remain when the surrounding neighborhood changed racial and class composition during the white flight of the 1960s and 1970s. Next, Meridian Street United Methodist and St. Paul Episcopal were the first essentially "suburban" churches surrounded by suburban-style yards in the third important area. A residential quietude marks the atmosphere around them. It is where one first notices how street life is essentially confined to the automobile, having left behind commercial buildings and pedestrian traffic in the old city center.

Even these churches were overtaken by the fourth suburban area — even newer and wealthier — at the very edge of the city, where St. Luke Catholic, Second Presbyterian, Indianapolis Hebrew Congregation, St. Luke's United Methodist, and First Baptist Church are located. These congregations flourish in sprawling, weighty campuses near the very desirable neighborhoods of Williams Creek and Meridian Hills. Their buildings are especially large and imposing, conveying awe but also suggesting privacy. Fifth and finally, the northward exodus crossed the county line into Carmel. Here, the mixed congregations of an older, stand-alone town are mixed with the newer congregations spawned by upwardly mobile growth. St. Mark's United Methodist congregation sits in a residential district that marks its difference from the large brick structure of Carmel UMC, the older congregation on the main drag. Even more striking is the distinction between the old, in-town Catholic parish — Our Lady of Mt. Carmel — and the newer subdivision parish, Elizabeth Seton, the latter so defiantly modern in design that it might at first glance appear to be a library or museum.

Wealthy congregations, like all congregations, must work continuously to attract new members. Three of the northernmost churches near the county line have strong and growing memberships: St. Luke's UMC, St. Luke Catholic, and Second Presbyterian. Nearby is the largest and wealthiest of the city's five synagogues, Indianapolis Hebrew Congregation. All except St. Luke Catholic, whose members live largely within the parish, attract members from across the city's northern region and its northern suburbs.

St. Luke's UMC paces the area's constant growth. The church recently completed a large building project that expands the church structures like a telescope, reaching into the back of their campus near 86th Street. They offer ten weekend worship services, including one on Sunday evening in the popular local musical theater dinner auditorium, Beef and Boards. Some of their success can be attributed to the collegial style of St. Luke's pastor, who eschews a heavy doctrinal hand and releases members to pursue ideas that appeal to them, a practice forged at megachurches like Willow Creek, outside of Chicago.

But much can also be attributed to the booming suburban location on the county line. As we have seen, Second Presbyterian, with a somewhat more traditional style, has also added an informal Sunday evening service to attract younger, less institutionally committed members. St. Luke Catholic Church benefits similarly from its location, a fact most evident in the growing parochial school of more than 500 students that is also undergoing a building expansion. Indianapolis Hebrew Congregation has the triple advantage of a prestigious Meridian Street address, proximity to the city's

"Jewish" neighborhood around Meridian Hills, and proximity to Carmel, where many affluent Jews, alongside every other kind of affluent resident, have recently moved.

Many of the congregations on the booming end of the Meridian Street religious district are skilled at *customer service*, but they are also driven by *community outreach*. These groups are filled with members who live in areas of high material and social capital. They seek to cement existing community relationships and to build on those strengths in their mission to the rest of the metropolis. And while most congregations practice some form of community outreach, those with high levels of resources, whether material or social, tend to make the biggest splash.

Meanwhile, many of the churches further down Meridian Street in the "good neighborhoods" of earlier generations are under stress, despite relatively large memberships and budgets. Even with upwards of 1,000 members — very large compared to the average congregation — it can be hard to support large physical plants and full-time staffs. While membership loss does not threaten these churches with closure, it reveals some organizational vulnerabilities. Congregations in the early suburbs remember the boom years of the 1950s and 1960s, and their identity is closely tied to an older image of institutional success. Many of these congregations have turned to traditional forms of community outreach in social service and racial reconciliation as responses to their changed environment.

Sts. Peter and Paul Cathedral is not the home of most of the Catholic elite, many of whom attend St. Luke Church on the northern end of the district. The Cathedral is instead an "urban" church that appeals to participants with a broadly metropolitan social vision. It draws a mixed-race and mixed-income membership that is the smallest of the Meridian Street "big" congregations. One parishioner suggested that the parish "came alive" when the diocese closed the African American parish, St. Bridget, and its members merged into the Cathedral's congregation. But downtown diversity is also the result of an increasingly suburbanized white Catholic population, which has left the central areas of town and settled around the perimeters of Indianapolis and in Carmel. While not all such parishes are socially mixed, the Cathedral worked deliberately at creating liturgical and social inclusion, sponsoring an intentional, if occasionally uncomfortable, "dialogue on race."

North United Methodist Church is one of the few other Meridian Street congregations to be racially "diverse," with a non-white population of about 10 percent. It was the first among the three Methodist congregations on Meridian Street to hire African American staff members. The difficulties of bridging racial and ethnic groups generally appear greater among mainline denominations than among either Catholic parishes or evangelical congregations. This is not unique to Indianapolis, as a recent national survey has evidenced.[11] Class and historic differences have played their roles. For instance, St. Philip's, the African American Episcopal congregation in Indianapolis, was founded in the nineteenth century and supported as a mission by St. Paul's Church. Joint worshipping was not permitted by the rectors of an earlier era, however, and the two congregations now have cordial but not close relationships. While it is easy today to observe a sprinkling of non-whites in most of the Meridian Street congregations, including the synagogue, most are quick to acknowledge the difficulty of creating a liturgically and culturally inclusive congregation. "Race is the defining conflict in our culture," confided one mainline clergyman, "and the religious community could latch on to one part of it." Left unspoken was the admission that this usually proves hard to do.

There are important differences among congregations on the northern and southern ends of this important urban district, but one characteristic bonds them: the extensive and intensive participation of the laity in church outreach activities. Highly educated members bring resources into their congregations that their clergy encourage and cultivate, even to the point of sometimes having to step aside. In accounting for the extensive involvement of North United Methodist's members, a staff member explained that the laity "expect you to let go because this is [their] ministry." Other pastors are seeking an appropriate balance from parishioners accustomed to leadership roles in their work lives. "From Monday through Friday, the members of this church are their own bosses. They think they can be in charge on Saturday and Sunday as well," related a Catholic staff member. Precisely for these reasons, the human capital and commitments of the members of these churches result in extensive community and social service outreach projects.

These outreach activities serve the purpose of "doing good" in the city, but they also provide an outlet for parishioners to participate in mission. It would be difficult to overestimate the depth of responsibility these wealthy congregations feel regarding their financial stewardship. During our research, the endowments at the three Episcopal churches on Meridian Street exceeded $100 million, as related in Chapter 4. While the other congregations have less financial capital and disperse less in programmatic mission activities, each reports a wide array of volunteer activities and services, from free, high-quality music concerts and tutoring projects in Indianapolis public schools to senior citizen and homeless services.

Different congregations prefer different projects for channeling their outreach funds. Moreover, civic influence requires collaboration, not just money. The three churches around Mapleton–Fall Creek — Tabernacle Presbyterian, North United Methodist, and Trinity Episcopal — have formed the strongest bond with other churches and organizations in the community, the Mid-North Church Council, the multichurch partnership mentioned at the opening of this chapter. The network is extensive, including secular organizations and several nearby non-elite churches including another UMC congregation, an ELCA Lutheran church, a nearby Catholic parish, three small African American congregations, the Mapleton–Fall Creek neighborhood association, the MFC development corporation, and health care and legal clinic. A complex web of support and depth in local leadership has enabled the Council to persevere in its mission of service to the local neighborhood.

The practices of customer service have taken hold in the finest suburbs in the city, as they have in other urban neighborhoods, but *community outreach* remains the congregational type most closely associated with *parlor* areas. The Meridian Street congregations maintain a strong sense of responsibility for the greater welfare of the community, but today they use different, more lay-led, methods than in the past. There is a growing view that they no longer want "to be stuck in charity," as a member of Trinity Episcopal put it.

Geography matters, but it is unclear just how it will matter in the future because both the congregations and the geography itself are changing. Some congregations are comfortable in the public eye, as for example, Second Presbyterian and North United Methodist. Yet their different styles and social commitments owe much to the details of their particular environments, and those are subject to change. A Starbuck's coffee shop is opening across the street from North Church where an auto alarm service center had been. This development is a barometer of changes occurring in that neighborhood, raising the question about how this will affect North's sense of itself and the kind of church it will become. In sum, the very visibility of the Meridian Street congregations creates heightened public expectations about their role in the city. Their financial and symbolic resources, their prominence and their aesthetics, and their sense of *noblesse oblige*—all these confer a rich range of choices about what they present to the larger public and how they view their missions. In 1999, Indianapolis elected another member of Second Presbyterian as mayor. When noted African American theologian and social critic Cornel West came to Indianapolis in 2001, he spent his Sunday morning preaching at North UMC. These are still congregations with "pop."

And yet these congregations do not comprise the city's cultural and social core in the way they once did. Although they tend to be key institutions within their own denominations, the congregations stand astride some significant gulfs, both demographic and historical. On the northern end of the corridor, the congregations bridge the gap between community outreach and customer service. They must seek new ways of taking care of their own and taking care of others. The congregations on the lower end of the Meridian corridor bridge the gap between the city's relatively poor downtown and its affluent northern suburbs. They draw their members from a world of privilege, but often serve a world of need outside the doors of their house of worship and outside their own neighborhood. Finally, all of these congregations symbolically bridge the gap between an era when the white, Protestant elite ran the city and a period of multiculturalism in which those same white Protestants play a smaller, though still substantial, role.

THE "KITCHEN" OF MARS HILL

South of U.S. 40, the city's literal and symbolic dividing line, the picture is much different. The northern suburbs have been shaped by a relatively recent influx of young, mostly white, professionals, but the south side was shaped by earlier white migration from Appalachia and other southern states into the Midwest's industrial cities. Mars Hill is the most distinctive such enclave, its residents among the poorest in Indianapolis. So much attention is paid to non-white impoverished people in the United States that Americans can forget that the majority of poor people are white.[12] Many cities have a stratum of whites living in poverty that are not concentrated in any particular locality, diluting their potential political power and making them practically invisible to policy makers.[13] Noted one local observer, "There is a tendency for city officials to tell poor blacks they need programs but to tell poor whites to get a job."

A southwest side pocket, named after a slight elevation in the land owned by farmer Marr and donated by him at the time of the platting of the area in 1911, became "little Kentucky." Some census tracts of the area show median family income as low as $16,000. Unlike some other poor areas that are socially isolated as well as economically depressed, Mars Hill is a mixture of working poor and working class, with a middle-class enclave tucked into the southernmost section.

The outstanding fact of Mars Hill neighborhood life is the near absence of institutions. The churches are something of an exception but even they, as we shall see, are not able to support adequately the needs of these residents. The commercial streets contain small stores that meet the basic needs of lower-income people — grocery and drug stores, smaller retail shops, a barber shop, day care facilities, auto and appliance repair, check-cashing services, loan agencies, liquor and tobacco stores, pet care establishments. Missing are traditional places for congregating and socializing. Even the public library branch has been closed for several years. Also missing are the minor extravagances like flower shops, coffee shops, bookstores, entertainment centers, or music stores. The schools have athletic facilities, and some appear well-used with new equipment. Others have overgrown baseball diamonds and netless basketball hoops. As in many other Indianapolis neighborhoods, public space for meeting, gathering, and rubbing shoulders with strangers is limited. Yet Mars Hill is more limited than most. The area is only partially served by municipal services because of its late incorporation into Indianapolis by Unigov in 1970.

The area grew haphazardly, without planning or centralized leadership. It was decentered almost from the start and has maintained much of its original rural flavor. Many residents still use wells for their drinking water and septic tanks for drainage, though stories continue of houses without indoor toilets. But like many poor areas, the neighborhood tends to be both "isolated and denied" within the larger city. Residents relate the story of former Mayor Goldsmith's response when he was asked why all his target neighborhoods for reform were in the north of the city: "because there are no poor people on the south side." Whether Mayor Goldsmith ever said such a thing or not, Mars Hill residents believe he did and it fits their preconceptions. As the director of a local community center put it, "The poor in Mars Hill get cheated because they are not in the inner city."

Many residents have transmigratory patterns and often bring their poverty with them as they move periodically but inconsistently between families living in their rural counties of origin and Indianapolis. These patterns sometimes contribute to local political amnesia because they tend to hide the extent of social needs. Such patterns also contribute to a lack of commitment to a local area by part-time residents, whose material and emotional resources are partly directed elsewhere. Despite the mobility, many families have passed down their houses from one generation to the next. As one observer summed up, "The neighborhood doesn't complain much and the city doesn't pay much attention."

One informant claimed her reasons for leaving the neighborhood were drugs, gangs, and crime. She named a gang, the Mars Hill Dogs, that controls the northern portion of the neighborhood and brought in big-city crime. She went so far as to assert that Mars Hill has the "worst of both worlds," the problems of a big city, but the mindset and resources of a small town. According to one counselor, "These are good people, but it's hard to get them out of their junk." The director of a nearby youth club noted how misogynist attitudes still fester, where "barefoot and pregnant" is still an active idea. In fact, a young woman in one of his counseling sessions blurted out, "The only thing girls are good for is to have babies." Not surprisingly, there is a high proportion of single mothers and female-headed households, the largest group of the impoverished in national statistics. "Kids are an afterthought" in the lives of these residents, reported the counselor. One of the scoutmasters of a local Boy Scout troop reported that about half of their twenty boys do not live with their families, many having been abandoned by their parents. Of the rest, only two come from intact families.

There are several social service outreach programs that include Mars Hill residents, but none exclusively from or for the neighborhood. Residents receive fragmentary attention at best, and they are also easily manipulated by political powers. But job placement for Mars Hill clients is a challenge, reports one social worker who claims that her clients are "shockingly lazy" and that she is losing credibility because many employees she provides to "merciful" employers cannot hold down their jobs for more than a few days or weeks. Her most successful program involves picking up senior citizens, bringing them to the center for socializing, exercise, and lunch, and then dropping them off.

While there is widespread agreement about the neglect of the area by the city, the inward, non-political focus and parochial views of most of the residents, and the external reputation as an area dominated by "rednecks" and "hicks," Mars Hill residents do not operate with a single cognitive map. Rather, they carry competing images of what their style of life is, as well as different meanings these lifestyles have for them. Some residents exhibit fierce pride in their neighborhood. Many of the houses and yards are neat and well-cared-for, adorned with American flags, wind socks, ornate decorations, and plants. Others "escape" if they can, even attempting to sell their homes at below their assessed value in their desperation to leave. Some residents claim the area has a friendliness that allows them to know their neighbors. Yet others report they do not socialize with their neighbors at all. In fact, they barely know them and limit their associations to family who live nearby. Some residents deny being from Mars Hill because of its perceived negative identity. Yet others who have moved outside the area, some not very far, return to work there. These poignant but contradictory meanings suggest there is no single neighborhood identity.

Religious Responses to Social Dislocation

Of the twenty-five churches in the greater Mars Hill area, most are Pentecostal and Baptist with one mainline Methodist church and a Catholic parish. Church facilities are varied. Some structures are less well-cared-for, but several, especially interiors, are surprisingly well-appointed. Many churches reported that they located in Mars Hill because of cheap, available land. On average, 75 percent of the church members drive in from outside the neighborhood by the local pastors' own accounts. In terms of social orientation, the churches in Mars Hill are generally inward looking and fiercely independent — in our terms, they are cloistered.

Most of the Protestant churches in Mars Hill have only tenuous ties to the local neighborhood, preferring to focus on the community within their church walls. Some Mars Hill churches cooperate in their missions to those outside their membership, but most do not, and only a few have outreach programs of any kind. In Mars Hill, many churches view the surrounding territory with some disdain.

An example of such a thwarted impulse is Charity Tabernacle — a large, active Pentecostal church. The site for Charity Tabernacle was originally selected by an earlier generation for missionary purposes rather than land costs or even historical ties to the area. The church has an extensive social service outreach component, yet its teaching supports an inward focus.

Members are admonished to tithe to support a hierarchy of beneficiaries that includes God, church, and family. While the church runs food and clothing pantries, provides emergency cash assistance and labor and supplies for housing needs, few of these services are devoted to the local area. The church's commitments are primarily extra-local — missionary societies, metropolitan help lines for people in need, other churches in their denominational network, and organizations such as Promise Keepers, the national men's group. This pattern is consistent with a membership three-quarters of which comes from outside of Mars Hill. Long and bitter memories also affect this church's relationships with neighbors. When the church suffered a major fire thirteen years ago, local people offered little assistance. Some within the congregation yearn to make connections to the surrounding neighborhood. But most do not think it will be possible because "society is too poised against conservative, Christ-centered Christianity," as one put it, in favor of a more liberal, love-centered Christianity of which they are suspicious.

The historic strength of the Catholic parish provides some continuing community resources, but even that is eroding as the theme of inward focus is played out in the story of St. Ann Catholic Church. St. Ann's was once a very active parish with a school that lost about half its members, especially young families, during the 1980s. Their membership now stands at fewer than 900, which is small given the amount of territory the parish covers and the population within it. The closing of the school and the selling of school and parish center buildings by the archdiocese created a "defeatist attitude," in the words of one parishioner, "with unspoken bitterness directed downtown for abandoning us." She went on, "The parish lost a community center that provided activities, including the weekly bingo game, that brought folks together in an ecumenical atmosphere, giving folks a chance to talk about neighborhood happenings." The members of the parish are aging and too few young adults are available to step into lay leadership roles. Lay leadership is especially crucial because the parish shares its pastor with neighboring St. Joseph Church, where the pastor resides, leaving many tasks of oversight to the leaders of the congregation itself. The parishioners have had to learn not to "let Father do it," because Father is not always around. The commitment to the community and to the elderly members for whom traveling to a distant church would be difficult has until now prevented the decision to merge with St. Joseph. St. Ann's perseveres in its efforts to develop community involvement through revitalizing the parish festival, keeping its remaining church facilities open to the local residents, studying demographic trends in the larger southwest side, and communicating information about the area to the local residents. The current pastor sits on the board of the Southwest Multi-Service Center but is not a member of the Decatur Township Ministerial Alliance.

The Decatur Ministerial Alliance is an important resource for Mars Hill churches, but it retains the same structural limitations as other local groups. Decatur and Wayne Township boundaries cut Mars Hill into two segments, and the clergy association follows these territories rather than using the neighborhood boundaries of Mars Hill in bringing clergy together. This decentering reflects the fragmented nature of association at another level. Mars Hill could benefit from coordinated attention by the churches, a coordination that could potentially challenge political and social agencies. Instead, the alliance denies itself the opportunity to speak for the whole neighborhood, which could create important internal coherence, and remains another institution that is inadequate in the face of local conditions.

As the saying goes, however, there are exceptions that prove the bleak rule just described. Two conservative Protestant churches, one relatively wealthy, the other operating on the financial margins, have taken different approaches toward the neighborhood. They have each put down roots and claimed the space and people of Mars Hill as their responsibility. The larger of the two, Seerley Creek Christian Church, is an independent, evangelical church with about 450 members. The church is a Protestant "parish" with a well-educated pastor exclusively serving the low-income area surrounding its location. To reinforce the parish model, the pastor refers supplicants from outside the two Zip code areas in which the church ministers to services closer to their homes when they approach the church for assistance. Two-thirds of the congregation's membership comes from Mars Hill. The church has outreach programs in banking, health care, and in serving youth. It holds seminars on topics ranging from Alzheimer's to smoking cessation to business and life skills training. "Churches need to adapt to the culture around them," asserted a longtime staffer who grew up in Mars Hill. Seerley Creek has a web page and a high-tech audiovisual system for their worship services. Yet the pastor was also trying to make clear that adaptation meant parishioners and clergy of Mars Hill churches needed to resist the fears stimulated by the problems of the neighborhood people, particularly youth's ungovernable behavior, their attitudes toward sex, and their parents' inability to hold a job.

Meanwhile, on the other side of Mars Hill, a bread line forms every Tuesday morning at the front porch of a small clapboard house in need of repair. In the line are elderly persons as well as teenage mothers carrying newborns; many walk to the house while some come in pickup trucks. At 10:30 sharp the youth minister picks up her guitar and perches on the stool in front of the waiting group, asking them to "heat things up a bit this morning." For ten or so minutes they sing, rap, and pray. A teenaged boy with an embarrassed smile endeared himself to the crowd with the tune, "I Don't Have Time for You, Devil." Then the grocery bags filled with an assortment of bread donated by Kroger's grocery chain are passed out.

The Community Caring and Sharing Mission is a singular faith-based social service outreach program, supported by several area churches and businesses. Some Mars Hill clergy automatically refer requests for assistance by the poor to the Community Mission. Even congregations with programs in place admit they do not want to have to screen requests for financial help, nor do they want to be taken advantage of by needy folks who make the rounds of as many churches as possible. The Mission, however, is less cynical in its dealings with the poor. Said the founding pastor, whose own father worked the strip mines in Tennessee, "I know what hunger is." The predominantly female leadership keeps the mission open to all, "no matter who they were or where they came from" and offers material assistance, mostly in the form of food, clothing, and other goods, especially for children. These pastors' religious presentation is so muted that our researchers were initially unaware they held regular worship services at all. While the mission has been operating since the mid-1980s, and they offer informal, outdoor, non-denominational worship on Saturday nights, formal worship on Sunday mornings began only in 1996.

The mission has been able to attract a steady group of teenagers who help with the outreach programs and are regular attenders at worship. The teens add energy to the already outgoing and open pastoral style of the three leaders — two women and one man. The bible study revealed their commitment to volunteerism when the speaker concluded, "We must decide we are servants instead of consumers." The mission keeps no membership records, although they count who comes for assistance. During the month of our observation, the mission served an average of 445 people each week. The leaders estimate that about one-fourth of the people come from outside of Mars Hill. The founding pastor is searching for a larger space within the neighborhood but the church has been turned down at a promising site. New space would allow the church to add day care as well as practical health and financial education for their "members."

In sum, Mars Hill is a neighborhood in need, but one whose heritage reflects autonomy and independence more than communal cooperation. It is neither a centered nor a defended neighborhood, and its residents live there more by default than by demand. Its Appalachian ties have loosened over the years, save for the link of poverty itself.

The cloister congregations of Mars Hill reflect these conditions and provide few community-building resources that residents can draw on. Some of these churches have among the tightest internal social bonds of any church members we observed. But individual social capital is different from community social capital, which consists of economic and political resources.[14] The cultural traditions of the residents, "cultural poverty" as one put it, and the attitudes expressed within the churches work against such involvement. Indianapolis sponsors community development corporations for areas identified by the municipal government, but Mars Hill has yet to develop — let alone demand — one.

The area hosts a wide range of churches, mostly Pentecostal and evangelical with a struggling Catholic parish. Most of the mainline Protestant traditions are notably absent. And with few exceptions, local religion reproduces, or at least subtly supports, a culture of separatism, poverty, and mistrust. As examples of what we have termed cloister congregations, they are models of and models for a way of life isolated from urban transactions across a multi-centered city. In fact, they tend to see themselves as centered communities writ small in a larger neighborhood that is decidedly decentered.

THE UNITED NORTHWEST AREA "PORCH"

Just north of the mile square, a little west of Meridian Street, is our neighborhood of porches. The United Northwest Area (UNWA) is among the poorest communities in the city, but it was not always so. It became poor as a result of middle-class white and black flight from the 1950s to the 1970s, a time during which Interstate 65 was routed and built through the center — some would say the heart — of the area.

Many neighborhood residents are quick to recall a prosperous and orderly neighborhood life "before the interstate highway came" and before jobs became harder to find. "When the highway came," recalled a long-time resident, "we lost a lot of good neighbors." The neighbors whose homes were razed to make room for construction were both white and black. Some felt they didn't get as much money as they thought they would for their properties. "The city did what it wanted to do and the people did what they had to do," reflected one of the residents on the conflicting interests of broad civic improvement and the integrity of local community life. Residents reported how the highway planners changed the route several times before construction began, seemingly oblivious to the effect of such indecision on local lives. One resident recounted how, at one time, the route went through their living room, another time through their church. "The residents had no say-so about what route it would take," recalled another. "Most of the people were unsure about what to do, but that didn't seem to matter 'to the powers that be.' " Whether the highway construction actually *caused* the neighborhood's decline, the community was weakened when residents perceived that their place, both physically and psychically, was considered expendable. The perception continues among residents that "their neighborhood was destroyed by the highway," even though the road was finished more than twenty-five years ago.

The post–World War II demographic and economic changes that affected inner-city neighborhoods in the larger northern industrial cities predated changes in Indianapolis by almost two decades.[15] In Indianapolis, the housing settlements remained mostly stable and segregated, creating two cities. The city had a brief but rich history of civil rights activism during the 1960s, led by African American clergy, most notably Rev. Andrew J. Brown, an

Indiana representative of Martin Luther King, Jr.'s Southern Christian Leadership Conference. He was also a member of Concerned Clergy, a local group founded in 1960 by African American pastors that continues to raise concerns on behalf of African Americans in the city. Although Concerned Clergy is mostly Protestant, Catholics are also represented.

Compared to that of many larger or more southern cities, black activism in Indianapolis has been limited. There are many reasons this might be so, though one black activist pastor was quick to charge that "the general media does not promote the work of black churches and tries to suppress it." During the changes to UNWA because of the interstate highway, there was no large-scale protest. Nonetheless, a disturbance along UNWA's Indiana Avenue was not reported by the press, according to some sources, because "it wouldn't be good for the city" if it were known.[16] A local priest who publicly criticized the police received limited public support from the archdiocese. By the 1980s, any activism in Indianapolis diminished as it did elsewhere around the country. One mainline pastor suggested that "an excess of rhetoric in the 60s and 70s caused church leadership to get too far ahead of its members." By the 1980s, it was clear that compromise and accommodation — the city's clear inclination to go along to get along — was again the norm.

African Americans remembered "being allowed to live" in the original black settlement along Indiana Avenue, in parts of UNWA just to the north, and in two neighborhoods on the east side. They attended segregated schools and were largely ignored by white Indianapolis. However, the availability of both skilled and unskilled jobs provided general economic stability.

Originally a middle-class white neighborhood at the turn of the previous century, UNWA began including some middle-class and working-class blacks into the segregated center of the neighborhood in the 1930s and 1940s. During the 1950s the starkest racial turnover occurred, and after the 1960s UNWA became significantly poor, its residents mostly African American. New housing opportunities opened up for African Americans with the passage of civil rights legislation, and many of those who could afford it moved to the outer townships.

Although still significantly poor, the African Americans of UNWA are no longer ignored. In many of the churches, members are middle-class people who once lived in UNWA but joined in the post-1960s flight to the suburbs and now drive in to worship. There are more than seventy churches in UNWA, but they have a cumulative 65 percent commuting rate, higher than the average in the city. Yet UNWA has strategic advantages because of its location, quartered as it is between the recently developed Indiana University–Purdue University Indianapolis (IUPUI) close on its southern border and historic Crown Hill Cemetery, the Indianapolis Art Museum, and the Children's Museum on the north end. There are two major parks and several golf courses. Middle-class housing redevelopment is occurring on the western edge along the White River, not far from a historic upper-middle-class enclave known as "Golden Hill." UNWA as a neighborhood is still very much shaped by its institutions, as are its residents' identities.

But "since the deterioration of the neighborhood, the children are not respectful," noted one resident with dismay. To underscore the contrast, UNWA is still an area of sturdy single-family brick and frame bungalows and duplexes. But as the middle-class left, so did most of the social resources and male role models.[17] The median family income reported in the 1990 U.S. census was $19,504, with 30 percent of the residents living below the poverty line. As property values have fallen relative to other areas in the city and as the racial stigma persists, UNWA is a neighborhood occupied by a double default.

Today, newer adult residents are renters. They are younger, fairly impoverished, and distrustful, especially of the youths hanging around the street corners, even when the children are their own. But there are other newcomers to the neighborhood as well who are described by a former UNWA resident as "a new breed of people . . . who don't care, and who are involved in drugs big time." There is now a pervasive fear of youth and the drug culture associated with them. This is both cause and consequence of a lack of reliable information about programs and organizations. It is also shown by the relinquishing of public space to criminal activity.

The key social dynamic in many African American urban neighborhoods is their relationship to the street.[18] All institutions — the family, the church, civil and educational authorities — are forced to contend with demands, codes, risks, and structures posed by the control of the streets. "People are afraid to take back their neighborhood," asserted a resident. "They are so afraid that [although] they 'see things,' they allow things to happen." Another resident reported on a neighborhood meeting at the school, IPS 42, about the drug activity. They claimed that "residents had to be careful when pointing out users and deals. Some residents choose to turn their heads while being afraid in their homes and on the streets." Another told the story of a small businessman who was shut down "because of the activity the owner allowed to occur in his business, even though he was not involved with it."

Deep discontinuities exist between various community groups and their potential clientele. "The problem in this area," exclaimed a long-time resident, "is that people don't know what's available to them." Residents repeated how little they knew about the social, educational, or recreational opportunities within their reach. The new principal of the recently remodeled IPS 42 shut down a popular after-school and evening athletic, training, and mentoring program for youth after two incidents of vandalism and marijuana use. Frustrated program organizers and staff members accused the principal of overreacting. "Do [the administrators] not think that youth recreation and parenting classes are programs worth fighting for?" they asked incredulously.

Although UNWA has many of the same liabilities as Mars Hill, most notably a lack of material capital, it has a much larger stock of social capital.
The community institutions of UNWA are considerable, and they exist to
serve the local residents. They include the UNWA Neighborhood Association, Riverside Civic League, UNWA Development Corporation, Crown Hill
Neighborhood Association, North West Way Civic Association, North West
Planning Development Corporation, and more recently the UNWA Weed
and Seed Initiative. Some of the groups limit their activities to subsections of
the neighborhood — Riverside or Crown Hill — while others are umbrella
groups attempting to take in the entire area. Most of the groups have been
active for more than twenty years with stable leadership. The groups are
predominantly represented by a generation of black women leaders who
have developed tight-knit relationships and who closely control the activities
of their organizations. Some significant gains have been made in housing
rehabilitation and community policing, yet the groups have been criticized
for slow progress, insufficient communication, and self-protective attitudes
toward new and younger activists. One community administrator was especially critical of local leaders. "The churches and community leaders do not
seek out advice from one another or sit down to communicate ideas. There
is a void between the leaders of UNWA and the residents, who want changes
but cannot get past the political, old line, rhetoric." Said another, "Fragmentation is the worst enemy of UNWA area residents and their leaders."

The Black Church Tradition in Flux

Using older categories and common stereotypes, UNWA might seem
to be the easiest of our neighborhoods to align with our congregational
types. African American neighborhoods have long contained congregations
marked as "evangelical," so the dominant trend here might well be toward
conversion congregations. Conversion congregations encourage others not
just to join the church or sect in organizational terms, but to join the heav-
enly procession in theological terms. Using richly stylized pulpit rhetoric
and gospel music, theirs is a call to religious arms that has long characterized both the great African American Baptist and Methodist Episcopal denominations as well as hundreds of storefront churches, of which UNWA
has its share.

As elsewhere in the U.S., the African American proselytizing congregations in UNWA sport unusually expressive names, often containing deep
emotional connotations of hope, fervency, and an expansive spirituality:
True Tried Missionary Baptist Church, Greater Love Temple, Pleasant
Union Baptist Church, or God's Temple of Deliverance.[19] This trait of spiritual emotionalism among storefront and other small, freestanding congregations correlates with a disengagement from secular affairs, because in the
words of one pastor, religion is the "only true source for changing the

attitudes of people." In fact, chided another pastor, his colleagues who have "too much of a political aspect" are missing their calling. Religious goals are sometimes combined with religious competition and unabashed rejection of other forms of belief. "Allah can't do nothing for you. The Jews don't have the true faith. Forget what [mortal] man can do for you. We got to know God for ourselves."

This disengaged model of a storefront church — balanced between conversion and cloister — treats questions about community involvement with suspicion. The members of one Pentecostal congregation asserted that their church is "not related to worldly values." In another frame house in which the living room was converted into worship space, twenty-one Pentecostal congregants were warned by their pastor against "worldly" guidance about religion and faith. Unknown visitors were singled out when the pastor suggested that "sometimes the devil can be among us; he can come into the church to see what's wrong with the church!"

Nonetheless, these independent and vocal traditions do not mask the genuinely interactive forms of worship that all comers, regulars and visitors alike, experience. There is no way for average visitors to enter most of these sanctuaries on a Sunday morning and be passive in their worship. Warm, intimate, often energetic communal worship is expected and generally achieved. Seeking release from and help for life's trials, such worship is seen as compensatory in some analytic frameworks. However, storefront religiosity serves other purposes as well. The church may be the last remaining avenue through which underemployed men (and sometimes women) can meet their economic needs and exercise their own entrepreneurial inclinations. The historical alienation of lower-class African Americans from mainstream economies may also help explain the proliferation of these small organizations in poor neighborhoods. Storefront rent is cheap and volunteer family support systems emerge to help build a gifted speaker's platform. One pastor in his late thirties recounted the limits of opportunity for him as a young black male, even as he described God's urgent call: "It was either preaching or the penitentiary or the cemetery," he exclaimed. "I chose preaching!"

Many of the congregations in UNWA appear cloistered; except for differences in race, they look much like the congregations of Mars Hill. But as anyone familiar with the tradition of the Black Church already knows, many of these congregations are also more likely to reach out into the community, both in evangelism (conversion) and in social services (community outreach). Although it would make correspondence between our congregational and neighborhood typologies neater if the dominant trend here was toward conversion, as stereotypes might suggest they would be, the truth is that the congregations of this neighborhood represent the most varied assortment.

Some African American congregations, especially larger, better-off ones, are historic leaders in social outreach. But smaller congregations have more recently heeded the call symbolized by Mayor Goldsmith's Front Porch Alliance, later echoed by President George W. Bush's "armies of compassion." Early research evidence[20] suggests that many of the white congregations most experienced with service delivery—for example, the high-status mainline churches in the upper Meridian parlor—regard a relationship with the government as both financially unnecessary and constitutionally suspect. Moreover, the white evangelical churches that seemed the most likely political ally of the Bush effort—including the kind in Mars Hill and Greenwood—have limited social service experience and little interest in entering a relationship with a governmental watchdog. But African American churches in at-risk neighborhoods have shown the most interest in a joint venture between religion and government. This makes it especially timely to reflect on the experiences of one group of such churches in this neighborhood where such services would be most welcome.

At the conclusion of our UNWA fieldwork, our researchers made a presentation to the UNWA neighborhood that stimulated some vigorous discussion about the role of the academy in the life of the neighborhood. One consequence of the discussion was the acknowledgment of several of the pastors attending that they did not know one another despite driving past each other's churches on a regular basis. A group of four resolved to continue meeting. The following year, a visit from Boston's widely known "Ten Point Coalition" team—a hands-on, clergy-based, local neighborhood action group focusing particularly on youth crime—stimulated a similar effort by the UNWA group. Many complex issues about credibility, leadership strategies, and divergent interests were raised as the program began in Indianapolis.

An alliance of eight churches was formed from the original four, including part of the adjacent Mapleton–Fall Creek neighborhood in its territory. In January 1999, Indianapolis's version of the Ten Point Coalition was established. Its signature activity is the Friday night "walk-arounds" in the neighborhoods from 9 P.M. to midnight as a signal to drug dealers and residents alike that some spaces in the neighborhood will be shielded from illicit traffic. The clergy and several other male leaders approach local residents, particularly men and boys, offering support while warning against drug-related and other criminal behavior. Over time, the walkers learn the routines of the neighborhood, helping police, for example, distinguish between the hard-core criminal types and the vulnerable kids who need assistance they can offer. The dramatic decline in Boston's homicide rate among youth in its beleaguered Dorchester neighborhood has been credited to the presence of the clergy coalition there.[21] Now about thirty churches, some from outside of UNWA, participate in a series of projects aimed at youth and anchored by the Friday night walk-arounds. Of course, the local coalition has not been able to convince most of the other pastors to join in. Said one dismissively, "These 'walk-arounds' are just not for me."

The key to this program, in Indianapolis as in Boston, is the collaborative relationships that are formed with the police, sheriff, fire department, court system, and other city agencies to address youthful offenders or youths who need counseling or training. In Indianapolis, a surprising number of clergy brought the relationships with them. For example, the president of the Coalition is a chaplain with the sheriff's department and the Coalition's secretary was formerly on staff at the governor's office. The activists have employed their connections to obtain resources such as surplus walkie-talkies, free cellular phones, and the subsidized erection of a radio tower in the area. After being active for only a year, they raised sufficient funds to begin the process of purchasing their own building.

The connection between Ten Point and the mayor's office was particularly visible because the organization began under former Mayor Steven Goldsmith and his Front Porch Alliance. The local Ten Point clergy wanted to establish its power and legitimacy by working with the authorities — be they the mayor, the police, the chamber of commerce — and maintaining a non-critical, or at least less critical, relationship with them. This stance is in contrast to that of the other organization of black ministers in Indianapolis, including the aforementioned Concerned Clergy, the activist civil rights group with which Ten Point is sometimes compared. "I just don't think black churches should be working with the mayor's office," stated Rev. Mel Girton, a member of Concerned Clergy and pastor of an active UNWA church.[22] "It was partisan to start with."

Concerned Clergy takes a more confrontational position in regard to the city, the police, and other authorities. They built their reputation through being critics, and they maintain their legitimacy at least in part by defining themselves against government authorities. Additionally, whereas Ten Point sees itself as dealing with issues caused in large measure by the loss of church influence in people's lives, Concerned Clergy looks more at racial and economic inequity as the cause of social ills. Said the group's president, "You still got a serious problem in Indianapolis in terms of racial discrimination and prejudice . . . we've still got a job on our hands."

Today many of Indianapolis's churches search for what Robert Hope Franklin has called "pragmatic accommodation" with government and business.[23] No longer wishing to remain on the margins, exhorting and challenging secular institutions to live by principles of social and economic justice, churches today negotiate and compromise in order to be on the same side of the table as government and business. Expanding into broader partnerships with one another, such as with the Ten Point Coalition, raises an opportunity for establishing an effective power base, constituency, and voice in the larger city. The caution to be noted here is that the official sanction Ten Point has received may be a double-edged sword and might generate suspicion and perhaps even hostility from other quarters, perhaps most directly the communities and groups Ten Point wants to assist.

Residents of UNWA have a memory of a centered and bounded community. But there can be little question that this is now an area primarily defined by others, especially by an urban political administration trying desperately to deal with social problems caused by continuing relocation both of population and resources. In a city defined by multiple centers that are sometimes economic, sometimes political, and only occasionally geographic, UNWA is working hard to be defined as a place deserving of greater attention and an infusion of needed resources. There can be no question that UNWA has low material capital. But it has multiple forms of social capital and so is socially centered in a way that imprints the community on its residents in ways that separate it from other poor places.

UNWA has a full range of congregational types, as does every neighborhood. There are many small, conservative, often Pentecostal churches that chastise the world around them and seek to withdraw from it in a cloistering fashion. The conversion tradition remains strong, and it is fair to say that there is a correspondence between *porch* neighborhoods and *conversion* congregations. But the historic Black Church in America has never separated conversion from community outreach, so it would be wrong for us to separate the two here, despite the temptation to do so in the interest of conceptual clarity. The churches of UNWA bridge our congregational types just as the members of those congregations often bridge urban neighborhoods — living in higher-status places but commuting "home" to worship. They are "for" the neighborhood, even when they are not always "of" it. In a society so highly mobile in both status and geography, people's lives are shaped by the evolution of multiple centers, because they continue to participate in the precincts of their past as well as of their present.

Some suburban churches have adapted to a multicentered world by providing spiritual and material service to families creating their own centers, but UNWA's emerging model of urban religion offers a counterweight. Its congregations have learned to lobby for their own combination of race, class, and place in a multicentered city. But UNWA also alerts theorists, planners, and civic leaders alike to take heed. With so many members living elsewhere, these are not purely indigenous organizations feeding romantic notions of grassroots revival. And while they are steeped in the tradition of self-help, they are very aware of the need to use political leverage — starting with existing social capital — to get what they need. Finally, anyone interested in urban religion must be wary of consigning congregations either to the heap of inconsequential organizations that seek only sanctuary and escape in heaven's future rewards or of defining them as one more kind of urban social service agency. Many urban congregations work hard to balance their vertical and horizontal concerns, a strategy especially well-suited to merging the historic role of the Black Church as a community institution with new, multicentered urban realities.

THE GREENWOOD "GARAGE"

Greenwood is contiguous with the southern border of Indianapolis and exemplifies the largely white, middle-class, booming suburbs that cities all over the U.S. have spawned, especially in the last quarter-century. The movement outward from metropolitan cores has paradoxically decentered both the cities and their surrounding environments. As urban refugees have pushed into once rural areas in search of new centers of domesticity, security, and stability, they have radically altered the small towns and farming environments of once bucolic landscapes. Greenwood remains the seat of Johnson County, but it has also become one of the many pit stops in the elaborate highway system that now rings Indianapolis. Even within the town itself, the action has been recentered to the outlying mall and to the busy interstate highway that connects the larger metropolis to south central Indiana.

Demographic and economic changes have taken their toll in the past. As one resident put it, "Greenwood has become a bedroom community . . . [although] through the churches and the schools, there is still a sense of community. The chamber of commerce also tries hard to keep the feel of community, [but] it is very difficult." Of course, the "bedroom" reference is a common cliché for such commuter areas. However, we prefer the "garage" reference, partly because it reflects the area's upscale housing standards but mostly because it indicates that these are people who seem constantly in car transit — to work, to school, to volunteer, to visit, to play, and, not surprisingly, to church.

In the last two decades, the rate of growth in the unincorporated areas abutting the town has outpaced that of Greenwood proper. White River Township, on the west border of Greenwood, is now larger than the town itself, and the residents of both White River Township and Clark Township to the east consider themselves part of Greenwood. The collective cognitive map of Greenwood also includes large sections of south side Indianapolis on the north, and Whiteland, a smaller town to the south. All of this produces a loose, unbounded and increasingly multicentered region. Nonetheless, there persists a firm notion for residents that this is the space they know and control. The cultural script describes a secure and familiar small town, despite its changing shape and character. This script was largely written by exurbanites seeking a way to adjust to the complex demands of corporate and professional lifestyles; it is enacted within political and cultural institutions that have evolved to meet those needs.

During the 1980s, Greenwood's pro-growth mayor incorporated adjacent land. She attracted new capital investment, renovated landmark buildings, and sunk new infrastructure. "[Former] Mayor Surina was not timid," recalled a council member. "She knew how to get things done, including how to go above everyone else." This was offered as both a commendation and a critique. Roads, water and drainage pipes, and schools are being constructed so fast that little attention is paid to the long-term durability or feasibility of the structures. "In five to ten years, everything will be run down because the city was more focused on a quantity effort than a quality one," predicted one pastor. Meanwhile, the residents of outside areas such as White River Township expect to receive their municipal services from Greenwood and are surprised when voting, police services, and tree limb removals are denied. "They want all these things but they do not want to pay for them," complained the council member.

The proponents of growth on the Greenwood city council have prevailed over the no-growth traditionalists, continuing a course that American cities have followed since the colonial era. "I think the more progress there is, the better," asserted one of the longest-standing council members, expressing a reliable formula. Change is inevitable, she thought, and she welcomed the increasing cosmopolitanism of the town, helped by the new high-tech workers. Asians, many of whom were recruited by Eli Lilly and Co., have seen their numbers increase fourfold in less than forty years, from 7,000 in 1960 to more than 30,000 by the mid-1990s. Nonetheless, tensions over growth strategies continue among residents as well as among council members. "[Growth] needs to be organized so it can continue to happen, but at a controllable rate," worried the pastor. As centers proliferate geographically, they also change over time. This adds to a palpable sense of deracinated unease — a sense that the churches themselves have confronted in their own fashion.

Religion on the Move

Residents of Greenwood remember when Main Street contained all the churches as well as all the principal commercial establishments. Today, all but one of the churches experiencing membership growth have been founded, or relocated, along with the stores, to the town's outskirts. More than half the membership in the Greenwood Ministerial Alliance comes from churches outside Greenwood proper, many from White River Township.

Several large and growing "evangelical" churches have created a different religious landscape in the Greenwood area, one that displays the rising economic well-being of many who are participating in the resurgent interest in biblically conservative, intimately spiritual Christianity. These churches are currently leading the local ministerial alliance — though "ministers don't flock there," according to one. Many churches attract newcomers to the area through their extensive programming. The largest of these is Community Church of Greenwood, with activities from day care to recreational facilities, twelve-step programs, tailored discussion groups, structured teenage activities, food and clothing provision, world travel tours, bible study, etc. When successful, programs like these lead to large membership increases for the congregations that offer them. Over time, they change the way churches do their work and the way they measure success.

As in many other suburban neighborhoods across America, this large community church highlights congregational adaptation to garage neighborhoods as it leads from the front. At its twentieth anniversary celebration, the senior pastor's mentor praised their leadership. "The bigger churches lead the smaller churches, since the local churches rarely think bigger than their own community. Key churches, and key people, keep Satan at bay better than those looking at their own congregations." The multiplication of congregations, the ability of the group to create a Christian community and to reproduce it, is one of its "hallmarks of faithfulness."

Another form of adaptation by congregations in garage neighborhoods is teaching church members to *cope* with the demands of high-pressure work and family lifestyles rather than trying to *change* them. One of the consequences of suburban and urban dispersal is that the activities of work, school, and home, including religious activities, are often separated and far from one another, especially in the *garage* suburb. This has resulted in constant efforts by parents to find ways to save time and has caused some churches to make activities fit the requirements of these overly busy families.

One member in a local Baptist church reported her exhaustion from the pressures of keeping up with the needs of her dual-income family in a competitive, activity-loaded environment. But she was reminded that exactly for these reasons she needed to learn to put the pressures of suburban life "second to one's relationship to God." Repeated the deacon, "That's why our church stresses spending time each day with God." In this way the church helps one put one's work and scheduling demands into a perspective that will prevent one's being totally absorbed by them. Yet the church seems to stop short of a deeper understanding of the member's crisis. The church has not asked her to consider the personal or familial sacrifices she may be making in order to achieve the affluence of her new position. It does not suggest a strategy of change that would challenge her lifestyle by pointing out how affluence imposes unforeseen burdens. Ultimately, the member herself must make the adjustment. Unspoken is how the church benefits from the affluence of its members and, therefore, participates in the stresses that affluence produces for them.

Other adapting newcomers find garage neighborhoods like Greenwood fertile ground. At the Vineyard Fellowship in Greenwood, one of several "new paradigm" congregations in the Indianapolis suburbs, a favorite community activity among the substantial adolescent segment of the congregation — about 30 percent of members — is the "Coke outreach." The youths distribute Coke cans to passing motorists stopped at intersections with labels that read "Just because" along with the church's location and times of service. If the garage motif befits the ministry to local drivers, it also befits the informal system of administration, where no membership rolls are kept and no long-term commitments required. Jeans and T-shirts predominate among this youthful congregation, who come to hear uplifting teachings on Sunday mornings, where the leader suggests that they sit back, theater style, and enjoy the service.

Though the customer service strategy for centering has produced phenomenal growth in many cases, some of the locals are concerned about its ramifications. Even rapidly growing, rapidly changing organizations cannot resist all rationalizing and bureaucratizing currents, streams readily articulated by those who have watched from outside. It is not uncommon to hear someone say of a fast-growing independent congregation, "This church has become everything that they were against when they started. They started as a bible study and they have grown into this large, institutional church." Indeed, not even every member of a customer service congregation likes the growth metaphor overlaid on their vision of a "small-town" church.

On the other side of the coin, some members of a liturgical, mainline congregation want to change some of the "stagnant" worship traditions that, they fear, make the worship service seem irrelevant or esoteric to too many residents. "The candles," one said, "are an unnecessary part of the church. They are a part of the tradition that people are afraid to let go of and now have imbued with an inappropriate symbolism." "The sanctuary lamp is similar," he went on, "in that it is not an eternal light. It was left lit during a time when it was dark in the church and they simply provided the direction to where the holy book was kept." A staff member suggested that the newer churches astutely criticize the "rules and regulations" of inherited traditions that no longer provide the meaning sought by believers who are themselves now removed from the inherited culture that originally sparked the traditions. But that same staffer still lamented the customer service that contemporary parishioners seem to require. He explained that "several people have come to our congregation and considered attending, but when they found out we did not offer a nursery during worship, they did not come back. We've changed and now offer a nursery." However, he noted that putting children into nursery during worship services prevents a family-based worship: ". . . services should be fun for them. It cannot be more fun elsewhere or they will never come here."

These liturgical traditionalists are not alone among mainline churches challenged by the new customer service model.[24] New churches have found it easier to adopt a consumer orientation, despite their tendency toward some kinds of conservatism. The older mainline and "liberal" traditions have found it difficult to change liturgical and ritual practices that have been embedded for some time, however much they may have been part of their surrounding culture in some earlier period. The process of reinterpreting these practices *for* a new generation, or even *by* a new generation, remains difficult. Mainline churches are conscious of the pressures to adapt to the new environment and find ways to rebuild their religious traditions into meaningful contemporary idioms.

As another example, consider the stately Greenwood Presbyterian Church, located in a 100-year-old historic building with a much admired stained glass window overlooking the town's main thoroughfare. The church is regularly sought out for weddings, yet members feel their loss of membership is tied to their "old town" location, an area where "no one comes anymore." But in a "garage" area so overrun with cars moving in every direction, transportation and access are not the problem. Greenwood Presbyterian offers a relatively formal worship service that, judging from membership statistics, has limited appeal for young children or younger adults.

Catholic churches have grown substantially in the nation's expanding suburbs and exurbs as white, ethnic Catholics have moved away from downtown. Our Lady of the Greenwood Catholic Church is no exception. At the same time, Catholicism itself has changed to accommodate these shifts. The tradition has become more customer-sensitive; for example, adherents are no longer restricted to their parish church but are increasingly free to explore and attend elsewhere.

Our Lady of the Greenwood is both family- and school-oriented, meeting the needs of growing suburban families in both traditional and nontraditional — sacred and secular — ways. Founded as a chapel in 1949, it is now the largest church in town with more than 4,000 members and an elementary school of 500 children, 95 percent of whom are Catholic. Four hundred children are taught in the religious education program for public school students. As the only Catholic church in town, Our Lady of the Greenwood is now bursting the walls of its present buildings. Some of the overcrowding will be relieved by the opening of a new, suburban parish that will support the expansion in the White River Township area. But Greenwood's old-town church has begun planning for a new sanctuary and auxiliary buildings to meet the needs of their extensive activities.

The largest portion of the church's almost $2 million annual budget supports the school and its ancillary activities, such as some two dozen basketball and volleyball teams in its youth group programs. Events such as the popular annual summer community festival not only raise money but raise a degree of community consciousness in Greenwood. The latter function is also served by making the church's limited facilities accessible to any community group requesting meeting space.

Meanwhile, in the words of one Sunday morning homilist, "Catholics can be sure that in matters of faith and morals the Church will lead so that Catholics know how to act and believe. The Church will be kept from error."

Church teachings and Catholic education retain the authoritative manner of a hierarchical church, though there is also respect for religious diversity within the parish and provision for a variety of Catholic subtraditions. Pietist devotions are popular, and the perpetual adoration of the Eucharist attracts a small but regular knot of daily mass attenders. Recently, the church began an annual celebration of Our Lady of Guadalupe, complete with a mariachi band and native dress. The youth group attracts about sixty fairly regular participants to do the variety of things that teenagers enjoy, but mostly discussing with one another the topical issues of peer pressure, sex, and drugs. There are retreats, charismatic renewal groups, and marriage preparation classes ("to prepare young people to have the right ideals, both realistic and spiritual," noted a liturgical leader). While some Catholics have criticized their own churches for lackluster liturgy and preaching that does not address members in personal ways, Catholicism's combination of inherited traditions and a new focus on program variety continues to draw — and, more importantly, retain — members.

Nor are Catholics wholly isolated from Protestant and other faith traditions in the community. Ecumenical organizations such as the Greenwood Ministerial Alliance and the newer Samaritan Services bridge the divides between conservative and mainline Protestant and Catholic churches. Samaritan Services was founded in 1989 as an offspring of the Ministerial Alliance to serve the needy in the greater Greenwood area with emergency and short-term assistance and to provide limited help for transitory migrant laborers and carnival workers. Its funds come from both public and private sources, including many of the churches themselves.

Greenwood United Methodist Church is a particularly important source of support. It also has its own unusually active social outreach program that cuts across typical liberal-conservative distinctions. Founded more than a century and a half ago at a time when Indianapolis itself was little more than a town as opposed to a city, the church now has 800 members, with about half coming from White River Township and the rest from Greenwood and southern Indianapolis. In addition to Samaritan Services, the church supports Jeremiah Agency, the non-denominational home for unwed mothers, the Crisis Pregnancy Center, and a shelter next door to the church for victims of domestic abuse and temporary homelessness. The church staff includes a parish nurse and makes hearing aids available during services as well as counseling and support programs for members. A major initiative with the new pastor has been to diversify their outreach efforts to include international mission projects to Zaire and Mexico for health clinics, housing, and other basic needs. A staff member articulates the church's mix of horizontal and vertical theology, linked to local commitment, when he states, "To those who love the Lord, we would invite to love our neighbors both here and across the world." More a community outreach than a customer service congregation, Greenwood United Methodist has managed to find its center in combining the two.

The growing Greenwood area provides a window into the changes shaping the realigned metropolis. The growing churches that benefit from these trends fit well with the changing lifestyles of the residents. They seek to provide centering to the decentered as much as faith to the faithless, but they do so in different ways. While the religious marketplace continues to foster a pluralism of religious styles,[25] it is impossible to ignore the affinity between the customer service congregations and the garage areas they serve.

Whatever else it may be, Greenwood is both a rising middle-class residential destination in demand and a sprawling congeries of subdivisions and malls that sometimes seems inchoate. Residents in these newer subdivisions adapt to a multicentered city by creating centers of their own. These newly constructed centers depend in turn on the centering capacities of a vast array of organizations and institutions, both public and private, secular and sacred. Each family draws for itself a mental map of its landscape, creating for itself "places" or "communities" that include shopping districts, schools, recreational choices, and — for at least half of them — congregations. Work may or may not be nearby. As likely as not their jobs are in downtown Indianapolis or even on the city's north side. In mental maps that designate places both by function and by spheres within one's life, this spatial disjuncture is not considered odd.

In booming suburbs such as Greenwood, the uprooted pursue a sense of place and security that confers a sense of communal likemindedness.[26] In the midst of family pressures, technological changes, job uncertainty, and sometimes a pervasive sense of meaninglessness, certain kinds of churches respond to their needs more directly and overtly than others. Such churches do not necessarily provide proximate comfort in sharing the questions, whatever ultimate answers they may or may not provide. Programs built around members' schedules are helpful, but so is an exaggerated friendliness. People moving for job reasons, divorce and family separations, or even just the desire to get a bigger house in a better neighborhood because they can now afford it, do not have time to carefully build intimacy within a new community. They need places where their strangeness is quickly overcome by welcoming styles of churches designed with exactly this in mind. The pursuit of certainty in typically (but not entirely or simply) conservative churches fits well with American suburbanites' pursuit of a centered groundedness, even in a familiarity that seems, from another perspective, too programmatic and mass-produced.

It is important to recognize just how different the multiple places that make up Indianapolis can be. Despite all the talk about the commercial homogenization of America, these neighborhoods and districts are more different than they are similar. There is, for instance, no McDonald's in either UNWA or Mars Hill. Houses along the Meridian Street corridor cost several times the Indianapolis median house price; in UNWA and Mars Hill many houses sell for less than half the median.

Of course, residents of these different areas still share many other things in common. They often vote for the same elected officials and generally follow the same laws. They feel the positive or negative effects — admittedly to different degrees — of dominant economic trends. They drive downtown if they want to watch the professional sports teams, visit a museum, or view a parade. Each of the places described here has been affected differently by urban realignment. The Meridian Street corridor has not only witnessed the outward pressure moving north, it has been its main thoroughfare. The "best neighborhoods" in the city have moved successively north, with the city's most prestigious and most expensive neighborhoods now located just on either side of the county line. UNWA felt that same pressure from the other side, as its population declined during the flight of the middle class — both black and white — to the townships and to the suburban counties. The interstates that made urban dispersal possible cut right through the heart of UNWA, and its residents are still stinging. In many ways, Mars Hill seems the least affected by the changes, clinging to its Appalachian roots and relatively unaffected so far by transportation changes. But in fact the neighborhood has changed despite itself; it is now defined by the urban institutions and social programs that it lacks. As the rest of the metropolis tried to rethink what it means to be the inner city and to respond appropriately with changes both in culture and in institutions, Mars Hill was defined by what it was not. Finally, Greenwood experienced the same shift that happened to small towns on the edges of big cities everywhere: it became the quaint "old town" hub of a sprawling mass of subdivisions and commercial developments. Its future was determined by the outward forces of suburbanization, and yet, in another sense, it was drawn inward toward identification with the metropolis as a whole. Fifty years ago, Greenwood was a small town *near* Indianapolis. Today, it is the southern portion *of* Indianapolis.

Each of these urban places is host to a range of religious organizations, but there is a marked affinity between congregation and community. The Meridian Street corridor has congregations oriented toward *community outreach*. Here, mission means using one's own resources to help others. Mars Hill is dominated by *cloister* congregations, places where mission often means sustaining internal identity in the face of overwhelming change. In Greenwood, mission is most often linked to *customer service*. Churches seek to create a religious community for suburbanites who have a wide array of choices but few ascribed social prerequisites. UNWA, finally, is home to the mix of congregational missions that characterize the Black Church in America, displaying a unique blend of *conversion*-oriented evangelism and an emphasis on social justice.

Even in our porch neighborhoods with mostly white residents, *conversion* congregations do not dominate. While virtually every congregation practices some form of outreach, and most of those have some spiritual, even other-worldly, dimension, it is fair to say that soul-winning, conversion-oriented, proselytizing evangelization of strangers is the primary mission goal of relatively few congregations. No doubt such activity can be a larger or smaller piece of the pie depending on the tradition and on the local group, but any concept of "evangelical" that does not see this activity in the context of character development, internal community building, and social service provision is probably caricaturing the believers who are so designated.

There is a very real sense in which religion, as an imagined sacred canopy, was decentered insofar as it lost its ability to define the city's establishment symbolized in its downtown core. It is also fair to say that religion was recentered in the multiple religious traditions that make up the city's culture. Moreover, religion was recentered in particular urban places. But it would be wrong to see this process as a simple matter of privatization. Religion still plays a public, if to some degree more local, role in every community within the metropolis. When we see the ways that congregations shape their missions to respond to multiple, particular social environments, then we understand better how both the city and its religion have become multicentered.

7

CONCLUSION: RELIGION
AND URBAN CULTURE

The basic story of Indianapolis and its religion can be quickly recounted. Indiana needed a new capital, so it planted and platted that capital in its very center. The town around it expanded first into a city and then one hundred years later into a metropolitan area. Indianapolis was centered from the start, and not merely in its geography and political-economic structure. Religion provided a cultural center in the form of a mainline Protestant establishment represented by the clutch of tall-steepled churches clustered around the city's center circle.

Over the course of the twentieth century, the city experienced repeated movement outward, creating a number of overlapping social and cultural centers. By century's end, power and the powerful had moved north from Monument Circle along Meridian Street, stretching that wealthy corridor all the way to one of the country's most affluent suburbs, Carmel. The city's economy had diversified, shaped increasingly by national companies run by highly mobile executives coming from outside the state. The city's cultural center had also changed. Religion lost a good deal of its pride of public place, although religious practice — especially in congregations — continued to play an important role. The city's "sacred" unifiers gradually shifted toward civic commitments, such as the patriotic war memorials and, more recently, sports. The Lilly Endowment provided support for local religious life out in the multiple centers, even as it also supported redevelopment of a new, common center founded on a new civic infrastructure of sports arenas, museums, and performance venues linked to downtown shopping.

Indianapolis housed religious diversity from its founding, but during the second half of the twentieth century the city shifted from a mainline Protestant religious establishment to a profuse religious pluralism. Although the older "liberal" denominations continued to attract and wield influence, they no longer had presumptive civic control. Black churches, evangelical white Protestant groups, Catholics, and even the city's small Jewish community all gained in both numbers and prominence. But it was not just the city's overarching religious scene that was decentered, only to be recentered in multiple faith communities; a similar process was occurring within each religious tradition. Every denomination was becoming multicentered, and in the process the action and the authority was shifting downward and outward from the central denominational offices to the enormous variety of local congregations.

To chart the diverse ways that these congregations were responding to their shifting social environments, we derived four congregational types from the intersection of two basic mission distinctions: vertical versus horizontal and internal versus external. We called the four resulting combinations "community outreach," "cloister," "conversion," and "customer service." It is important to note one last time that these differences are more relative than absolute — especially since most congregations are themselves multicentered.

A multicentered religious scene within a multicentered metropolis suggests that lives are now increasingly gathered in the myriad localities of neighborhoods, regions, and districts. But here too there is change and diversity. Once again we used two distinctions to define four types. Some areas are centered and centering for their residents; other areas are more de-centered and de-stabilizing. Some areas are in demand, while others are lived in by default. We gave the names "parlors," "kitchens," "porches," and "garages" to the resulting neighborhood models. Each of these neighborhood models has an affinity for a particular congregational type. Parlor areas have an affinity with community outreach congregations that seek to render services to other areas of the city where they are needed. However, the low-status kitchen neighborhoods have more cloistered congregations that reflect the tendency among many older residents to hunker down, to separate themselves both from a neighborhood in decay and from a city whose progress excludes them. Our garage neighborhoods are sprawling areas where almost as much time is spent in the car as in the home; churches there respond by becoming mini-communities and quasi-malls offering various sorts of customer service to residents who define themselves primarily as consumers. Finally, porch neighborhoods have considerable social capital and many organizations meant to build community, but they lack financial resources. The example we chose is an African American area whose traditional churches and storefront sects exhibit the conversion tendency but also reflect the complex mixture of congregational types that characterize the Black Church. This mixture is especially important in places where persistent problems have led many former residents to move away, returning only for Sunday services. In fact, this tendency for congregations to serve a commuting membership is increasingly common among all congregations in all urban places. Neither congregations nor neighborhoods are as locally centered or as bound together as some contemporary stereotypes suggest.

Both the city and the role of religion within it have changed over Indianapolis's 180 years. It is true that Indianapolis locals once called the city "Naptown" to reflect a sleepy—not to say boring—quality. But as Susan Walcott illustrates in the title of her account of Indianapolis's shift "from Bustbelt to Boomtown,"[1] the city's images have changed over the years. Not merely keyed to a city at sleep and at play, they also reflect a city hard at work. With massive suburbanization[2] came an unprecedented merging of city and county, a shift from an industrial base to a service economy, and the global effect of transnational movements of people and money over the course of the last half-century.

Today, we have argued, most Indianapolis citizens live the bulk of their lives in multiple small communities: their side of the city, their small suburban town or urban district, their subdivision or neighborhood, and often their church, synagogue, or mosque. They have, literally, multiple social identities located in multiple social centers. But the metropolitan area is not just the amalgamation of 1.6 million multicentered individuals. Indianapolis has a recognizable center that shapes the character of each of those smaller centers and the interplay among them.

The story of urban religion we have recounted here is about changes in both the one and the many centers of the city. The churches and their overtly Christian symbols gradually receded from the downtown mile square, replaced by the structures and symbols of patriotism, commerce, government, and sport. But traditional, specific religion flourished in the many centers, in the regions, towns, neighborhoods, districts, and elective communities that together constitute the rest of the metropolitan area. This is the sense in which religion truly became multicentered.

Thinking about the city in this way—understanding that it was shaped by both inward and outward forces that created multiple urban centers—offers new ways to think about many of the themes that animate our lives together. It provides a new lens for viewing some big-picture community issues such as social capital, church-state relations, cultural pluralism, civil religion, and secularization. It also stimulates much more practical reflection about the role of religious organizations — especially congregations — and their relationship to their external environment. A multicentered view of the city has firm policy implications, for public officials as well as religious planners. In what follows we start with a fresh look at some abiding civic concerns, leading toward new ways to think about the civic relationship between religion and urban culture.

Social Capital

Anyone reading this book is likely to be well-familiar with James Coleman's term "social capital," especially as it was used by Robert Putnam in his *Bowling Alone*. Putnam highlighted concerns that Americans were exhibiting less community-oriented behavior by voting less, failing to join civic clubs, and bowling alone rather than in leagues. Like so much analysis of American community, social capital harks back to Frenchman Alexis de Tocqueville's observations concerning voluntary organizations. From his earliest observations of American behavior to the present, debating the community-building capacity of different organizations has become something of an obsession. Many people fear that we are becoming more individualistic and losing some older sense of community. They want to know where community comes from and how we can get some more. There is widespread agreement that community is generated in small groups containing people who share common interests linked to race, social class, and education. Their geographic proximity to one another still matters, but it seems to matter less than it once did as our society becomes increasingly mobile, with daily thirty-minute work commutes the norm.

Much has been written about mediating institutions or about civil society that treats certain organizations as crucial to moderating between the isolated individual and the large but impersonal forces of the polity and economy. Putnam himself stands in that breach. Peter Berger and Richard John Neuhaus[3] tried, in an earlier period, to bridge that same divide from a different angle with their book on mediating institutions.

Recent concerns about social capital are in many ways only new conceptualizations of much older worries about the relationship between individuals and their communities in an increasingly complex, pluralistic society. Over the years, observers from the social sciences have periodically lamented America's loss of community. This was an important theme of sociology's best-selling work of all time by David Riesman and his colleagues with the brilliant title *The Lonely Crowd*. Others in the tradition include Philip Slater's *The Pursuit of Loneliness;* Christopher Lasch's *The Culture of Narcissism;* and more recently Robert Bellah et al.'s *Habits of the Heart*, as well as Putnam's *Bowling Alone*.[4] Each of these authors has a somewhat different explanation of the problem. Putnam's account is more structural in that it focuses, as Tocqueville did himself, on rates of associational participation; Bellah, despite a title drawn from Tocqueville, draws from a tradition dating back to the early French sociologist Emile Durkheim. He is more attuned to cultural nuance, concerned that we are increasingly betrayed by a value commitment to "individualism" that has surged out of control.

Our story of a multicentered city is, in its own small way, part of this tradition. And yet it is different in at least three respects. First, whereas the works named above depend mostly on interviews with and surveys of individuals, we have focused on the civic context in which individuals live, work, play, and sometimes worship. The great advantage of studying only one city rather than all of urban America or the society at large is that it allowed us to focus on details.

Second, rather than choose either a structural or a cultural explanation for what we have found, we tried to have it both ways and portray the two perspectives as complementary. Essentially, culture has been forced to diversify and decenter as a way of coping with underlying structural changes. This pattern would not surprise early theorists like Durkheim, who believed that societies oscillated between periods of intense group solidarity and relative isolation, between intense coming together and gradual drifting apart. The twenty-first century will likely have to cope with a new and multicentered structure and culture, providing perhaps the sternest test yet of American cohesion and coherence.

And yet there is a third difference between this work and its predecessors, which is that our views are not nearly as pessimistic. Chronic or permanent loss of community, or decenteredness, is one thing; what we have called "multicenteredness" is quite another. The term has a certain oxymoronic quality: anything with multiple centers can never be truly centered; at the same time, anything with multiple centers can never be wholly uncentered. Even the simplest societies have a variety of centers and centering principles, and it is rare indeed for them to all coincide and overlap perfectly. Multicenteredness is the rule rather than the exception, but the kind of centering combination can make a difference in the quality of both the life of the community and the lives of its individuals.

One important pattern for Indianapolis involves an increasing disjuncture between the city's structural properties and its cultural resources. The city has tried repeatedly to buttress its structural center with inward, centering forces such as Unigov, the development of the IUPUI campus, and repeated attempts to revive downtown shopping. But the outward force of suburbanization has already given way to exurbanization, for working as well as non-working hours. Although this sort of structural spread is now far advanced, culture has begun to follow, if unevenly. A few areas are both structurally and culturally centered, many have one without the other, but only a few with no centeredness at all confirm the worst prophecies of both Bellah and Putnam.

Since Putnam's dire evaluation, much has been said about religion's ability to build and to sustain a social stock of trust, good will, communication, and the other human connections that make up social capital.[5] But the story of Indianapolis suggests that if we truly want to understand religion's role in social capital, then we will have to be very conscious of, and very careful about, the level of social interaction if we are to understand its effect. For instance, it is absolutely clear even to casual observers that religion builds commitment and community among members within religious congregations and, to a lesser degree, within religious traditions. But the overall social effects of that community building are tricky to evaluate. Our community outreach congregations invest their social capital to try to build social ties to a wider environment. Cloister congregations, on the other hand, use their stock of capital to protect themselves from that environment. Customer service congregations do not always maintain tight internal bonds, nor do they necessarily build bridges to their surrounding environment, though they sometimes do both. Like conversion congregations, they frequently expend their efforts on bringing individuals *in* more than on reaching *out*.

The same kind of reasoning applies to neighborhoods and other local centers within the city. Places with high levels of social and material capital — our parlor neighborhoods or districts — can use those resources either to improve their connections to the whole metropolis or to maintain high property values and enhance personal safety. Neighborhoods that have high levels of one capital but not the other — our porch and garage neighborhoods — may find it very difficult to use one kind of resource as leverage to gain the other kind. No matter how much financial capital a place has, it cannot necessarily purchase communication, trust, and a sense of belonging. Just as true, a place with a strong social infrastructure but few material resources may have a leg up on other poor neighborhoods, but even a larder filled with social "assets" does not mean prosperity.

The kind of social capital that comes from the broadest metropolitan identity symbolized in the downtown core is different still. It doubtless says something about community when citizens of the city and of the state share a common reverence for the war memorials. The state capitol building symbolizes another shared identity. Even the excitement surrounding sports teams like the Colts or the Pacers signifies a community link. But if these human connections are social capital, then they are very different from one another, and more different still from the kind of social bonds formed in congregations where members share historical ties, demographic characteristics, and intimate personal connections.

Does religion, then, build social capital in the city? It does, but in particular ways in particular places. We must be careful to recognize that for all the ways that religion reaches out and joins diverse communities — from parochial schools that welcome other neighborhood children outside their faith to the racial reconciliation of the Celebration of Hope — it can also serve to

isolate and insulate specific communities that use it as a mechanism to separate the sheep from the goats, insiders from outsiders, "us" from "them."

Church and State: Faith-Based Initiatives

Seeing religious change in the light of multiple centers created by countervailing inward and outward pressures helps us to understand other kinds
of social change as well. Recently, questions about church and state have
resurfaced as questions about "faith-based initiatives," known also as "charitable choice" or "faith-based welfare reform."[6] Although this is not the
place to attempt a sustained analysis of these proposed reforms, our understanding of religion as multicentered offers a new perspective on the issue.

Put most simply, the faith-based welfare reform movement highlights the
enormous shift from a central, de facto religious establishment to religious
pluralism as the accepted societal norm. As faith-based reformers like to
point out, there is nothing novel about government partnering with religious organizations to provide social services. Government has long worked
through groups like Lutheran Child and Family Services, Catholic Charities,
Jewish Welfare Federations, and the Salvation Army, in some cases providing
the majority of their funding. It was always understood that those groups
would be religiously affiliated, but that they would operate as stand-alone
enterprises subject to applicable federal regulations. In essence, those charitable organizations were either drawn from the mainline religious establishment or were themselves established as the providers of choice for specific
clients (i.e., Catholic Charities for Catholics, Jewish Welfare Federation for
Jews, etc.). It is not the religion-government partnership that is new, but the
fact that reformers want to include smaller, more local groups that behave in
a more sectarian fashion.

The reforms begun in 1996 are not about using government money to
fund religiously affiliated charities, which has long been standard practice,
but about government's expectations that religiously affiliated groups limit
their sectarian nature and behave as component parts of the federal social
welfare bureaucracy. Reformers claim that government has discriminated
against the truly faith-based groups that manifest specific religious ideas
and moral codes in their delivery of services. Under new laws and new presidential executive directives, religious groups are allowed to maintain their
essential religious character. They cannot use federal funds to evangelize or
proselytize and they cannot discriminate against those from outside their
religion, but they can continue to display religious symbols, to read from religious texts in the overall delivery of services, and to hire only coreligionists.

The practical effect of these changes is that government support for religious groups is moving *down* a level, from charities affiliated with denominations to local services affiliated with congregations. When former Mayor
Goldsmith began his Front Porch Alliance in Indianapolis, he was not seek-

ing more help from the Jewish Welfare Federation or Catholic Charities—he was hoping to enlist congregations as neighborhood assets. When the local homelessness coalition began a faith-based program, it was looking to engage *congregations* as partners in transitional housing. When the Juvenile Court judge wanted to enlist religious counselors for juvenile offenders, he turned to pastors and to congregations.[7]

The real effect of welfare reform is to move government partnership down to the most local level, down to specific congregations working in their particular urban environments. This movement is premised on the understanding that religion now operates mostly at the local level, that its primary effects are in the diverse, multiple centers of the city. The days of turning to denominational officials or diocesan leaders to generate religious involvement in public life are past. Whatever one thinks about the constitutionality or the effectiveness of faith-based initiatives, the impetus for these new changes fits our reading of religion as multicentered. If congregations are the primary religious organizations and if they act in ways that make sense in and make sense of their specific urban environments, then it is easy to see why reformers are eager to move government's partnerships with religion down to a more local level.

Ours is one of several recent studies finding that most congregations do some form of social service, but that few congregations have experience with program administration or an eagerness to enter into government partnership to advance the cause. Of course, many congregations collect moneys and supplies for relief and refugee services run by their denominations—mostly abroad; many also have small funds available for the disabled and disadvantaged in their immediate midst, and few indeed would turn down the subsistence requests of the needy at their doorstep. Yet it is the rare congregation that has a major program up and running on a large-scale basis. Rarer still are those that enter into a cooperative arrangement with local government to extend the program at the risk of losing some control over it. Poor neighborhoods are often more likely to find assistance from affluent congregations across town than from the congregations in their own vicinity, unless those congregations are filled with members who drive in from wealthier precincts. This is partly because many congregations are not tightly bound to their own neighborhoods and depend heavily on members who have moved elsewhere but return for Sunday services. The commonly reported exception in other studies as well as our own is the Black Church. Many African American congregations have long-standing service and political responsibilities in their neighborhoods, and they are on record as the group most interested in exploring government partnerships to further their efforts.

Many procedural, constitutional questions about faith-based reforms remain, as do questions about congregations' efficacy as government contractors and organized service providers (their own considerable, if sometimes ad hoc, service provision is never in question). But if we can see these reforms in the context of religious and social multicentering, if we can recognize their relationship to changes both in cultural ideas about religion and about the structural changes in religious organizations themselves, then perhaps we can make better sense of what seems, at times, an intractable problem.

Pluralism

Ideas about church and state, or about individualism and community, seem at times to percolate at a high level of abstraction. But here as elsewhere, religious practice goes on at the very local level. And at that local level, multicenteredness is the norm. It is just one more way of acknowledging cultural pluralism. Indianapolis is not, in the end, a melting pot, any more than America as a nation is.

Viewed through the lens of contemporary American society, Indianapolis may look relatively homogeneous, and pluralism may seem correspondingly less important. After all, about three-quarters of the city's residents — and about 90 percent of those in the whole metropolitan area — are white. The huge majority are culturally Christian. From a broad enough perspective, that looks like homogeneity. But Indianapolis has always had its own, less dramatic, pluralism, as meaningful to its residents as any more dramatic variety. Indianapolis has long been home to Protestant, Catholic, and Jew. It has never been dominated by one ethnic group. It was once much more strongly shaped by one religious tradition, but never to the total exclusion of the others.

This pluralism grew steadily throughout the twentieth century. Indianapolis itself has a small yet growing Muslim community anchored by the headquarters of the Islamic Society of North America. It has modest numbers of Sikhs and Buddhists. At the beginning of the twenty-first century, it is experiencing rapid growth among Hispanic immigrants, many of whom are Catholic. Indeed, after leveling off during the 1970s, 1980s, and 1990s, the number of Catholics is growing again. Indianapolis could yet come to look more like other midwestern cities in which Catholics constitute a majority, though this is unlikely to happen soon.

This reading of Indianapolis fits well with assumption of pluralism that has become a master concept in the contemporary sociology of religion. Half a century ago, professional sociologists of religion invoked "sacred canopies," to use Peter Berger's famous term, when considering religion's social role. They considered the impact of religious ideas on the whole of culture. They looked for ways that religion influenced the social construction of meaning and public order. Robert Bellah considered "civil religion"[8] and Will Herberg described Protestant, Catholic, and Jew as three ways of being American.[9]

Today, talk about sacred canopies, denominations, and deviance is out of vogue. If there is any discussion of truly overarching civil religion, it centers more on religious abstraction, invoking patriotism, politics, or the totemic significance of sports teams more than what we used to call religion. The emphasis in the study of religion, traditionally understood, has shifted to the plurality of belief and practice. Some faith groups are understood as older and more established, while others are "new religious movements," but there is less discussion about where these fit in some overarching, prevailing culture. The energy in the social study of religion surrounds ethnographies and case studies of small groups, often of religious congregations. Nancy Ammerman et al.'s *Congregation and Community*,[10] Robert Wuthnow's *I Come Away Stronger*,[11] and R. Stephen Warner's *New Wine in Old Wineskins*[12] exemplify the trend.

Warner summed up this shift in his "Work in Progress toward a New Paradigm for the Sociological Study of Religion in the United States."[13] As the abstract states, "a new paradigm is emerging in that field, the crux of which is that organized religion thrives in the United States in an open market system, an observation anomalous to the older paradigm's monopoly concept." The new paradigm characterizes *Sacred Canopy*-ist Peter Berger as the bogeyman. Berger's "old paradigm" is said to have developed to describe "the European experience" where real *churches,* in the monopolistic, normative sense that Troeltsch used, were one with the dominant culture and everything else was either sectarian deviance or individual mysticism by comparison. The old paradigm more accurately described Catholicism in Italy or Anglicanism in England. The new paradigm, by contrast, draws from the unique character of American history. Religion is best described not as a property that applies to society as a whole, at least not to highly pluralistic American society, but as particular practices and ideas belonging to specific subcultures.

American religion is, on this reading, distinctly pluralistic and competitive. A number of scholars — Roger Finke, Rodney Stark, and Laurence Iannaccone[14] among them — developed elaborate market descriptions of American religion but, as Warner says, that is not the crux of the matter. The axis on which the new paradigm turns is an understanding of *disestablishment* as the central feature of American religion, a realization that pluralism and competition and even marketing are the norm, not deviations from a given, dominant culture that require elaborate explanation. In Warner's new paradigm, the master function of religion is the provision of "social space for cultural pluralism." Structurally, religion is infinitely adaptive as it empowers both groups and the individuals within them.

The story we have told about Indianapolis both acknowledges and challenges certain elements in this intellectual trend toward pluralism and disestablishment as dominant metaphors. On the one hand, there can be little question that our concept of *multicentering* fits well with both pluralism and disestablishment as explanations for religious change. Religion really *has* created the social space for pluralism in Indianapolis. But to the degree that new paradigm thinkers discount the existence of a real establishment, or insist on seeing its decline as relevant only to specific elites, then our story calls theirs into question. From 1820 to the present, Indianapolis has had a real religious establishment linked to political and economic power. Although pluralism always existed in the city, it was shaped, even defined, by the establishment's role. Put another way, Indianapolis had a very real "sacred canopy" that defined urban culture for everyone, even if different people viewed that canopy from different perspectives. To refuse to see the city's culture prominently formed by this elite force, to suggest that decentering only matters from one group's point of view, is to misinterpret historical reality. Therefore, we happily acknowledge our indebtedness to an evolving discussion about religious pluralism, but respectfully disagree with certain pronouncements about secularization, to which we now turn.

Secularization

Just a few generations ago, scholars — especially sociologists — thought religion's influence would recede as rational, scientific worldviews explained more and more of the world. Today, many are arguing that secularization never happened, that contemporary society is just as religious as it ever was.

The story we have told here clearly establishes religion's ongoing vitality. Not only are individuals still religious — very possibly at about the same rate they ever were — but religion continues to have important public effects. Many of the city's hospitals have religious roots. The parochial schools continue to work in concert with public schools to provide universal education. Many of the city's social service agencies have either religious roots, current religious affiliation, or both. Even more to the point, individuals of faith bring their values and beliefs to the table when they lead and participate in an unlimited range of civic activities. Their *character*, and thus the character of the organizations they compose, is shaped by their faith commitments.

Despite these many public religious influences, however, the fact remains that many *specific* religious practices have receded from Indianapolis's civic center and that religion has thus ceded some of its public authority. Religion is still vital in many ways, but changes in religion's social role are clear evidence of *secularization* properly defined, as for instance when sociologist Mark Chaves[15] defined it as "declining religious authority."

The current argument among scholars and practitioners about whether American religion is experiencing secularization is stoked by certain historical mischaracterizations. Secularization's detractors sometimes inflate the concept so that it refers to the transition between a past era when religion was all-powerful and an approaching era when religion will completely disappear. But neither the beginning nor the end of that scenario is historically realistic. Hence the popular conclusion that secularization cannot exist unless both of these fanciful eras also exist does a disservice to more nuanced explanations that clearly operate between these poles. Religious expression obviously experiences changes, even losses, far short of death. At the same time, society may also experience occasional "sacralization" that occurs when new forms of the sacred develop in response to changing circumstances. These may involve whole new religious systems imported from elsewhere; they may also involve processes by which once ordinary or secular aspects of life take on sacred significance under changing circumstances.

While it may seem that multicentering is always secularizing in its consequences, it actually provides conditions favoring both secularization and sacralization in different ways. As religion's older, more traditionally centered, influence is pulled apart and scattered by decentering social processes at work, the results can involve both bad and good news for religion overall. Fragmentation and differentiation can leave older institutions exposed to secularizing influences. But at the same time, some of the newer configurations of faith communities that result from these divisions have an opportunity to define or redefine their own beliefs and practices in a way that assures greater sacred significance. Each newly developing religious community is given greater latitude to shape its own religious program in response to its own particular needs — whether these are defined for example by ethnicity, gender, or social class. Thus, the religious change involved in multicentering involves gains and losses. Some changes in the public role of religion and must be viewed as secularization; others may actually increase religious commitment of a more local, decentered type.

In the "new paradigm" for religion described above, Warner and others have challenged the very notion of secularization by saying that America never had a true religious establishment, or a true sacred canopy, to be "secularized." Religion, in this account, was always creating the "social space for pluralism." We fully agree that religion both defines and is defined by pluralism. In Indianapolis, religion is both cause and consequence of the development of multiple social centers, and the city has been home to many religious traditions since its founding. *But it is simply wrong* to think that those traditions have existed side by side as separate equals, to imagine that the city did not have a de facto religious establishment, even if that establishment was not codified in law as it was in Old World Europe. Indianapolis evolved as the city it is today because of the mainline Protestant linkage among its political and economic elites. From the original churches on the Circle to the role played by the Lilly Endowment to the mayors from Second Presbyterian, Indianapolis had a de facto religious establishment that still plays a formative role in the city. Gradually, over time, the pluralism of religious traditions that had always existed in an officially disestablished city gained a stronger voice. Gradually, the city's central symbols and even its central landscape came to reflect that pluralism by decreasing the role of mainline Protestants in defining the city center.

Civil Religion

When those mainline Protestants held sway, their version of Christianity served as the civil religion that shaped the entire metropolitan community. Even though others — Catholics Jews, sectarian groups — may not have agreed with the establishment, their activities were defined over against that establishment and often circumscribed by it. Today, a different, less explicitly religious, set of symbols and ideas dominate Indianapolis's public square. As we have argued repeatedly, patriotism, government, commerce, and sport now serve as the foundation for metropolitan identity.

As we conclude our conceptual analysis, it is worth considering how Indianapolis's evolving civil religion fits with America's own self-perception. Decades ago Robert Bellah described an American civil religion of patriotism and nationalism.[16] In a later analysis that more clearly foreshadows our multicenteredness, Robert Wuthnow[17] argued that there are now actually *two* civil religions in America — one conservative and other liberal; the first expressed by the Pledge of Allegiance's phrase "one nation under God," and the second conveyed by the words that follow, "with liberty and justice for all." Although both of these new civil religions are centered in their own right, there is no longer a single religious center for the nation as a whole. In fact, having two civil religions raises the question of whether we have a civil religion at all, since the whole point is to gather the country in a single cultural embrace. Under these multicentered conditions, the nation's civil religious core may be giving way to a more secular "religion of the civil." This involves a doctrine that reaches out to every citizen and is sacred if not religious. It is anchored in the democratic faith expressed in the U.S. Constitution and other founding texts.[18]

Certainly these changes and ambiguities in the national civil religion fit the story we have told about Indianapolis, the story of *civic* religion at the community level. As we have shown, the city's symbolic sense of itself as a unified whole has undergone a series of transformations over the years in both content and cohesion. The shift from a centering religious consensus to a series of multicentered alternative gatherings has transformed the city's original core. Lives have moved from the center to the periphery as suburbanization and economic sprawl have produced both gains and losses. For many members of the city's elite, a center not holding is a problem to be solved. But for many residents of the area's many neighborhoods and municipalities, a multicentered life has its own compensations for being closely attuned to local issues and local needs. At the same time, cities like Indianapolis also have their own versions of civil religion that support both the good life and the common good.

We have no special stake in the nomenclature and no wish to debate the definition of the terms "civil" or "religion." But it is clear enough that a mixture of patriotism, commerce, politics, and sport are what identify Indianapolis in the minds of its citizens and in the minds of outsiders as well. When people throughout the state think of Indianapolis, they think of the home office of statewide businesses, as the seat of state government, and as the location of our pro sports teams. Visitors from outside the state and even outside the U.S. think first of the Indianapolis 500.

Although we have argued consistently that specific, traditional religion flourished in the many centers yet gave way to more generalized values in the one center, we should not lose sight of the fact that the faith traditions themselves have not necessarily voluntarily conceded that central influence. Mainline Protestants have, in one sense, been forced to acknowledge their role as one tradition among many. Catholics and Jews have good reason to welcome an acknowledgment of pluralism in Indianapolis and a broadening of civic values. But biblically conservative Christians — those most commonly referred to as "evangelical" — are the least likely to be happy with a generalization, and inevitable secularization, of *shared* social values.

Is there room, then, for a conservative Christian revolution in Indianapolis capable of changing the relationship between the one and the many centers? It is still too early to judge, but two facts merit our ongoing attention. First, religious growth is now paced by customer service congregations that are frequently biblically conservative. Second, the city's civic identification with patriotism provides a fertile seedbed for other kinds of conservative, pro-American ideas. Patriotism as a shared value may be more readily accessible to all of the population than more specific religious values, but it plays better in some religious venues than others. The tighter the identification of religion and patriotism, the greater the chances for a shift in the multicentered character of modern urban culture, at least in cities like Indianapolis.

There are good reasons to think that the shift from establishment Protestantism to other, more general, symbols and values offered several long-term benefits to the city. Throughout the twentieth century, Catholics and Jews moved closer and closer to the city's cultural core, not least through a common commitment to defeat Nazism in World War II and a shared anti-communist sentiment thereafter. The fact that the city's symbols could be shared by these groups, and the related recognition that what joined people was qualitatively different from what separated them, made it possible for the many and the one to coexist. Whether this system will make it easier for new religious groups such as Muslims, Sikhs, and Hindus to maintain their own identities and to become part of the unified metropolis remains to be seen, but Indianapolis has consistently applied an inward pressure that emphasizes shared values and resists balkanization.

Congregational Studies

Another benefit of our multicentered approach both to urban environments and to religious practice within them is that it puts the rise of congregational studies as an academic field into better perspective. Over the past couple of decades, students of religion have spent much more time observing specific religious groups and correspondingly less time studying religion as a system of action or belief.

Some of the reasons for the change follow from trends we have already discussed. For instance, the focus on pluralism embodied in the "new paradigm" point toward the many individual instances of religion and away from overarching sacred canopies. Interest in social capital, and in the organizations that create and sustain it, also resonated with a developing interest in congregations. A third intellectual trend joined these when organizational studies, already important in schools of business or public affairs, made its way gradually into the field of religion. A developing interest in congregations recognized advantages in borrowing arrows from the organizational studies quiver. Terms like "institutional isomorphism" and "resource mobilization" began dribbling into the vocabulary of those whose primary interest was religion. Perhaps most importantly, the emerging field of "non-profit studies" began to blur over into the sociology of religion, and vice versa. Congregations were considered alongside those other institutions of civil society such as charities, social service organizations, and service fraternities. Congregations began, at least in some circles, to be seen as "neighborhood-based groups."

Paul Dimaggio, Carl Milofsky, and Walter Powell, among others, argued that a place — a neighborhood — could be understood as an ecology of organizations. Congregations played an important role, but one that was dependent on other factors in the environment.

One of the strongest links between the developing field of non-profit organizational analysis and the sociology of religion was through the Program on Non-Profit Organizations (PONPO) at Yale University. That linkage jelled in the publication of *Sacred Companies: Organizational Aspects of Religion and Religious Aspects of Organizations* (1998). In that book, Demerath et al. brought together organizational theorists to challenge the notion that religious organizations and religious expression needed to be treated as unique.

> A common theme throughout this literature involves the singularity of the religious experience and the organizations that serve it. Rarely are other societal spheres or sectors invoked for congenial or instructive compari-

sons. For some, even admitting the presence of a secular dimension to the sacred experience is akin to profanation. Rather than treat religious organizations as sharing some basic characteristics with all organizations, there is a tendency to treat them more as the exception than as the rule. (vii)

By the late 1990s, students of congregations such as Nancy Ammerman, Penny Edgell, and Nancy Eiesland were not only working within the new paradigm, emphasizing pluralism over sacred canopies, but they were doing organizational studies. Ammerman's conclusion to *Congregation and Community* makes clear her debt to the field.

> The metaphor of ecology has been helpful here. . . . We can think about the community in which a congregation is lodged as an ecology of resources and organizations in which people seek out social support for everything from the most basic survival needs to sociability, aesthetic pleasure, meaning making, and community improvement. . . . We should pay attention then, not so much to the decline of any given social organization but to the whole inventory of organizations and the available social capital that may lie dormant outside officially organized structures. (Ammerman et al., 346–47)

Here the competitive, interactive, particular notions embodied in the new paradigm, the structural elements of organizational studies, and the cultural interest in social capital were drawn together. The confluence of these intellectual streams meant a major shift toward thinking of religious practice as embodied in local organizations which were themselves embedded in particular places.

Our analysis has obviously also been shaped by these converging trends. We see religious organizations as constituent pieces of a much larger urban ecology and think of their activities not only in terms of theological ideas or even in terms of their member's demographic characteristics, but in a larger context of urban realignment. The same intellectual forces that continue to push analysis of religious practice down to the local, grass-roots level have caused us to focus on the particular communities created by outward urban forces, though we have tried never to lose sight of the inward forces aiming to create a unified metropolitan community. Any analysis that sees only the congregations and their members, somehow ignoring religion's wider social influence, truly cannot see the forest for the trees.

It bears noting at this point that congregational studies did not simply evolve organically from the happy confluence of related intellectual streams. The field was constructed very deliberately with the support of the Lilly Endowment. Many of the intellectuals named here in each of the streams, especially those writing in the last twenty years, received Endowment support for their work. Beyond their intellectual efforts, though, the Endowment helped develop the field of practical congregational consulting, populated by those who had one foot in the academic world but the other in the world of religious practice. People like Loren Mead, founder of the Alban Institute, and Carl Dudley of Hartford Seminary bridged the gap between academia and religious practice. *The Congregational Studies Handbook* and its sequel, *Studying Congregations*,[19] were written by intellectuals who shared academic interests, but they were funded by the very practical interests of the Endowment. The present volume stands in that same tradition.

So the same family foundation that supported the mainline Protestant establishment in Indianapolis, and that now supports the daily life of the city's many congregations, was crucial to the national development of the academic field that studies it. In 2000, the Religion Division of the Lilly Endowment spent $141.5 million on religion and approved another $140.9 million. In 1999, it spent $104 million on American religion and approved a further $88 million. In 1998 it spent $89 million and approved $101 million. In 1997 it paid $66 million and approved $50 million.[20] (Money approved in any given year may be paid out over the multiple years of any program's life, making a direct year-to-year correlation impossible.) These are large sums. Although they were not all earmarked for the study of congregations, they helped shape the academic field enormously, both in terms of what kinds of research were possible, but also in terms of what graduate students might consider worthwhile.

But the Lilly Endowment is clear—clearer just now than in past years— that they do not fund research for its own sake. The Endowment's primary objective is "to deepen and enrich the religious lives of American Christians, primarily by helping to strengthen their churches." Further, it wishes "to strengthen the contributions that religious ideas, practices, values, and institutions make to the common good of our society."[21] Thus they spend their money in the interest of improving religious life in America and of building better organizations and institutions, especially in the churches of the old liberal establishment. Catholics came to be included about fifteen years ago, but the liberal mainline still dominates Endowment grant-making, and its staff and board members are drawn from those groups, all tied to the powerful Protestant establishment in Indianapolis.

There is no need to suggest that any scholar's findings or judgment is swayed by the Endowment's influence. But it would be folly to think that the research subjects chosen and the methods employed were not shaped by the Endowment's pragmatic approach, oriented as it is toward the goal of enhancing and improving American congregational life. Scholars and dissertation students are often keen to make sure that their research results in something that will be useful and beneficial for people of faith and their congregations. Without practical, applied consequences, there will not be any money.

It would be wrong to suggest that any amount of intellectual activity, or even the money invested in it, contributed very much to the rising profile of congregations as the pre-eminent form of American religious organizations. But at the confluence of these intellectual streams highlights the stark recognition that congregations have, in fact, become the primary vehicle for religious community in America. There has been a seismic shift from top-down to bottom-up patterns of religious activity.

The rise of congregations did not occur, of course, inside a religious cocoon, but in the context of other important urban changes. In our terms, religious expression developed this multicentered organizational pattern in response to other urban changes. Our attempt to link the congregational ideal types of Chapter 5 to the neighborhood ideal types of Chapter 6 is intended to establish basic linkages between religious practice and urban place. We believe this provides a better frame of reference, and a better vocabulary, for thinking about contemporary religious change.

For instance, in recent years much has been made of an evangelical re-surgence.[22] The term "evangelical" remains useful for generalizing about a large group of American Christians who emphasize personal transformation and are biblically conservative, which is how we use the word ourselves in Chapter 4 and elsewhere. But taken down to the congregational level, "evangelical" fails to do justice to the variety of religious responses to urban realignment. Every one of our congregational types could, in some instances, fit under the "evangelical" umbrella. The conversion congregations are the most plainly evangelical, because their mission is driven by traditional evangelization, the goal of converting and recruiting strangers. But the cloister congregations emphasize personal transformation and biblical conservatism, both of which are usually offered as evangelical traits. Many congregations, especially those that have growth as a goal, emphasize customer service. The many megachurches and community churches that excel at customer service are generally classified as evangelical. Finally, community outreach is a common characteristic of many evangelicals. Theology cannot, in and of itself, tell us how congregations relate to their environments because religion is about doing, not just about thinking. Given the city's multiple social and cultural centers, we found it helpful to link dominant trends within religious "doing" to specific kinds of neighborhoods, regions, and districts within the city. This helps us use the different intellectual traditions from which we have drawn not only to think about religion in the city, but to think about what it has to do with urban culture and, ultimately, urban community.

Our idea of religious multicentering not only improves concepts like "evangelical" by contextualizing them in relationship to their specific environment, it gives us a way to think about other policies and strategies — both public and private — meant to improve the nature of urban community. Perhaps the most important implication, for civic leaders as well as religious ones, is that we must never underestimate differences among the various parts of the city in our attempts to understand or to enhance urban community. Even places that appear quite similar can house very different social arrangements, with religious organizations playing quite different roles.

The example of the Martindale-Brightwood and Mapleton–Fall Creek neighborhoods from Chapter 6 makes the point nicely. In the 1980s and early 1990s the neighborhoods looked very similar on paper, but the role of religious organizations within them was very different. The churches of Mapleton–Fall Creek—some of which were also mentioned in our discussion of the Meridian Street corridor—were where they were for specific historical reasons. This neighborhood was once in high demand; many of its houses are large and fancy. Several important institutions, including the Lilly Endowment, sit on its westward edge on Meridian Street. For other, equally concrete, historical reasons, the churches of Martindale-Brightwood were quite different. This neighborhood was the amalgam of two working-class neighborhoods, one white, the other black. Both Mapleton–Fall Creek and Martindale-Brightwood experienced white flight, but the whites who fled Martindale-Brightwood simply left their churches behind. The impressive limestone churches of Mapleton–Fall Creek were not so easily abandoned. Today, these churches offer their respective neighborhoods very different kinds of resources, one more oriented toward material capital, the other toward social capital.

Observers from outside the university often complain that academic research intentionally makes matters more complex. But is clear to us that a sufficiently complex understanding of the city, and of religious life within it, is required if we hope to understand a diverse urban community. Both the forces that drew people out to the suburbs and the forces that bring them back downtown shaped the neighborhoods in question. The specific public roles of the congregations within them are intimately related to differences in the social environment, including differences in their histories. To the degree that we can see the city as multicentered, we can make better decisions about what kinds of programs or organizations are most likely to be community assets in any given "center" of the city.

Big differences, like those between Carmel and Mars Hill, for instance, are easy enough to discern from a distance. But unless we are able to read the historical and cultural details of a place alongside the demographic statistics that tend to dominate social policy, we will never really understand the intersection of religion and community. Policy makers and church planners alike benefit when they consider the environmental context of religious activity.

A second, related implication of this multicentered understanding is that civic leaders, especially, must learn to appreciate variation among religious traditions and among the congregations within them. Too often, important religious differences are boiled down to difference in belief. Catholics believe this, Methodists believe that. Christians have this theology, Jews have that one. Our point is not that theological difference is insignificant, but that other kinds of difference are usually more important to understanding religion's social role, even when those differences have theological roots.

Differences in polity, for instance, are crucial. Congregations that exist within recognized, established hierarchies, in religious organizations often referred to as "episcopal," are different from those that make all decisions locally, usually referred to as "congregational." When the mayor's office or a philanthropic foundation seeks to encourage religious involvement, knowing whom to talk to and what to talk about can hinge on appreciating that distinction.

But our framework points to other differences that go far beyond these large, structural ones. The degree to which congregations are likely to be active civic participants depends both on their own, internal sense of mission *and* on the environment that surrounds them. Although it would not be necessary, or even possible, for civic and philanthropic leaders to place every congregation squarely in a pigeonhole marked "community outreach" or "customer service," it would behoove any such leader to understand those different tendencies and the history, ideas, and practices that lie behind them. Anyone hoping to increase the overlap between civic ideals and religious ones — as contemporary faith-based welfare reformers do — must have a sufficiently complex, nuanced view of just what those religious ideas are and how they fit into the larger urban context.

Attempts in the mid-1990s by various civic, secular organizations in Indianapolis to contract with congregations to provide social services bear this out. Seen from a distance, the facts were simple: relatively few congregations took up the offer to apply for these funds and many of those who did found the administration burdensome. But closer to the ground, other differences emerged. African American congregations were much more likely to apply for external funding. The community outreach congregations of the Protestant mainline were very unlikely to apply, though they were by far the *most* likely to get involved in other voluntary efforts like Faith and Families or the Interfaith Housing Network. A few white conversion congregations applied for government or United Way funding, but conversion congregations — white or black — did not join the voluntary networks. The large, independent customer service congregations were unlikely to participate in either kind of venture, although most sponsored their own missions that sometimes worked with partners of their choosing. Not surprisingly, the cloister congregations were not in the loop at all.

This is the kind of difference that matters when thinking about religion and community in its urban context. The concept of multicentering, by itself, does not provide all the details for every case. Civic and religious leaders in cities across the country will have to supply those details for themselves. But it is important to have a sound conceptual framework in which context-specific information makes best sense and is most useful.

This means that all of us must assume a different posture toward the idea of religious gain or loss when we think about changes in the city. In meetings from the mayor's office to local neighborhood block groups, people ask, "How can we get the churches more involved?" From time to time people lament what they interpret as the loss of a more powerful public role for churches. "Whatever happened to Easter sunrise services on the Circle?" they might ask, or "Where are the churches of the civil rights movement?"

Our view, as by now is obvious, is that churches, synagogues, and mosques are deeply involved in a whole range of public activities, but that the range of these has changed through the years. It is true that religious leaders are less likely to be prominent public figures unless, as in the case of former mayor and former Second Presbyterian pastor William Hudnut, they actually run for office. Sermons are not usually printed in the newspaper today. In Indianapolis, neither the archbishop nor prominent conservative Protestant clergy make loud public pronouncements about abortion or school prayer. Even African American leaders who double as political leaders maintain relatively low public profiles except in times of civil rights crisis.

But congregations are involved in a wide range of community-building and community-serving activities out in the multiple centers of the city. And those congregations' members still take part in the civic life of the larger community defined by its downtown center. Religion is an integral part of community life, but its activities and its effects are diffuse. This diffusion means a *loss* of religious influence at the center, but no such loss is apparent in the many other centers. There may even be a corresponding religious *gain*, as many religious traditions share a more roughly equal relationship to the civic center.

All of this suggests that we must also assume a different posture toward the idea of "community" itself. Undoubtedly the city has experienced the loss of some sorts of community, but these too are offset by gains in other kinds because, in the end, Indianapolis is composed of multiple communities. Whether the net effect is positive or negative depends on what kind of community *you* think is most important and what relationship *you* think religion should bear to it. If community is about the bonds that link everyone in the city, and indeed everyone in the society, then there have been significant changes linked to increasing pluralism. Traditional religion, insofar as it is about specific texts and beliefs, necessarily plays a diluted, or at least muted, role. If community is about many smaller, overlapping groups that together make up the urban mosaic, then religion plays a vital role.

This bilevel understanding of religion and community also applies to social capital. Indianapolis is awash in social capital, formed through shared interests linked to social class, neighborhood geography, ethnicity, and religion. But the many kinds of social capital do not always overlap nor are they always oriented toward greater *overall* social cooperation. Beliefs, practices, and interests that bind one ethnic group, one neighborhood, one congregation, or one religious tradition are often the very things that separate these groups — both consciously and unconsciously — from others. Strong social capital in one community may mean weaker social capital for the city as a whole.

When a neighborhood works hard to establish its identity and to build internal cohesion, it usually begins by defining who is in and who is out. Strong "neighborhood watch" groups build internal trust and communication, but they are also invested in identifying, and usually excluding, those who are unfamiliar. The same principle applies to religious groups. Emphasizing uniqueness in a way that builds trust among members, and perhaps even between members and local residents, may also generate distrust of strangers and foreigners. This need not be a zero-sum game. What is good for the many need not be bad for the one, or vice versa. But it is wrong to assume that "community," "religion," or "social capital" are monolithic and that gains or losses can easily be aggregated.

The social situation we have described is neither fixed nor immutable. Whether the many religious traditions will continue to thrive in many local centers remains to be seen, though all available evidence portends their ongoing strength. The past century suggests that some groups will wax while others wane, not least because of the fit, or lack thereof, between their organizational missions and the environment to which they respond. Neither is it a foregone conclusion that specific religious values rooted in specific traditions can never again play leading roles in the public square. Indianapolis's metropolitan core is not values-free. If one tradition can lay special claim to the mix of patriotism, commerce, and government that animates it, that tradition could emerge as the new establishment. The new Christian right has been relatively muted in Indianapolis, but future social circumstances are impossible to predict. Similarly, other kinds of demographic changes created by inward or outward migration could tilt the table toward a different tradition. After thirty years of stability, the number of Catholics in the city is rising again, due in part to recent Hispanic in-migration. Who can say what the next several decades hold?

It is possible, of course, that our story of Indianapolis is unique. After all, Indianapolis has never experienced the overwhelming racial and ethnic and religious pluralism experienced by New York, Chicago, or Los Angeles. No other city has a Lilly Endowment to mold its Protestant heritage or to reinforce metropolitan identity through strategic downtown development. Maybe this story of religion's changing role in the city is idiosyncratic.

Not surprisingly, though, we do not think so. It is not difficult to see America as multicentered. How many times, for instance, do we hear that the "melting pot" metaphor has given way to the "salad bowl" or to some similar new catchphrase meant to suggest that the pieces exist side by side and work together without being fully identified with one another through complete assimilation. Protestant, Catholic, and Jew are still three ways of being American;[23] so are black, white, and Hispanic. Each of these groups separately, and all of them together, seek to define their common citizenship in ways that emphasize both their special, particular interests and their common, overlapping ones.

Anyone who believes that America was not shaped by an elite cultural core of its own is willfully ignoring the historical facts. From presidents to U.S. senators to Supreme Court justices to corporate CEOs, white males from the mainline Protestant traditions have wielded enormously disproportionate cultural power in defining what it means to be American. The symbols and rituals of that Protestant establishment have infused our nation just as they infused Indianapolis.

But anyone who has not seen that situation begin to change since the mid-twentieth century is just as willfully ignoring contemporary reality. The many centers of American life — separated by gender, race, ethnicity, social class, and religion — each now speak with stronger voices of their own. And, of course, the centers overlap in a multitude of ways, not in neat, concentric circles. No one is only defined by any one of these characteristics, but by very particular combinations thereof.

The question is not whether these disparate pieces can all be gradually "melted" into one unified culture, or whether there is a traditionally religious "sacred canopy" capable of covering them all. The question is whether the "many" can define what they have in common as the "one" in ways that make cooperation and progress possible amidst obvious difference.

The story of Indianapolis offers grounds for cautious optimism. True, there are still significant divisions among races, ethnic groups, and socio-economic classes in the city. The inner city and suburbs are still worlds apart in many ways. And it is not clear whether everyone is content to live with a common center that is more religiously neutral. Christian conservatives may continue to insist that their values deserve greater attention; members of religions outside the Judeo-Christian tradition may find the common values at the city's core less neutral, even more hostile, than they would like. But Indianapolis seems to have found a way to acknowledge both common citizenship and important cultural differences. It is consciously managing the tension between the outward and inward forces shaping the city.

Neither in Indianapolis nor in the broader United States is religion *the* single key to understanding changes in our shared identity. Religious ideas by themselves, separated from other contextual, environmental variables, cannot even fully explain changes in religious responses as our culture races to catch up to a society that has been structurally multicentered for some time. But religion is one important variable that helps us think more creatively about what it means to live in community. It is impossible to see something as ephemeral as "culture" change, but in religion we can see those changes embodied and personified. In observing the interplay between religion and urban culture, we get a glimpse of the tensions that animate our pluralism, and understand that we live our lives both in community and in communities.

NOTES

1. INTRODUCTION

1. Stephen Goldsmith, "Providing Social Services: The Role of Church and Synagogue," speech to the Columbia School of Law, March 12, 1998.

2. Robert Putnam, *Bowling Alone: The Collapse and Revival of American Community* (New York: Simon and Schuster, 2000).

3. Nancy T. Ammerman, "Bowling Together: Congregations and the American Civic Order," University Lecture in Religion, Arizona State University, 1996.

4. Mark Chaves, "Secularization as Declining Religious Authority," *Social Forces* 72, no. 3 (March 1994): 749–74.

5. John Kretzmann and John McKnight, *Building Communities from the Inside Out: A Path toward Finding and Mobilizing Community Assets* (Chicago: ACTA Publications, 1997).

6. For more information, see the brief methodological appendix or view both methodological information and the data itself at: www.thepoliscenter.iupui.edu.

7. Robert and Helen Lynd, *Middletown: A Study in Modern American Culture* (New York: Harcourt, Brace, Jovanovich, 1929); idem, *Middletown in Transition* (New York: Harcourt, Brace, Jovanovich, 1935). For the experience of yet another Hoosier city, see James Lewis, *The Protestant Experience in Gary, Indiana, 1906–1975* (Knoxville: University of Tennessee Press, 1992).

8. Robert Orsi, ed., *Gods of the City: Religion and the American Urban Landscape* (Bloomington: Indiana University Press, 1999). Other urban religion books that shaped our thinking include Harvey Cox, *The Secular City* (New York: Macmillan, 1965); idem, *Religion in the Secular City* (New York: Simon and Schuster, 1984); and, more recently, Lowell Livezey, ed., *Public Religion and Urban Transformation* (New York: NYU Press, 2000).

9. Martin Bradley et al., *Churches and Church Membership in the U.S. 1990: An Enumeration by Region, State and County Based on Data Reported for 133 Church Groupings* (Atlanta, Ga.: Glenmary Research Center, 1992).

2. THE CIRCLE CITY ON THE PLAINS

1. Post-War Planning Committee, *The Post War Plan for Indianapolis* (Indianapolis, Ind.: Post-War Planning Committee, 1944), p. 12.

2. Robert Fishman, "Megalopolis Unbound: America's New City," *Wilson Quarterly* 16 (Winter 1990): 24–45.

3. Charles Leven, "Distance, Space, and the Organisation of Urban Life," *Urban Studies* 28 (1991): 319–25.

4. Kevin Lynch, *The Image of a City* (Cambridge, Mass.: MIT Press, 1960).

5. Seminal articles that influenced our understanding of urban alignment include Louis Wirth's classic "Urbanism as a Way of Life," *American Journal of Sociology* 44 (1938): 3–24, and Claude Fischer's "Ambivalent Communities: How Americans Understand Their Localities," in Alan Wolfe, ed., *America at Century's End* (Berkeley and Los Angeles: University of California Press, 1991).

6. David Bodenhamer and Robert Barrows, *Encyclopedia of Indianapolis* (Bloomington: Indiana University Press, 1994), Appendix 3, Table 36.

7. "Consumer Analysis of the Indianapolis Metropolitan Market" (Indianapolis: Indianapolis Newspapers, 1957), 19.

8. Homer Hoyt Associates, "Market Survey of the Meadows, 38th and Rural Streets, Indianapolis, Indiana, for Leo A. Lippman" (New York: Homer Hoyt Associates, September 1952), 2–3, 6.

9. Richard Hebert, *Highways to Nowhere: The Politics of City Transportation* (New York: Bobbs-Merrill Co., 1972).

10. Lizabeth Cohen, *Making a New Deal: Industrial Workers in Chicago, 1919–1939* (Cambridge: Cambridge University Press, 1990).

11. "Gregory & Appel, Inc.," *Bank Notes* 7 (December 1952): 4.

12. *Indianapolis News*, July 11, 1941.

13. Bureau of the Census, Table 27: Composition of the Rural-Farm Population, by Counties: 1940; Table 49: Characteristics of the Rural-Farm Population, for Counties: 1950.

14. *Indianapolis Star Magazine*, December 29, 1957.

15. *Indianapolis Star*, March 10, 1940.

16. *Indianapolis Times*, March 25, 1962.

17. Jon Teaford, *City and Suburb: The Political Fragmentation of Metropolitan America, 1850–1970* (Baltimore, Md.: Johns Hopkins University Press, 1979).

18. *Indianapolis Star*, November 24, 1968.

19. *Indianapolis Star*, November 28, 1968; December 29, 1968.

20. William Blomquist, "Unigov and Political Participation," in Bodenhamer and Barrows, *Encyclopedia of Indianapolis*, 1355–58.

21. "Indianapolis for Journalists: Unigov," http://www.indy.org/unigov.htm (accessed April 8, 1998); William Hudnut, *Indianapolis: Past, Present and Future* (Philadelphia: Newcomen Society, 1986).

22. Blomquist, "Unigov and Political Participation."

23. Randy Roberts, "Sports," in Bodenhamer and Barrows, *Encyclopedia of Indianapolis*, 182–88.

3. RELIGIOUS CIVILITY, CIVIL RELIGION

1. *Indianapolis News,* June 12, 1915.

2. *Indianapolis Star,* August 14, 1990.

3. David O'Brien, *Public Catholicism* (New York: Macmillan, 1989), 2.

4. Carl Smith, *Disorder and the Shape of Belief: The Great Chicago Fire, the Haymarket Bomb, and the Model Town of Pullman* (Chicago: University of Chicago Press, 1995).

5. David Bodenhamer and Robert Barrows, *Encyclopedia of Indianapolis* (Bloomington: Indiana University Press, 1994), 55.

6. *Indianapolis News,* January 4, 1916.

7. Bodenhamer and Barrows, *Encyclopedia of Indianapolis,* 1310.

8. *Indianapolis Star,* February 24, 1911.

9. *Indianapolis News,* February 23, 1912.

10. *Indianapolis Star,* January 1, 1910.

11. For a history of the Church Federation, see Edwin Becker, *From Sovereign to Servant: The Church Federation of Greater Indianapolis, 1912–1987* (Indianapolis, Ind.: Church Federation of Greater Indianapolis, 1987).

12. *Indianapolis News,* June 12, 1915.

13. *Indianapolis News,* October 9, 1914.

14. Ruth Crocker, *Social Work and Social Order: The Settlement Movement in Two Industrial Cities, 1889–1930* (Urbana: University of Illinois Press, 1992).

15. Bodenhamer and Barrows, *Encyclopedia of Indianapolis,* 879.

16. Leonard Moore, *Citizen Klansmen: The Ku Klux Klan in Indiana, 1921–1928* (Chapel Hill: University of North Carolina Press, 1991).

17. Deborah Markisohn, "Ministers of the Klan: Indianapolis Clergy Involvement with the 1920s Ku Klux Klan" (M.A. thesis, Indiana University, 1992), 28.

18. Ibid., 45–46.

19. Bodenhamer and Barrows, *Encyclopedia of Indianapolis,* 801.

20. Mary Ryan, "The American Parade: Representations of the Nineteenth Century Social Order," in Raymond Mohl, ed., *The Making of Urban America* (Wilmington, Del.: Scholarly Research, 1997), 74.

21. David Vanderstel, "A City of Churches: The Development and Role of Religious Institutions in Indianapolis, 1905–1926" (unpublished manuscript, 2001), 62.

22. Ibid., 69.

23. *Indiana Catholic and Record,* December 8, 1916.

24. Sister Angela Horan, *The Story of Old St. John's: A Parish Rooted in Pioneer Indianapolis* (Indianapolis, Ind.: Litho Press, 1971), 113–28.

25. James Divita, *Slaves to No One: A History of the Holy Trinity Catholic Congregation in Indianapolis in the Diamond Jubilee of the Founding of Holy Trinity Parish* (Indianapolis, Ind.: Holy Trinity Parish; Ethnic History Project of the Indiana Historical Society, 1981), 20–21.

26. Ibid., 24.

27. *Indiana Catholic and Record,* June 30, 1911.

28. Becker, *From Sovereign to Servant,* 51.

29. Ibid.

30. *Weekly Religious Education in Indianapolis: A Manual of Policy and Procedures by Member Denominations* (Weekly Religious Education Association, 1960), p. iv.

31. *Indianapolis Star,* October 31, 1954.
32. *Indianapolis Star,* March 10, 1948.
33. *Indianapolis Star,* October 31, 1954.
34. *Indianapolis Times,* February 17, 1949.
35. Becker, *From Sovereign to Servant,* 46.
36. Marian Towne, *That All May Be One: Centennial History of Church Women United in Indianapolis, 1898–1998* (Indianapolis, Ind.: Church Women United in Indianapolis, 1998), 92.
37. Ibid., 93.
38. *Indianapolis News,* May 6, 1963. Cited in Becker, *From Sovereign to Servant,* 96–97.
39. Becker, *From Sovereign to Servant,* 96.
40. *Indianapolis News,* May 6, 1963. Cited in Becker, *From Sovereign to Servant,* 96–97.
41. Towne, *That All May Be One,* 99.
42. Becker, *From Sovereign to Servant,* 104.
43. William McLoughlin, "Faith," *American Quarterly* 35 (Spring–Summer 1983): 102.
44. *Indianapolis Star,* March 29, 1981.
45. Ibid.
46. Ibid.
47. Quoted in Michael Katz, *In the Shadow of the Poorhouse: A Social History of Welfare in America* (New York: Basic Books, 1996), 330.
48. Arthur Farnsley, *Rising Expectations: Urban Congregations, Welfare Reform, and Civic Life* (Bloomington: Indiana University Press, 2003).
49. Stanley Carlson-Theis, *A Guide to Charitable Choice* (Washington, D.C.: Center for Public Justice, 1997).
50. Arthur Farnsley, *Ten Good Questions about Faith-Based Partnerships and Welfare Reform* (Indianapolis, Ind.: The Polis Center, 2000).
51. Arthur Farnsley, "Can Faith-Based Organizations Compete?" *Non-Profit and Voluntary Sector Quarterly* (March 2001): 99–111.
52. Becker, *From Sovereign to Servant,* 114.
53. Ibid., 131.

4. RELIGIOUS TRADITIONS DIVERSIFIED AND DOMESTICATED

1. See, for instance, Nancy T. Ammerman, *Baptist Battles* (New Brunswick, N.J.: Rutgers University Press, 1990), or James Hunter, *Culture Wars* (New York: Basic Books, 1991).
2. William R. Hutchison, *Religious Pluralism in America* (New Haven, Conn.: Yale University Press, 2003).
3. It is worth mentioning that Columbus, Ohio, has a religious makeup more like Indianapolis's. This may well have to do with the fact that like Indianapolis, it arose as an intentional government and administrative center chosen for its geographic centrality. The other midwestern cities grew as trade centers located on major river or lake ports. These comparative numbers, like the others used throughout this chapter, come from Martin Bradley, Norman Green, Jr., Dale Jones, Mac Lynn, and Lou McNeill, *Churches and Church Membership in the U.S. 1990: An Enumeration by Region, State and County Based on Data Reported for 133 Church Groupings* (Atlanta, Ga.: Glenmary Research Center, 1992).
4. In March of 1999, Eli Lilly and Company stock reached what was then a peak

of $97.31 before settling back down into the $60 to $70 range. Then in August of 2000 it peaked at $108.56. As the Lilly Endowment is nearly fully invested in Eli Lilly stock, the funds with which it makes grants are dependent on these prices. Although the next year's available funds are pegged on a given calendar day and so not dependent solely on the price peak, 1999 and 2000 were the years in which the Endowment had the most money to disperse.

5. As has been noted already, it also invested roughly $6 million in a multifaceted project on public religion from which this volume is drawn.

6. David Bodenhamer and Robert Barrows, *Encyclopedia of Indianapolis* (Bloomington: Indiana University Press, 1994).

7. Nancy T. Ammerman with Arthur E. Farnsley et al., *Congregation and Community* (New Brunswick, N.J.: Rutgers University Press, 1997).

8. From research by James Duke as reported in the *New York Times*, June 14, 1998.

9. Edwin Becker, *From Sovereign to Servant: The Church Federation of Greater Indianapolis, 1912–1987* (Indianapolis, Ind.: The Church Federation of Greater Indianapolis, 1987).

10. For more on the history of Catholics in Indianapolis, see James Divita, *Slaves to No One: A History of the Holy Trinity Catholic Congregation in Indianapolis in the Diamond Jubilee of the Founding of Holy Trinity Parish* (Indianapolis, Ind.: Holy Trinity Parish; Ethnic History Project of the Indiana Historical Society, 1981).

11. See N. J. Demerath III et al., *Sacred Companies: Organizational Aspects of Religion and Religious Aspects of Organizations* (New York: Oxford University Press, 1997).

12. John McGreevey, *Parish Boundaries: The Catholic Encounter with Race in the Twentieth-Century Urban North* (Chicago: University of Chicago Press, 1996).

13. Judith Endelman, *The Jewish Community of Indianapolis, 1849 to the Present* (Bloomington: Indiana University Press, 1984).

14. Background research on these synagogues was done by Kevin Corn, a graduate researcher at Indiana University working under the direction of social historian and team member Etan Diamond.

15. On the Black Church, see especially C. Eric Lincoln and Lawrence Mamiya, *The Black Church in the African-American Experience* (Durham, N.C.: Duke University Press, 1990).

16. These numbers, like the other population numbers offered throughout the book, are from the U.S. Census.

17. On the authority and power distinction, see Paul Harrison, *Authority and Power in the Free Church Tradition* (Princeton, N.J.: Princeton University Press, 1959), and Arthur Farnsley, *Southern Baptist Politics: Authority and Power in the Making of an American Denomination* (State College, Pa.: Pennsylvania State University Press, 1994).

18. Survey of Indianapolis residents, directed by William Mirola and Arthur Farnsley for The Polis Center, and conducted by the Indiana University Center for Survey Research, 1999.

19. From a study by Marvin Scott and Dulce Scott, conducted in conjunction with The Polis Center, 1998.

5. TYPES AND TENSIONS OF CONGREGATIONAL LIFE

1. It is worth noting that budget figures were usually provided by larger, better-off congregations. The actual median is likely to be lower still. Arthur Farnsley, "What Do You Mean by Average?" *Research Notes from the Project on Religion and Urban Culture* 2, no. 6 (The Polis Center, 2000). These numbers come from data collected directly by field researchers in the Project on Religion and Urban Culture.

2. William Mirola, "Indianapolis Clergy: Private Ministries, Public Figures," *Research Notes from the Project on Religion and Urban Culture* 2, no. 9 (2000).

3. R. Stephen Warner, "Work in Progress toward a New Paradigm for the Sociological Study of Religion in the U.S.," *American Journal of Sociology* 98, no. 5 (1993): 1044–93.

4. See Roger Finke and Rodney Starke, *The Churching of America, 1776–1990: Winners and Losers in Our Religious Economy* (New Brunswick, N.J.: Rutgers University Press, 1992).

5. Ibid.

6. Nancy T. Ammerman with Arthur E. Farnsley et al., *Congregation and Community* (New Brunswick, N.J.: Rutgers University Press, 1997); R. Stephen Warner, *New Wine in Old Wineskins: Evangelicals and Liberals in a Small-Town Church* (Berkeley: University of California Press, 1988); James Wind and James Lewis, *American Congregations* (Chicago: University of Chicago Press, 1994); Nancy Eiesland, *A Particular Place: Urban Restructuring and Religious Ecology in a Southern Exurb* (New Brunswick, N.J.: Rutgers University Press, 2000); Penny Becker, *Congregations in Conflict: Cultural Models of Local Religious Life* (Cambridge: Cambridge University Press, 2000).

7. Arthur Farnsley, *Rising Expectations: Urban Congregations, Welfare Reform, and Civic Life* (Bloomington: Indiana University Press, 2003).

8. Mark Chaves, *Congregations in America* (Cambridge, Mass.: Harvard University Press, 2004).

9. Robert Wuthnow, *Producing the Sacred: An Essay on Public Religion* (Urbana and Chicago: University of Illinois Press, 1994).

10. Peter Berger and Richard Neuhaus, *To Empower People* (New York: American Enterprise Institute, 1977).

11. Robert Putnam, *Bowling Alone: The Collapse and Revival of American Community* (New York: Simon and Schuster, 2000).

12. There are many typologies of congregational life, but we are especially indebted to David A. Roozen et al., *Varieties of Religious Presence* (New York: Pilgrim Press, 1984). We have also been influenced by Ammerman et al., *Congregation and Community*, and Becker, *Congregations in Conflict*.

13. This distinction was first helpfully suggested to me by Rev. Richard Hamilton, retired minister of North United Methodist Church, Indianapolis.

14. Mirola, "Indianapolis Clergy: Private Ministries, Public Figures."

15. We defined a congregation as "integrated" if 10 percent or more of its members came from a second race. We considered any group that was racially homogeneous at a level of 90 percent or above to be of one race for our statistical purposes.

16. Henry Cisneros, *Higher Ground: Faith Communities and Community Building* (Washington, D.C.: Department of Housing and Urban Development, 1996).

17. William Mirola, "Religious Attitudes in Indianapolis: A Survey," *Research Notes from the Project on Religion and Urban Culture* (Indianapolis, Ind.: The Polis Center, 2000). Arthur Farnsley, "Can Faith-Based Organizations Compete?" *Non-Profit and Voluntary Sector Quarterly* 30, no. 1 (2001): 99–111.

18. It is precisely this distinction which led the authors of *Varieties of Religious Presence* to choose "sanctuary" as one of their ideal types, distinguishing it from "evangelical." But "evangelical" has become a too-broad catchall term covering all who profess salvation as an individual experience.

19. Donald Miller, *Reinventing American Protestantism: Christianity in the New Millennium* (Berkeley: University of California Press, 1997).

20. *Indianapolis Star,* November 7, 2002.

21. Mirola, "Indianapolis Clergy: Private Ministries, Public Figures."

22. Ibid.

6. BACK HOME AGAIN

1. Henry Cisneros, *Higher Ground: Faith Communities and Community Building* (Washington, D.C.: Department of Housing and Urban Development, 1996).

2. The demographics have changed slightly since our analysis was conducted in the 1990s. No doubt in part because of its border on Meridian Street and its history as an early upper-class suburb with fine homes, Mapleton–Fall Creek has experienced a "gentrification" that has brought in more white residents and more money.

3. Arthur Farnsley, "Congregations, Local Knowledge, and Devolution," *Review of Religious Research* 42 (2000): 96–110.

4. Sharon Zukin, *Landscapes of Power: From Detroit to Disney World* (Berkeley: University of California Press, 1991), p. 20; and Charles Jencks, *What Is Postmodernism?* (New York: St. Martin's Press, 1986), p. 25.

5. Daniel Monti, Jr., *The American City: A Social and Cultural History* (Malden, Mass., and Oxford: Blackwell, 2000), p. 42.

6. Robert E. Park, *The City: Suggestions for the Investigation of Human Behavior in the Social Environment* (Chicago and London: University of Chicago Press, 1967 [1925]).

7. Ibid.

8. Morris Janowitz, *The Community Press in an Urban Setting* (Chicago: University of Chicago Press, 1967); Gerald Suttles, *Social Construction of Communities* (Chicago: University of Chicago Press, 1972).

9. Elfriede Wedam, "The 'Religious District' of Elite Congregations: Reproducing Spatial Centrality and Redefining Mission," *Sociology of Religion* 64, no. 1 (Spring 2003): 47–64.

10. David Bodenhamer with Lamont Hulse and Elizabeth Monroe, *The Main Stem: The History and Architecture of North Meridian Street* (Indianapolis, Ind.: Historic Landmarks Foundation of Indiana, 1992).

11. Mark Chaves, *The National Congregations Survey*, Machine Readable File, 1999; Michael O. Emerson, "Beyond Ethnic Composition: Are Multiracial Congregations Unique?" paper presented at the annual meetings of the Society for the Scientific Study of Religion, Houston, Texas, 2000.

12. U.S. Bureau of the Census, *Statistical Abstract of the United States* (Washington, D.C.: U.S. Government Printing Office, 1995), cited in David Newman, *Sociology: Exploring the Architecture of Everyday Life* (Thousand Oaks, Calif.: Pine Forge Press, 1997).

13. William Julius Wilson, *The Truly Disadvantaged: The Inner City, the Underclass, and Public Policy* (Chicago: University of Chicago Press, 1988).

14. Alejandro Portes, "Social Capital: Origins and Applications," *Annual Review of Sociology* 24 (1998): 1–24.

15. Robert Barrows, "Indianapolis: Silver Buckle on the Rustbelt." In Richard Bernard, ed., *Snowbelt Cities: Metropolitan Politics in the Northeast and Midwest Since WWII* (Bloomington: Indiana University Press, 1990).

16. Susan McKee, private correspondence, 1999.

17. Wilson, *The Truly Disadvantaged*.

18. Elijah Anderson, *Streetwise: Race, Class, and Change in an Urban Community* (Chicago: University of Chicago Press, 1990); idem, "The Code of the Streets," *Atlantic Monthly* (May 1994): 81–94; Omar M. McRoberts, *Streets of Glory: Church and Community in a Black Urban Neighborhood* (Chicago: University of Chicago Press, 2003).

19. Wilbur Zelinsky, "The Names of Chicago's Churches: A Tale of at Least Two Cultures" (unpublished manuscript, 2002).

20. Arthur Farnsley, *Rising Expectations: Urban Congregations, Welfare Reform, and Civic Life* (Bloomington: Indiana University Press, 2003); Mark Chaves, "Religious Congregations and Welfare Reform," *Society* 38, no. 2 (2001): 21–27; Ram Cnaan et al., *The Newer Deal: Social Work and Religion in Partnership* (New York: Columbia University Press, 1999); Robert Wineburg, *A Limited Partnership: The Politics of Religion, Welfare, and Social Service* (New York: Columbia University Press, 2001).

21. McRoberts, *Streets of Glory*.

22. "Something to Prove," *Indianapolis Star*, January 30, 2000.

23. Robert M. Franklin, *Another Day's Journey: Black Churches Confronting the American Crisis* (Minneapolis, Minn.: Fortress Press, 1997).

24. Donald E. Miller, *Reinventing American Protestantism: Christianity in the New Millennium* (Berkeley: University of California Press, 1998), see Chapter 8.

25. R. Stephen Warner, "Work in Progress toward a New Paradigm for the Sociological Study of Religion in the United States," *American Journal of Sociology* 98, no. 5 (1993): 1044–93.

26. Anthony Cohen, *The Symbolic Construction of Community* (London: Routledge, 1985).

7. CONCLUSION

1. Susan M. Walcott, "From Bustbelt to Boomtown: Regime Succession and the Transformation of Downtown Indianapolis," *Urban Geography* 20, no. 7 (1999): 648–66.

2. For more on suburbanization of religion, see Etan Diamond, *Souls of the City* (Bloomington: Indiana University Press, 2003).

3. Peter Berger and R. J. Neuhaus, *To Empower People* (New York: American Enterprise Institute, 1977).

4. David Riesman, *The Lonely Crowd* (New Haven, Conn.: Yale University Press, 1961); Christopher Lasch, *The Culture of Narcissism* (New York: Warner Books, 1979); Philip Slater, *The Pursuit of Loneliness* (Boston: Beacon Press, 1970); R. Bellah, R. Madsen, W. Sullivan, A. Swidler, and S. Tipton, *Habits of the Heart: Individualism and Commitment in American Life* (Berkeley: University of California Press, 1985); Robert Putnam, *Bowling Alone: The Collapse and Revival of American Community* (New York: Simon and Schuster, 2000).

5. Nancy T. Ammerman, "Bowling Together," University Lecture on Religion, Arizona State University, 1996; James Coleman, "Social Capital in the Creation of Human Capital," *American Journal of Sociology* 94 (1988): S95–S120; Putnam, *Bowling Alone*.

6. Stanley Carlson-Theis, *Charitable Choice: The Charitable Choice Opportunity* (Washington, D.C.: Center for Public Justice, 2001).

7. Arthur Farnsley, *Rising Expectations: Urban Congregations, Welfare Reform, and Civic Life* (Bloomington: Indiana University Press, 2003).

8. Robert Bellah, "Civil Religion in America," *Daedalus* (Winter 1967): 1–21.

9. Will Herberg, *Protestant, Catholic, Jew* (Garden City, N.J.: Anchor Books, 1955).

10. Nancy T. Ammerman with Arthur E. Farnsley et al., *Congregation and Community* (New Brunswick, N.J.: Rutgers University Press, 1997).

11. Robert Wuthnow, *I Come Away Stronger: How Small Groups Are Shaping American Religion* (New York: Eerdmans Publishing, 1994).

12. R. Stephen Warner, *New Wine in Old Wineskins: Evangelicals and Liberals in a Small-Town Church* (Berkeley: University of California Press, 1988).

13. R. Stephen Warner, "Work in Progress toward a New Paradigm for the So-

ciological Study of Religion in the United States," *American Journal of Sociology* 98, no. 5 (1993): 1044–93.

14. Roger Finke and Rodney Stark, *The Churching of America, 1775–1990: Winners and Losers in Our Religious Economy* (New Brunswick, N.J.: Rutgers University Press, 1992); idem, "Religious Economies and Sacred Canopies: Religious Mobilization in American Cities," *American Sociological Review* 53 (1988): 41–49; Laurence Iannaccone, "A Formal Model of Church and Sect," *American Journal of Sociology* 94 (1988): S241–S268.

15. Mark Chaves, "Secularization as Declining Religious Authority," *Social Forces* 72, no. 3 (March 1994): 749–74.

16. Bellah, "Civil Religion in America."

17. Robert Wuthnow, *The Restructuring of American Religion* (Princeton, N.J.: Princeton University Press, 1988).

18. N. J. Demerath III, *Crossing the Gods* (New Brunswick, N.J.: Rutgers University Press, 2001).

19. C. Dudley et al., *Handbook for Congregational Studies* (Nashville, Tenn.: Abingdon Press, 1986); Nancy Ammerman et al., *Studying Congregations* (Nashville, Tenn.: Abingdon Press, 1998).

20. Lilly Endowment Incorporated Annual Reports for the relevant years.

21. Lilly Endowment Incorporated mission statement.

22. Christian Smith, *American Evangelicalism: Embattled and Thriving* (Chicago: University of Chicago Press, 1998).

23. Herberg, *Protestant, Catholic, Jew.*

BIBLIOGRAPHY

American Baptist Home Missionary Society. "Church and Community Study of Thirteen American Baptist Churches in Indianapolis, IN." 1955.

Ammerman, Nancy T. *Baptist Battles*. New Brunswick, N.J.: Rutgers University Press, 1990.

———. "Bowling Together: Congregations and the American Civic Order." University Lecture in Religion, Arizona State University, 1996.

Ammerman, Nancy T., with Arthur Farnsley et al. *Congregation and Community*. New Brunswick, N.J.: Rutgers University Press, 1997.

Ammerman, Nancy, et al. *Studying Congregations*. Nashville, Tenn.: Abingdon Press, 1998.

Anderson, Elijah. *Streetwise: Race, Class, and Change in an Urban Community*. Chicago: University of Chicago Press, 1990.

———. "The Code of the Streets." *Atlantic Monthly* (May 1994), 81–94.

Barrows, Robert. "Indianapolis: Silver Buckle on the Rustbelt." In *Snowbelt Cities: Metropolitan Politics in the Northeast and Midwest Since WWII*. Edited by Richard Bernard. Bloomington: Indiana University Press, 1990.

Becker, Edwin. *From Sovereign to Servant: The Church Federation of Greater Indianapolis, 1912–1987*. Indianapolis, Ind.: The Church Federation of Greater Indianapolis, 1987.

Becker, Penny Edgell. *Congregations in Conflict: Cultural Models of Local Religious Life*. Cambridge: Cambridge University Press, 2000.

Bellah, Robert. "Civil Religion in America." *Daedalus* (Winter 1967): 1–21.

Bellah, Robert, et al. *Habits of the Heart: Individualism and Commitment in American Life.* Berkeley: University of California Press, 1985.

Berger, Peter. *The Sacred Canopy.* Garden City, N.J.: Anchor Books, 1969.

Berger, Peter, and R. J. Neuhaus. *To Empower People.* New York: American Enterprise Institute, 1977.

Berner, Jerry, and Christopher Winship. "Should We Have Faith in the Churches? Ten-Point Coalition's Effect on Boston's Youth Violence." Northwestern University/University of Chicago Joint Center for Poverty Research Working Paper, 1999.

Bodenhamer, David J., and Robert G. Barrows. *Encyclopedia of Indianapolis.* Bloomington: Indiana University Press, 1994.

Bodenhamer, David, with Lamont Hulse and Elizabeth Monroe. *The Main Stem: The History and Architecture of North Meridian Street.* Indianapolis, Ind.: Historic Landmarks Foundation of Indiana, 1992.

Bradley, Martin, Norman Green, Jr., Dale Jones, Mac Lynn, and Lou McNeill. *Churches and Church Membership in the U.S. 1990: An Enumeration by Region, State and County Based on Data Reported for 133 Church Groupings.* Atlanta, Ga.: Glenmary Research Center, 1992.

Carlson-Theis, Stanley. *A Guide to Charitable Choice.* Washington, D.C.: Center for Public Justice, 1997.

———. *Charitable Choice: The Charitable Choice Opportunity.* Washington, D.C.: Center for Public Justice, 2001.

Chaves, Mark. "Secularization as Declining Religious Authority." *Social Forces* 72, no. 3 (March 1994): 749–74.

———. "Religious Congregations and Welfare Reform." *Society* 38, no. 2 (2001): 21–27.

———. *Congregations in America.* Cambridge, Mass.: Harvard University Press, 2004.

Cisneros, Henry. *Higher Ground: Faith Communities and Community Building.* Washington, D.C.: Department of Housing and Urban Development, 1996.

Cnaan, Ram, with Robert Wineburg and Stephanie Boddie. *The Newer Deal: Social Work and Religion in Partnership.* New York: Columbia University Press, 1999.

Cohen, Anthony. *The Symbolic Construction of Community.* London: Routledge, 1985.

Cohen, Lizabeth. *Making a New Deal: Industrial Workers in Chicago, 1919–1939.* Cambridge: Cambridge University Press, 1990.

Coleman, James. "Social Capital in the Creation of Human Capital." *American Journal of Sociology* 94 (1988): S95–S120.

Cox, Harvey. *The Secular City.* New York: Macmillan Publishing, 1965.

———. *Religion in the Secular City.* New York: Simon and Schuster, 1984.

Crocker, Ruth. *Social Work and Social Order: The Settlement Movement in Two Industrial Cities, 1889–1930.* Urbana: University of Illinois Press, 1992.

Demerath, N. J. III. *Crossing the Gods.* New Brunswick, N.J.: Rutgers University Press, 2001.

Demerath, N. J. III, and Rhys Williams. *A Bridging of Faiths: Religion and Politics in a New England City.* Princeton, N.J.: Princeton University Press, 1992.

Demerath, N. J. III, Peter Dobkin Hall, Terry Schmitt, and Rhys Williams, eds. *Sacred Companies: Organizational Aspects of Religion and Religious Aspects of Organizations.* New York: Oxford University Press, 1997.

Diamond, Etan. *Souls of the City: Religion and the Search for Community in Postwar America.* Bloomington: Indiana University Press, 2003.

Divita, James. *Slaves to No One: A History of the Holy Trinity Catholic Congregation in Indianapolis in the Diamond Jubilee of the Founding of Holy Trinity Parish.* Indianapolis, Ind.: Holy Trinity Parish; Ethnic History Project of the Indiana Historical Society, 1981.

Dudley, Carl, et al. *Handbook for Congregational Studies*. Nashville, Tenn.: Abingdon Press, 1986.

Eiesland, Nancy. *A Particular Place: Urban Restructuring and Religious Ecology in a Southern Exurb*. New Brunswick, N.J.: Rutgers University Press, 2000.

Emerson, Michael O. "Beyond Ethnic Composition: Are Multiracial Congregations Unique?" Paper presented at Society for Scientific Study of Religion annual meetings, Houston, Texas, 2000.

Endelman, Judith. *The Jewish Community of Indianapolis, 1849 to the Present*. Bloomington: Indiana University Press, 1984.

Farnsley, Arthur II. *Southern Baptist Politics: Authority and Power in the Restructuring of an American Denomination*. State College, Pa.: Pennsylvania State University Press, 1994.

———. *Ten Good Questions about Faith-Based Partnerships and Welfare Reform*. Indianapolis, Ind.: The Polis Center, 2000.

———. "Congregations, Local Knowledge, and Devolution." *Review of Religious Research* 42, no. 1 (2000): 96–110.

———. "What Do You Mean by Average?" *Research Notes from the Project on Religion and Urban Culture*. Indianapolis, Ind.: The Polis Center, 2000.

———. "Can Faith-Based Organizations Compete?" *Non-Profit and Voluntary Sector Quarterly* (March 2001).

———. *Rising Expectations: Urban Congregations, Welfare Reform, and Civic Life*. Bloomington: Indiana University Press, 2003.

Finke, Roger, and Rodney Stark. "Religious Economies and Sacred Canopies: Religious Mobilization in American Cities." *American Sociological Review* 53 (1988): 41–49.

———. *The Churching of America, 1776–1990: Winners and Losers in Our Religious Economy*. New Brunswick, N.J.: Rutgers University Press, 1992.

Fischer, Claude. "Ambivalent Communities: How Americans Understand Their Localities," in *America at Century's End*, ed. Alan Wolfe. Berkeley and Los Angeles: University of California Press, 1991.

Fishman, Robert. "Megalopolis Unbound: America's New City." *Wilson Quarterly* 16 (Winter 1990): 24–45.

Franklin, Robert M. *Another Day's Journey: Black Churches Confronting the American Crisis*. Minneapolis, Minn.: Fortress Press, 1997.

Gelder, Kenneth, and Sarah Thornton. *The Subcultures Reader*. London and New York: Routledge, 1997.

Harrison, Paul. *Authority and Power in the Free Church Tradition*. Princeton, N.J.: Princeton University Press, 1959.

Hebert, Richard. *Highways to Nowhere: The Politics of City Transportation*. New York: Bobbs-Merrill Co., 1972.

Herberg, Will. *Protestant, Catholic, Jew: An Essay in American Religious Sociology*. Garden City, N.J.: Anchor Books, 1955.

Homer Hoyt Associates. "Market Survey of the Meadows, 38th and Rural Streets, Indianapolis, Indiana, for Leo A. Lippman." New York: Homer Hoyt Associates, 1952.

Horan, Sister Angela. *The Story of Old St. John's: A Parish Rooted in Pioneer Indianapolis*. Indianapolis, Ind.: Litho Press, 1971.

Hunter, James. *American Evangelicalism*. New Brunswick, N.J.: Rutgers University Press, 1983.

———. *Culture Wars*. New York: Basic Books, 1991.

Hutchison, William. *Religious Pluralism in America*. New Haven, Conn.: Yale University Press, 2003.

Iannaccone, Laurence. "A Formal Model of Church and Sect." *American Journal of Sociology* 94 (1988): S241–S268.

Janowitz, Morris. *The Community Press in an Urban Setting*. Chicago: University of Chicago Press, 1967.

Jencks, Charles. *What Is Postmodernism?* New York: St. Martin's Press, 1986.

Katz, Michael. *In the Shadow of the Poorhouse: A Social History of Welfare in America*. New York: Basic Books, 1996.

Kretzmann, John, and John McKnight. *Building Communities from the Inside Out: A Path Toward Finding and Mobilizing Community Assets*. Chicago: ACTA Publications, 1997.

Lasch, Christopher. *The Culture of Narcissism*. New York: Warner Books, 1979.

Leven, Charles. "Distance, Space, and the Organisation of Urban Life." *Urban Studies* 28 (1991): 319–25.

Lewis, James. *The Protestant Experience in Gary, Indiana, 1906–1975*. Knoxville: University of Tennessee Press, 1992.

———. "Going Downtown: Historical Resources for Urban Ministry." *Word and World* 14, no. 4 (1994): 402–408.

Lilly Endowment Annual Report, 2000.

Lincoln, C. Eric, and Lawrence Mamiya. *The Black Church in the African-American Experience*. Durham, N.C.: Duke University Press, 1990.

Livezey, Lowell, ed. *Public Religion and Urban Transformation*. New York: NYU Press, 2000.

Lynch, Kevin. *The Image of a City*. Cambridge, Mass.: MIT Press, 1960.

Lynd, Robert and Helen. *Middletown: A Study in Modern American Culture*. New York: Harcourt, Brace, Jovanovich, 1929.

———. *Middletown in Transition*. New York: Harcourt, Brace, Jovanovich, 1935.

Markisohn, Deborah. "Ministers of the Klan: Indianapolis Clergy Involvement with the 1920s Ku Klux Klan." M.A. thesis, Indiana University, 1992.

May, Elaine. *Homeward Bound: American Families in the Cold War Era*. New York: Basic Books, 1988.

McGreevey, John. *Parish Boundaries: The Catholic Encounter with Race in the Twentieth-Century Urban North*. Chicago: University of Chicago Press, 1996.

McLoughlin, William. "Faith." *American Quarterly* 35 (Spring–Summer 1983): 101–15.

McRoberts, Omar M. *Streets of Glory: Church and Community in a Black Urban Neighborhood*. Chicago: University of Chicago Press, 2003.

Miller, Donald. *Reinventing American Protestantism: Christianity in the New Millennium*. Berkeley: University of California Press, 1997.

Mirola, William. "Religious Attitudes in Indianapolis: A Survey." *Research Notes from the Project on Religion and Urban Culture*. Indianapolis, Ind.: The Polis Center, 2000.

———. "Indianapolis Clergy: Private Ministries, Public Figures." *Research Notes from the Project on Religion and Urban Culture*. Indianapolis, Ind.: The Polis Center, 2000.

Monti, Daniel, Jr. *The American City: A Social and Cultural History*. Malden, Mass., and Oxford: Blackwell, 2000.

Moore, Leonard. *Citizen Klansmen: The Ku Klux Klan in Indiana, 1921–1928*. Chapel Hill: University of North Carolina Press, 1991.

Newman, David. *Sociology: Exploring the Architecture of Everyday Life*. Thousand Oaks, Calif.: Pine Forge Press, 1997.

O'Brien, David J. *Public Catholicism*. New York: Macmillan, 1989.

Orsi, Robert, ed. *Gods of the City: Religion and the American Urban Landscape.* Bloomington: Indiana University Press, 1999.

Park, Robert E. *The City: Suggestions for the Investigation of Human Behavior in the Urban Environment.* Chicago and London: University of Chicago Press, 1967 (originally published 1925).

Portes, Alejandro. "Social Capital: Origins and Applications." *Annual Review of Sociology* 24 (1998): 1–24.

Post-War Planning Committee. *The Post War Plan for Indianapolis.* Indiananapolis, Ind.: Post-War Planning Committee, 1944.

Putnam, Robert. *Bowling Alone: The Collapse and Revival of American Community.* New York: Simon and Schuster, 2000.

Ramsay, Meredith. "Redeeming the City: Exploring the Relationship Between Church and Metropolis." *Urban Affairs Review* 33, no. 5 (1998): 595–626.

Riesman, David. *The Lonely Crowd.* New Haven, Conn.: Yale University Press, 1961.

Roozen, David A., William McKinney, and Jackson Carroll. *Varieties of Religious Presence.* New York: Pilgrim Press, 1984.

Ryan, Mary. "The American Parade: Representations of the Nineteenth Century Social Order." In Raymond Mohl, ed., *The Making of Urban America.* Wilmington, Del.: Scholarly Research, 1997.

Slater, Phillip. *The Pursuit of Loneliness.* Boston: Beacon Press, 1970.

Smith, Carl. *Disorder and the Shape of Belief: The Great Chicago Fire, the Haymarket Bomb, and the Model Town of Pullman.* Chicago: University of Chicago Press, 1995.

Smith, Christian. *American Evangelicalism: Embattled and Thriving.* Chicago: University of Chicago Press, 1998.

Suttles, Gerald. *Social Construction of Communities.* Chicago: University of Chicago Press, 1972.

Swidler, Ann. "Culture in Action: Symbols and Strategies." *American Sociological Review* 51 (1986): 273–86.

Teaford, Jon. *City and Suburb: The Political Fragmentation of Metropolitan America, 1850–1970.* Baltimore, Md.: Johns Hopkins University Press, 1979.

Towne, Marian. *That All May Be One: Centennial History of Church Women United in Indianapolis, 1898–1998.* Indianapolis, Ind.: Church Women United in Indianapolis, 1998.

Vanderstel, David. "A City of Churches: The Development and Role of Religious Institutions in Indianapolis, 1905–1926." Unpublished manuscript, 2001.

Walcott, Susan M. "From Bustbelt to Boomtown: Regime Succession and the Transformation of Downtown Indianapolis." *Urban Geography* 20, no. 7 (1999): 648–66.

Warner, R. Stephen. *New Wine in Old Wineskins: Evangelicals and Liberals in a Small-Town Church.* Berkeley: University of California Press, 1988.

———. "Work in Progress toward a New Paradigm for the Sociological Study of Religion in the U.S." *American Journal of Sociology* 98, no. 5 (1993): 1044–93.

Wedam, Elfriede. "The 'Religious District' of Elite Congregations: Reproducing Spatial Centrality and Redefining Mission." *Sociology of Religion* 64, no. 1 (Spring 2003): 47–64.

Wilson, William Julius. *The Truly Disadvantaged: The Inner City, the Underclass, and Public Policy.* Chicago: University of Chicago Press, 1988.

Wind, James, and James Lewis. *American Congregations.* Vols. 1 and 2. Chicago: University of Chicago Press, 1994.

Wineburg, Robert. *A Limited Partnership: The Politics of Religion, Welfare, and Social Service.* New York: Columbia University Press, 2001.

Wirth, Louis. "Urbanism as a Way of Life." *American Journal of Sociology* 44 (July 1938): 3–24.

Wuthnow, Robert. *The Restructuring of American Religion*. Princeton, N.J.: Princeton University Press, 1988.

———. *I Come Away Stronger: How Small Groups Are Shaping American Religion*. New York: Eerdmans Publishing, 1994.

———. *Producing the Sacred: An Essay on Public Religion*. Urbana and Chicago: University of Illinois Press, 1994.

Zelinsky, Wilbur. "The Names of Chicago Churches: A Tale of at least Two Cultures." Unpublished manuscript, 2002.

Zukin, Sharon. *Landscapes of Power: From Detroit to Disney World*. Berkeley: University of California Press, 1991.

CONTRIBUTORS

Arthur E. Farnsley II is an independent researcher and consultant, as well as Adjunct Professor of Sociology and Religion at IUPUC. He is author of *Southern Baptist Politics: Authority and Power in the Restructuring of an American Denomination* and *Rising Expectations: Urban Congregations, Welfare Reform, and Civic Life* (Indiana University Press, 2003).

N. J. Demerath III is Professor of Sociology at the University of Massachusetts, Amherst. His books include *Crossing the Gods: World Religions and Worldly Politics; Sacred Companies: Organizational Aspects of Religion and Religious Aspects of Organizations* (edited with Peter Hall, Terry Schmitt, and Rhys Williams); and *A Bridging of Faiths: Religion and Politics in a New England City.*

Etan Diamond is a social historian whose research interests lie at the intersection of urban history and the history of religion. He is author of *And I Will Dwell in Their Midst: Orthodox Jews in Suburbia* and *Souls of the City: Religion and the Search for Community in Postwar America* (Indiana University Press, 2003).

Mary L. Mapes is Adjunct Professor of History at Lake Forest College and author of *A Public Charity: Religion and Social Welfare in Indianapolis* (Indiana University Press, 2004).

Elfriede Wedam is Visiting Lecturer in the Honors College at the University of Illinois–Chicago. She is a contributing author to *Religion in the New Urban Era* and a forthcoming book about Chicago, *Public Religion and Urban Transformation*. She has published several articles on religion in Indianapolis.

INDEX

Page numbers in italics indicate illustrations. An "m" following a page number indicates a map; a "t" following a page number indicates a table.

Adventists, 110
Affluence, 181, 188
African American community: cultural realignment, 29; Indiana Avenue congregations, 172; population density, 98, *102m*, 171–72; religiosity, 100–101; response to Unigov, 36–37, 98. *See also* Black churches; Civil Rights movement
African Methodist Episcopal (AME), 99
Aid to Families with Dependent Children, 72
Alban Institute, 100
Alignment/realignment: cultural, 27–29, 192, 196; inward/outward pressure dynamics, 12–14, 110–11, 118, 146, 203; metropolitan centers, 17, 29–39; neighborhoods, 39–44, 137, 140, 156t, 166, 169; population shifts, 33–34; religious

response, 2–9, 61–71, 74–80, 110–14, 186, 189, 203. *See also* Multicentering; Pluralism; Secularism/secularization; Suburbs/suburbanization
AME Zion, 99
American, identity as, 196, 197, 209–10
American Baptist, 77, 80. *See also* Baptists
American religion, 197, 198–99
Americanism movement, 48–55, 61–66, 86
Ammerman, Nancy, 9, 197, 203
Amusement parks, 25–26
Anti-communism, 61–65
Anti-crime crusade, 69
Appel, Fred G., 28
"Armies of compassion," 72, 176
Armstrong, A. James, 70
Asian immigrants, 180

Assemblies of God, 108
Assimilation, 61–66, 209–10
Authority. *See* Moral authority
Automobiles, 157–58

Baptist Alliance, 99
Baptists, 55–56, 77, 80, 99, 100, 104–105,
   108–109, 117, 127–29, 161, 167
Barton, John, 94
Baseball, 49
Bayne, F., 67
Bayt, Philip, 94
Bedroom communities, 179
Beecher, Henry Ward, 84, 86
Bellah, Robert, 191, 192, 196, 200
Benjamin, T. Garrott, 105
Berger, Peter, 191, 196, 197
Beth-El Zedeck synagogue, 96–97
Biblical conservatism, 201, 205
"Big tent" strategy, 117
Billy Graham Crusade, 108
Black Baptists, 77, 99, 100
Black churches: cloister congregations, 127–
   31; Concerned Clergy, 47, 99, 172, 177–
   78; congregations, 101–105, *103m;* Evan-
   gelicals, 105, 174–75, 186–87; external
   funding applications, 73–74, 126–27,
   207; growth and change in, 11, 33–34, 76,
   98–106, 174–79, 190; interracial worship,
   87, 99, 104, 117, 216n15; organizational
   authority, 99–100, 105; safety concerns,
   128; social services, 126–27, 174, 176,
   178, 195; storefront churches, 128. *See also*
   African American community; Civil Rights
   movement
Black Methodists, 77
Black Pentecostals, 77, 99
Block, Meier S., 15
Block grant program, 73–74
Blue laws. *See* Sunday closing laws/campaigns
B'nai Torah synagogue, 97
Born-again community, 107
Boston, 176
Bowling Alone (Putnam), 4, 191
Bowling leagues, 26
Brightwood Community Center, 123
Brightwood Congregational, 54
Broad Ripple Amusement Park, 26
Broad Ripple neighborhood, 153
Brolley bill, 49
Brown, Andrew J., 29, 67, 99, 171–72
Browning, James E., 28
Buddhists, 110, 196

Building Better Neighborhoods program, 3,
   39
Burton, Dan, 108
Bush, George W., 71–73, 126, 176
Busing, 92, 93, 108
Butler University, 153

"C Day," 65
Cadle, Howard, 54, 109
Cadle Tabernacle, *54,* 64, 109
Calvary Baptist Church, 55
Calvary Evangelical Church, 129–30
Campbell, Alexander, 79
Carmel, 159, 161, 188, 206
Carmel United Methodist, 161
Carroll, Michael, 94
Carson, Julia, 108
Carter, Vinson, 50
Cathedral High School, 60
Catholic Charities, 29, 58, 71, 72–73, 194
Catholic Conference, 71
Catholicism/Catholic community: Ameri-
   canism movement, 48–61, 64; bureau-
   cratic centralization, 92–93; civic roles,
   57–58, 201; confirmation class, *59;* as
   "Consumer congregations," 183–84;
   Diocesan boundaries, 91–93, 116, 141;
   discrimination against, 90; growth, 11, 29,
   60–61, 76–78, 80, 90–95; marginaliza-
   tion, 37, 58; Meridian Street congrega-
   tions, 81, 160; parishes, 90–95; social ser-
   vices, 29, 58–60, 91, 167, 183–84
Celebration of Hope, 87, 104, 117
Centennial celebration, 1, 46, 51
Centering and decentering: in neighbor-
   hoods, *156t,* 166, 169, 192; in religion,
   44–45, 66, 110–12, 127, 187, 189, 208.
   See also Alignment/realignment;
   Multicentering
Chamber of Commerce, 50–51
Change, theological approaches to, 119–22
"Charitable Choice," 4, 72–73, 118, 126,
   148, 194–96
Charity Tabernacle, 167–68
Chartrand, Joseph, 58, 60, 90
Chaves, Mark, 9, 198
Chavurah Shalom congregation, 97
Children's Aid Association, 60
Christ Church Cathedral, 67, 81, 88, 144,
   160
Christian Church, 11
Christian Church (Disciples of Christ), 79,
   89, 104, 108

"Christian Declaration of Loyalty," 66
Christian Independent Church (CIC), 138–40
Christian Inner City Association (CICA), 69
Christian Methodist Episcopal (CME), 99
Christian militia, 109
Christian Theological Seminary (CTS), 89, 106, 146
Christian Theological Society, 11
Church Federation. *See* Indianapolis Church Federation
Church membership, 76–80, 107, 115–16
Church of God, Anderson, Indiana, 79, 108
Church of Jesus Christ of Latter-day Saints (LDS/Mormons), 133–36
Church Women United, 65–66, 69
Church/state relationship, 5–7, 52–53, 61–64, 126, 194–96
Circle Center Mall, 25, 39
Circle Street, 1–2, *3*
Cisneros, Henry, 73, 125–26, 150
Citizenship, 49–53, 58, 61–63, 111, 113. *See also* Americanism movement
Civic identity: civic religion, 4, 200; multiple sources of, 189–90; patriotism, 101, 189, 193; public religious expression, 44–45, 55–56, 58, 74–75, 98; search for, 18–19, 30, 38, 118, 200–202, 209; as sports center, 18–19, 27, 38, 75, 94; symbolism of civic centers, 19–23. *See also* Americanism movement; Congregations; Neighborhoods
Civil religion: concept, 7–8, 45, 196, 197, 200–202; emergence, 53, 55–56; social capital, 75, 111
Civil Rights movement: clergy role, 46–47, 67–69; impact, 15; marchers, *68;* religious participation, 29, 74, 98, 99, 105, 126, 171–72. *See also* Race relations
Clark Township, 179
Class, sense of, 153
Clergy: Civil Rights movement, 46–47, 67–69; congregational consulting, 203; as entrepreneurs, 117, 146; response to fundamentalism, 70–71; roles of, 49–52, 145–48; Ten Point Coalition, 128. *See also* Ministerial associations
Cloister congregations, 127–31, 167–71, 178, 186, 189, 193, 205, 207. *See also* Evangelicals
Coalition for Homelessness Intervention and Prevention, 73–74, 105, 195
"Coke" outreach, 182

Coleman, James, 4
Columbia Club, 65
Columbus, Ohio, 214n3
"Come and See Tour," 69
Commerce. *See* Work and commerce
Common Council, 37
Communism, fear of, 61–65
Communities: bifocal understanding of, 135; common bonds, 19–23, 113–14, 116, 209; congregations as builders of, 8–10, 13, 110–18, 126, 136–37, 148, 190, 191, 193, 208; inward/outward pressure dynamics, 12–14, 110–11, 118; sense of, 4–5, 152, 179, 208, 210; types of, 110, 112, 140. *See also* Multicentering; Neighborhoods
Community Caring and Sharing Mission, 169–70
Community Chest, 50–51, 74
Community Church of Greenwood, 181
Community Development Block Grants, 72
Community Development Corporation (CDC), 154
Community outreach congregations, 121–25, 162–64, 170, 189
Concerned Clergy, 47, 99, 172, 177–78
Congregationalists/United Church of Christ, 77
Congregations, *103m, 115m,* 116–41; budget figures, 215n1; categories, 113–19, 148–49, 189–90, 193, 202–207; changing nature of, 78, 180–87; church membership, 76–80, 107, 115–16; as community builders, 4–5, 8–10, 13, 110–18, 126, 136–37, 148, 190, 191, 193, 208; as extended families, 116, 140; general views on, 122; inner-city, 125–29; interracial, 87, 99, 104, 117, 162–63, 216n15; Meridian Street corridor, 81–90, 96, 150–51; multicentering contexts, 141–49, 189–91; public partnerships, 73–74, 117–18, 125–27, 195; response to change, *121t;* sense of identity, 110–12, 209; studies of, 202–10; world religions, 110, 201. *See also* Black churches; Mission/mission types; Theology
Conseco Fieldhouse, 27
Conversion congregations, 130–36, 174–75, 178, 186–87, 193, 205, 207
Corporate Community Council (CCC), 32
Crime, 153, 166, 173, 177
Crisis Pregnancy Center, 184
Crocker, Ruth, 52

Cross burnings, 54–55
Crown Hill Cemetery, 172
Crown Hill Neighborhood Association, 174
Culturescapes: civic centers, 19–23; pluralism, 27–29, 165, 192, 196; poverty, 165,
  170; recreation, 8, 18–19, 21–23, 25–27,
  38, 74–75, 94; religion, 4, 27–29, 46–48,
  188
Cummins, Inc., 89
Customer service congregations, 136–41,
  162, 164, 182–84, 186, 190, 193, 205, 207

Decatur Township Ministerial Alliance, 168–
  69
Demand/Default neighborhoods, 155–56,
  206
Demerath, N. J., III, 202–203
Democracy. See Church/state relationship
Democratic Center Township, 36
Demographics: African American community, 98, 100, 102m, 103m, 171–72;
  church affiliation, 76–80, 78t, 82–85m,
  88, 91, 95, 107, 115m, 116; consumer
  spending habits, 24; Hamilton County,
  159; Indianapolis racial concentration,
  106–107; KKK membership, 54;
  Martindale-Brightwood neighborhood,
  151; Meridian Street changes, 217n2;
  neighborhoods, 42t, 43m, 165; population
  shifts, 33–34
Dignity movement, 125
Dillin, Hugh, 93
Dimaggio, Paul, 202
Diocesan boundaries, 91–93
Disciples of Christ (Christian Church), 79,
  89, 104, 108
Disestablishment, 101, 116, 197
"A Distant Thunder," 132–33
Diversity. See Race relations
Dixon, Greg, 70–71
Doliver, Louis, 65
Downtown Development Research Commit-
  tee, 38
Drug culture, 173
Dudley, Carl, 204
Durkheim, Emile, 192

Easter Sunday services, 5, 55–56, 67, 74, 208
Eastern Star Missionary Baptist, 73, 104–105
Ecumenism, 61–71, 87, 89, 117–18, 143. See
  also Ministerial associations
Edge cities. See Suburbs/suburbanization
Edgell, Penny, 203

Education: Americanism movement, 48–55,
  61–66, 86; busing, 92, 93, 108; Hebrew
  School students, 60; higher education,
  93–94, 105–106; home schooling, 106;
  parochial schools, 93–94, 58, 63, 91, 124;
  public school system, 37, 63, 94; religious
  instruction and public schools, 52–53,
  61–64; value of the month program, 134–
  35
Eiesland, Nancy, 203
ELCA Lutheran, 163
Elites: downtown revitalization, 38; networks,
  27–33, 50–51, 163–64; religious organiza-
  tions, 160, 163–64, 199–200; response to
  urban change, 51, 145
Elizabeth Seton Catholic church, 161
Emmis Communications, 95
Enright, William, 145
Episcopalians, 67, 77, 80, 81, 88
Eschatology, 133
Establishment/Established religion. See
  Mainline Protestantism
Ethnicity: religious expression, 91, 110, 153.
  See also Pluralism; Race relations
Etz Chaim synagogue, 97
European Union, 133
Evangelicals: defined, 129–30, 205, 216n18;
  "Garage" neighborhoods, 180; growth
  of, 11, 64–65, 69–71, 77, 80, 106–10;
  responses to pluralism, 201; revival meet-
  ings, 56. See also Black churches; Cloister
  congregations
Evolution, 86

Faith and Families initiative, 71–72, 207
Faith-based initiatives, 47, 71–74, 94, 118,
  148, 194–96, 207
Faith-based organizations, government atti-
  tudes toward, 2–4, 6. See also
  Congregations
Faith-based welfare reform, 105, 148, 194–
  96, 207
Falwell, Jerry, 70, 107
Families as focus, 62–65, 71–72, 126, 139,
  144–45, 194, 207
Federal employment discrimination laws,
  72–73
Feeney, Albert, 94
Feurlicht, Morris, 59, 60
Few Are Chosen Missionary Baptist Church,
  127–29
Field, Harold N., 62
Fincke, Roger, 197

Finney, Charles Grandison, 108
First Baptist Church, 161
First Baptist Church North, 117
First Baptist Mission, 56
First Methodist Mission, 56
Fishman, Robert, 17
Fletcher Place Community Center, 52, 123
Fordyce, Kirk, 71
Foreign House, 52
Foster Care homes, 58
Franklin, Robert Hope, 177
Freedom of religion, 56, 61
Frick, David, 28
Front Porch Alliance (FPA): and communities, 113, 127; creation and mission, 2, 39, 126, 176, 177, 194–95; welfare reform, 72, 74
Fundamentalism, 69–71, 86, 133
Funding sources, 72–74

Garage neighborhoods, 157–58, 179–86, 189–90, 193
Gentrification, 39, 151, 217n2
German Methodist Church, 56
GIPC. See Greater Indianapolis Progress Committee
Globalism, 30–31, 133, 190
God, relationships to, 120, *121t*, 127, 132, 178–79, 184
Goldsmith, Stephen: election, 39, 95; Faith and Families initiative, 71–74; religion and urban development, 2–3, 6, 106, 126, 166; support of diocesan schools, 94. See also Front Porch Alliance
Gospel music, 174
Government: church/state relationship, 5–7, 52–53, 61–64, 126, 194–96; faith-based initiatives, 118, 194–96; partnerships with congregations, 118, 125–27, 177, 195; Unigov, 33–37
Graham, Billy, 64, 94
Greater Indianapolis Progress Committee (GIPC), 31, 32
Greenwood Ministerial Alliance, 180, 184
Greenwood neighborhood, 179–86
Greenwood Presbyterian Church, 183
Greenwood United Methodist Church, 184–85
Gritz, Bo, 109
Gun control, 124

Halloween, 140
Hamilton County, 159

Haughville neighborhood, 57
Hebrew Congregation, 96
Herberg, Will, 196
Higher education, 93–94, 105–106
Hindus, 110, 201
Hispanic immigrants, 196, 209
Hofstadter, Richard, 152
Holiness churches, 108
Holy Trinity Catholic Church, 57, 58
Holy Week services, 5, 55–56, 67, 74
Home schooling, 106
Homer Hoyt Associates, 24–25
HOMES. See Housing Opportunities Multiplied Ecumenically
Hoosier Dome (RCA Dome), 27, 38
Horizontal relationships to God, 120, *121t*, 178–79, 184
Housing and Urban Development (HUD), 126
Housing Opportunities Multiplied Ecumenically (HOMES), 69
Housing settlements. See Low-income housing
Hudnut, William, 86, 208
Human Relations Task Force, 105
Hutchison, William, 77

Iannaccone, Laurence, 197
ICF. See Indianapolis Church Federation
Ideal-typical worldview, 120–21
Immigration/immigrants: Americanization of, 48–55, 61–66, 86; growth of Catholicism, 90–95; social welfare programs, 58–60, 123, 154; as threat, 52–53
Independent churches, 108, 137–41, 168–71, 180–82
Indiana Commission of Human Equality, 104
Indiana General Assembly, Unigov bill, 36–37
Indiana Pacers, 95
Indiana University School of Nursing, 123
Indiana University–Purdue University Indianapolis (IUPUI), 38, 172, 192
Indiana World War Memorial Plaza. See War Memorial Plaza
Indianapolis: Centennial celebration, 1, 46; downtown revitalization, 37–39; founding and growth, 1–4, 12, 15–19, 44–45, 188–89; globalism, 30–31, 133, 190; patriotic monuments, 8, *20*, *22*; post–World War II planning, 15–16; prohibition campaigns, 46–48, 50–52; recreation and sports facilities, 8, 18–19, 21–27, 38, 74–75, 94;

Indianapolis (*continued*)
    social register residences, *32m;* Unigov,
    33–37. *See also* Civic identity; Neighbor-
    hoods; Suburbs/suburbanization; Work
    and commerce
Indianapolis Art Museum, 172
Indianapolis Baptist Temple, 109
Indianapolis Center for Congregations, 100,
    117, 143–44
Indianapolis Children's Museum, 151, 172
Indianapolis Church Federation (ICF), 46–
    47, 50–53, 62, 65–66, 74, 89, 104, 106,
    117, 127
Indianapolis Colts, 27
Indianapolis 500, 21–22, 74, 94
Indianapolis Foundation, 32
Indianapolis Hebrew Congregation, 161–62
Indianapolis Motor Speedway, 21–22, 23
Indianapolis Neighborhood Resource Cen-
    ter, 41
Indianapolis Pacers, 27
Indianapolis Star, "Faith and Values" section,
    142, 146
Integration. *See* Civil Rights movement; Race
    relations
Interchurch Center, 89
Interfaith Hospitality Network, 123
Interfaith Housing, Inc., 69
Interfaith Housing Network, 207
Interracial worship, 87, 99, 104, 117, 162–
    63, 216n15. *See also* Race relations
Interstate highway construction, 92–93, 171,
    186
Irvington, 153
Islamic congregations, 7, 78, 110, 196, 201
Islamic Society of North America (ISNA), 7,
    196

Jacobs, Andy, 39
Jennings, Jonathan, 1
Jeremiah Agency, 184
Jewish Education Association (JEA), 63
Jewish Welfare Federations, 194
Jireh Sports, 74
John Birch Society, 66
Johnson, Jeffrey, 105
Johnson County, 179
Judaism/Jewish community: Americanism
    campaigns, 48, 52, 53, 56, 61; belief in
    public schools, 63; demographics, 95;
    Goldsmith election, 95; growth, 11, 60–
    61, 78, 95–98; Hebrew Academy, 29, 95,
    97; Hebrew School, *60;* Jewish Community

Center, 95, 96, 97–98; Jewish Federation,
    29, 59–60, 95; Ladies Hebrew Benevolent
    Society, 59; Meridian Street congregation,
    81, 160; reaction to pluralism, 201; social
    services, 58–60

Keystone at the Crossing, 24
"Kitchen" neighborhoods, 157, 165–71, 189
Kretzmann, John, 9
Ku Klux Klan, 7, 53–55, 90, 96, 107, 109
Kuhn, George A., 15–18

Ladies Hebrew Benevolent Society, 59
Lafayette, 34
Lafayette diocese, 91
Lafayette Square, 25
Lake, Thomas, 144
Lake Family Institute on Faith and Giving,
    144–45
Landscapes: civic centers, 19–23; recreation
    and sports facilities, 8, 18–19, 21–27, 38,
    74–75, 94; urban centers, 18–27; work
    and commerce, 23–25, 30. *See also*
    Culturescapes
Lasch, Christopher, 191
"Let Freedom Ring," 66
Leven, Charles, 17
Lewis, James, 9
Liberalism, 69–71, 108
Life skills training, 62–65, 169–70, 181–82,
    184
Light of the World Christian Church, 87,
    102, 104, 105, 117
Lilly, Eli, 81
Lilly Endowment: and Catholic community,
    94, 204; civic activism, 19, 32, 38, 82–83,
    144, 199, 209; ecumenism, 62, 99, 117–
    18, 143, 145, 189; funding availability, 81,
    214–15n4, 215n5; and Jewish community,
    96; mission, 11–12, 204; response to
    urban realignment, 143–45, 151, 203–
    204. *See also* Indianapolis Center for
    Congregations
Lilly pharmaceutical company, 19, 144, 180,
    214–15n4
"Little Kentucky," 165
Localism, 9–10, 30–31
Lockerbie Square, 39
Loomis, Samuel, 48
Low-income housing, 69, 153, 171, 207
Lugar, Richard, 5, 36, 74, 151
Lutheran Child and Family Services, 72, 126,
    194

Lutherans, 77
Lynch, Kevin, 17
Lynn, Robert, 144–45

Mainline Protestantism: community outreach, 207; denomination membership,
77, 78t; growth and decline of, 81–90;
influence, 2–4, 11, 28, 51–52, 71, 188,
200, 201, 208, 210; linkage with elites,
199–200; Meridian Street churches, 81–
90, 160; response to pluralism, 89, 110–
12, 142–45, 148, 189; Social register residences, 32m. See also Congregations;
Protestantism
Malls, 24–25, 39, 157
Mapleton–Fall Creek neighborhood, 150–
51, 160, 163–64, 206, 217n2
Marion County: church membership by
denomination, 79–80; suburbanization,
33–35, 41, 44, 112; Unigov, 33–37
Market Square Arena, 16
Mars Hill neighborhood, 153, 165–71, 186,
206
Martindale-Brightwood neighborhood, 74,
101, 114, 151, 206
Masonic Lodges, 31
The Matrix, 140
May, Elaine Tyler, 64
Mayer Neighborhood House, 52
McGowan, William K., Jr., 28
McKnight, John, 9
McPherson, Aimee Semple, 109
Mead, Loren, 204
The Meadows Shopping Center, 24–25
Megachurches, 138, 140–41, 205
Melting pot, 209, 210
Meridian Corridor congregations, 81–90,
96, 159–65, 186, 188, 206, 217n2
Meridian Hills neighborhood, 159, 161, 162
Meridian Street United Methodist, 160
Methodists, 77, 167
Metropolitan centers, 17, 29–39, 35–37
Metropolitan identity, 200–202, 209
Mid-North Church Council, 150–51, 163–64
Middletown studies, 10
Migrant workers, 184
Miller, Donald, 137, 138, 141
Miller, J. Irwin, 89
Milner, Jean, 86
Milofsky, Carl, 202
Ministerial associations: Concerned Clergy,
47, 99, 172, 177–78; Decatur Township
Ministerial Alliance, 168–69; Greenwood

Ministerial Alliance, 180, 184; Ten Point
Coalition, 128, 176–77
Misogynist attitudes, 166
Mission/mission types: consumer service,
136–41; conversion, 130–36; importance
of in Christianity, 130; International mis-
sion projects, 184; linkage with urban cen-
ters, 158; personal salvation, 127–41;
response to change, 121t, 122; service to
external community, 120–21, 139–40,
163–65
Mississippi, 71–72
Modernism, 107
Monument Circle, 19–21, 20, 55–56
Moral authority, 8, 53, 74, 189, 198
Moral Majority, 70, 106
Mormons (Church of Jesus Christ of Latter-
day Saints [LDS]), 133–36
Morris, James, 28
Moynihan, Daniel Patrick, 71
Multicentering: Black Churches, 174–79;
defined, 13–14, 41; growth of, 192, 209–
10; metropolitan, 12–14, 17, 29–39, 189–
91, 200; neighborhoods, 152–55, 185;
personal networks, 17; regional, 37–39;
religious response, 141–58, 185, 189, 190,
205–207, 210; urban alignment, 12–14,
29–39, 141–49, 189–91
Multiculturalism. See Culturescapes;
Pluralism
Muslims, 7, 78, 110, 196, 201
Myers-Briggs personality inventory, 120

Nathan Morris House, 59
Nation of Islam, 131
National Conference of Catholic Bishops, 71
National Council of Churches, 89
Nazarenes, 79
NCAA headquarters, 19
Neighborhood watch, 209
Neighborhoods: Building Better Neighborhoods program, 3, 39; church location,
127–36; commercial districts, 24–25;
defined, 15, 110–12, 114–18, 152–54,
202, 209; diversity, 153, 185–86; growth
and development, 3, 39–44, 119, 150–52,
154; inner-city, 171–72; interstate highway
construction, 92–93, 171, 186; Meridian
Street corridor, 159–65; as multiple centers, 152–55, 185; myths about, 152;
typologies, 41–44, 155–59, 156t, 166,
169, 189–90, 193. See also Congregations
Networks, 17, 27–33, 122

Neuhaus, Richard John, 191
New economy, 32–33
New paradigm congregations, 181–82, 197–98, 199, 202
New Protestants, 138, 141
New York Central Railroad, 24
Newton, Miller, 69
Noblesse oblige, 160–65
Nodes. *See* Networks
Nondenominational churches, 79, 99, 108–10, 137–41, 180–82
Non-profit organizations, study of, 202–203
North United Methodist, 160, 162, 163, 164
North West Planning Development Corporation, 174
North West Way Civic Association, 174

O'Brien, David J., 64
O'Meara, Edward, 92, 94
Operation Breadbasket, 67
Operation Classroom, 123
Orsi, Robert, 11
Our Lady of Guadalupe Catholic Church, 184
Our Lady of Mt. Carmel, 161
Our Lady of the Greenwood Catholic Church, 183–84
Outreach activities: by congregation type, 4, 121–25, 184–85, 186, 207; Meridian Corridor congregations, 163–65, 186. *See also* Social services

Pan American Games, 18–19
Parishes, 91–93
Park, Robert E., 152–53
Parlor neighborhoods, 156–57, 159–65, 189, 193
Parochial schools, 58, 63, 91, 93–94, 124, 161, 168, 183, 184
Parochialism, 131, 167
Partnership congregations, 163. *See also* Interracial worship
Patriotism: and civic identity, 101, 111, 201. *See also* Americanism movement
Pentecostals, 107, 108, 167, 178
Personal salvation, 127–41, 174–75
Peterson, Bart, 86
Pfeiderer, F. A., 62
Planted congregations, 139
Pledge of Allegiance, 200
Pluralism: defined, 7, 110–12; growth of, 67–71, 74–75, 77, 196–99; religious, 88–90, 101, 116–17, 201, 210; responses to, 130–31, 143–44, 185, 189, 194

Police violence, 46–47
Polis Center, website, 211n6
Popular culture, 138
Porch neighborhoods, 157, 171–79, 187, 193
Porchlight Summer Program, 72
Powell, Walter, 202
Pragmatic accommodation, 177–78
Pratt, James, 69
Presbyterians, 77, 80
Privatization of religion, 114, 187
Program on Non-Profit Organizations (PONPO), 202–203
Prohibition, 46–48, 50–52, 74
Project on Religion and Urban Culture (PRUC), 9–14
Promise Keepers, 105, 168
Proselytizing congregations, 131–36, 174–75, 187
Protestantism: Americanism campaigns, 48–55, 86; conservative nature, 107–109; Easter Sunday services, 5, 55–56, 67, 74, 208; Sunday closing laws/campaigns, 49–50, 65. *See also* Mainline Protestantism; Social services
Public Morals Committee, 50, 51
Public partnerships, 73–74, 117–18, 125–27, 195
Public policy, 146–47
Public school system. *See* Education
Putnam, Robert, 4, 191, 192–93

Quakers (Friends), 79, 110

Race relations: African American community demographics, 98, 100, *102m, 103m,* 171–72; interracial worship, 87, 99, 104, 117, 162–63, 216n15; neighborhood diversity, 124–25, 185–86; racial concentration, 106–107, 115, 124; racism, 153
Railroadmen's Savings & Loan, 28
Ralston, Alexander, 1, 12
Ransom, William B., 29
Ray, Esther, 19–20
RCA Dome (Hoosier Dome), 27, 38
Recreation and sports facilities, 8, 18–19, 21–27, 38, 74–75, 94, 139
Reform synagogues, 160
Regional Center Plans, 37–39. *See also* Shopping malls
Religion: church/state relationship, 5–7, 52–53, 61–64, 126, 194–96; and citizen-

ship, 49–53, 58, 61–63, 113; and city's public good(s), 9, 71–74, 98; faith-based initiatives, 47, 71–74, 94, 118, 148, 194–96, 207; freedom of, 56, 61; as moral authority, 8, 53, 74, 189, 198; multicentering, 141–49, 189–91, 199; and *noblesse oblige*, 160–65; premillennial vision, 64; public role, 46–48, 55–56, 66–71, 143, 176–77, 199, 208; response to social dislocation, 167–71; secularization, 8, 50, 51, 65–67, 111, 113, 198–200; and social capital, 4–5, 75, 191–94; and social dislocation, 167–71; vitality of, 197–200. *See also specific religions*

Religious Education Act, 62, 63

Religious entrepreneurship, 117, 141, 146

Religious expression: Easter Sunday services, 5, 55–56, 67, 74, 208; in public schools, 52–53, 61–64

Religious organizations. *See* Congregations

Religious practice: changes in, 180–87, 206–207; church membership, 76–80, 107, 115–16; importance of congregations, 205–207; inherited traditions, 182, 184, 187; localized nature, 108, 148–49, 196, 198; privatization, 114, 187

Repentance, 130

Republican Action Committee (RAC), 35–36

Republican Party, 35–36

Residential spaces. *See* Neighborhoods

Revival tent services, 56

Revolutionary change, 119

Riesman, David, 191

Riverside Amusement Park, 25–26

Riverside Civic League, 174

Riverside neighborhood, 174

Sacred canopies, 196–97, 198, 199, 202

Sacrilization, 199

St. Ann Catholic Church, 168

St. Christopher's parish, 16

St. Francis de Sales parish, 92

St. James United Methodist, 122–23

St. John's Baptist Church, 99

St. John's Missionary Baptist Church, 105

St. John's parish, 56–57

St. Joseph Catholic Church, 168

St. Luke Catholic, 161, 162

St. Luke's United Methodist, 161

St. Mark's United Methodist, 161

St. Paul Episcopal, 160

St. Paul's Church, 163

St. Philips African American Episcopal Church, 162–63

St. Stephen Catholic Church, 124–25

Sts. Peter and Paul Catholic, 160, 162

Salad bowl, 209

Salt Lake City, 134, 135

Salvation, 130

Salvation Army, 126, 194

Samaritan Services, 184

Sandburg, Carl, 18

Schools. *See* Education

SCLC. *See* Southern Christian Leadership Conference

"Second at Six," 142

Second Christian, 104

Second Presbyterian, 81–88, 117, 142, 161, 164; membership, *82–85m*

Sectarianism, 131

Secularism/secularization, 8, 50, 51, 65–67, 111, 113, 198–200

Seeker sensitive congregations, 138, 141

Seerley Creek Christian Church, 169

Self-help, 138

Sermons, 138, 147

Seventh Day Adventists, 79

Shaarey Tefilla synagogue, 97–98

Shalom Wellness Center, 123

Shelter House, 59

Shopping malls, 24–25, 39, 157

Sikhs, 110, 196, 201

Slater, Philip, 191

Small congregations, 127–31

Social activism: anti-poverty programs, 69, 123; social justice campaigns, 47, 125; urban ministry, 86–87, 117–18, 150, 160; vice campaigns, 46–48, 50–52. *See also* Civil Rights movement; Welfare reform

Social capital: Black Churches, 174, 178; building community, 75, 135, 147–48, 170, 191–94, 202; changing nature of, 111, 118, 208–209; Community outreach congregations, 162–64; defined, 4–5; "porch" neighborhoods, 157. *See also* Welfare reform

Social dislocation, 165–71, 183–84

Social Gospel, 107

Social register residences, *32m*

Social services: access to, 119, 195, 207; aid for immigrants, 52–53, 58–60; Black churches, 176, 195; Catholic, 91; cloister congregations, 167–71, 207; customer service congregations, 207; migrant workers, 184. *See also* Mission/mission types

Soldiers and Sailors Monument, *20*
Southern Baptists, 108
Southern Christian Leadership Conference (SCLC), 67, 105, 172
Southwest Multi-Service Center, 168
Soviet Union, 62, 64
Speedway (town), 16–17
Sports facilities, 8, 18–19, 26–27, 74, 111
Stark, Rodney, 197
State Board of Charities and Correction, 60
Stein, Jonathan, 70
Stone, Barton W., 79
Storefront churches, 128, 174–75
Strong, Josiah, 48
Suburbs/suburbanization: annexation efforts, 35; dependence on automobiles, 157–58, 179–80; edge cities, 134–35; growth, 2–3, 12, 16, 33–37, 41, 44, 66–67, 80, 112; highway construction, 186; housing developments, 153; multicentering, 190, 192; nondenominational and independent churches, 180–82; religious districts, 159
Summer youth programs, 72, 73
Sunday, Billy, 109
Sunday closing laws/campaigns, 49–50, 65
Sunday evening services, 161
Sunday sports events, 49
Surina, Jeanette, 180
Synagogues, 95–98, 160

Tabernacle Presbyterian, 160, 163
Tall-steeple churches, 117, 143, 150, 188. *See also* Mainline Protestantism
Taylor, Michael, 105
Temporary Assistance to Needy Families, 72
Ten Commandments, 106
Ten Point Coalition, 128, 176–77
Thanksgiving contributions, 130
Theology: approaches to change, 119–21, 125, 127, 131; relationships to God, 120, *121t*, 127, 132, 178–79, 184
Tithing, 135, 168
Tocqueville, Alexis de, 191, 192
Trader's Point, 34–35
Trinity Episcopal, 160, 163
Troeltsch, Ernst, 197

Unified Planning Program, 38
Unigov, 33–37, 98, 100, 192, 212n21
Union of American Hebrew Congregations, 71
United Methodists, 79, 81, 88, 99

United Nations Day, 65
United Northwest Area (UNWA) neighborhoods, 171–79
U.S. Congress: church affiliation, 88; Welfare Reform Act, 71–72, 118
U.S. Constitution, 200
United Way Charities, 50–51
UNWA Development Corporation, 174
UNWA Neighborhood Association, 174
UNWA Weed and Seed Initiative, 174
Urban centers, 18–27, 39–44
Urban change. *See* Alignment/realignment
Urban ministry, 86–87, 117–18, 150, 160
Urban places. *See* Neighborhoods

Value of the month program, 134–35
Values debate, 6, 70
Vatican II, 124
Veblen, Thorstein, 157
Vertical relationships to God, 120, *121t*, 127, 132, 178–79, 184
Vice campaigns, 46–48, 50–52
Victory Field, 27, 39
Vida Nueva, 123
Vineyard Fellowship, 181–82
Volz, Shirley, 16–18
Vonnegut, Kurt, 151

Walcott, Susan, 190
Walk-arounds, 176–77
Wanamaker, 34, 35
War Memorial Plaza, 21, 22, 64, 74, 86, 189, 193
War on Poverty, 69
Warner, R. Stephen, 197, 199
Weekday Religious Education Association (WREA), 61–63
Welfare reform: faith-based, 105, 148, 194–96, 207; religious presence in, 4, 6, 71–74, 75, 118, 126
Welfare Reform Act, 71–72, 118, 126
Wescslen, Judah, 59
West, Cornel, 164
Westminster Presbyterian, 87
Wetherell, W. D., 40
White Evangelicals. *See* Evangelicals
White flight, 108, 124, 151, 206
White River, 173
White River State Park, 39
White River Township, 179, 180, 183
Whiteland, 179
Widow's Mite Christian Fellowship Church, 132–33

Williams Creek, 159, 161
Willow Creek, 138
Wind, James, 9
Woodruff Place, 153
Work and commerce: central business district, 23–24; civic identity, 111; globalism, 30–31, 133, 190; industrial/manufacturing base, 18; neighborhood commercial districts, 24–25; "new" economy, 32–33; population shifts, 33–34; regional shopping centers, 24–25; religion, 177–78; religious collaboration, 177–78

World religions, 110, 201
Worship: alternative forms of, 137–39, 142, 161, 169–70, 181–82; communal styles, 175; interracial, 87, 99, 104, 117, 162–63, 216n15
WREA. See Weekday Religious Education Association
Wuthnow, Robert, 197, 200

Youth programs, 65, 72, 73, 170, 182, 183, 184

www.ingramcontent.com/pod-product-compliance
Lightning Source LLC
Chambersburg PA
CBHW050228270326
41914CB00003BA/611